Clean | Break

∤

KAREN STEWART'S

Guide to Divorce

book one

 **FriesenPress**

Suite 300 – 990 Fort Street
Victoria, BC, Canada V8V 3K2
www.friesenpress.com

Copyright © 2014 by Karen Stewart
First Edition — 2014

Edited by Stephen Lund

ISBN
978-1-4602-5556-8 (Paperback)
978-1-4602-5557-5 (eBook)

1. Family & Relationships, Divorce

Distributed to the trade by The Ingram Book Company

Table Of Contents

I dedicate this book to my beautiful children and to all children whose journeys take them across the path of their parents' divorce.

— *Karen Stewart*

No problem can be solved from the same level of consciousness that created it.

— Albert Einstein

Praise for Clean Break

"This is a vital book for anyone pondering divorce or about to go through the trauma of this life-changing event. Karen Stewart knows what she is talking about, having experienced a gut-wrenching termination to her own marriage. *Clean Break* provides a brilliant new alternative to resolving the dilemma of divorce. This practical step-by-step process will not only save considerable time, energy and money, but most of all it will provide a clear path for a hopeful future."

—Les Hewitt, co-author of the international bestseller,
The Power of Focus

"I have to tell you that I think your book, "Clean Break" is excellent! I planned to take it with me to Mexico this Saturday but since I stared reading it this past Saturday – I could not put it dwon, I was following your story like I was right there beside you watching everything unfold. I found it gripping"

—Bhairvi Johnstone, Author
The Business of Break Up – Your Personal Guide

"Your book is read, powerful, insightful and human – and I predict it will be a run away best seller.."

—Dr. June Donaldson (MBA, EdD),
Certified Mediator and Arbitrator

"Because of her important new book, Karen Stewart has advanced the debate on divorce into a new realm where the sadistic, exploitative, adversarial system can give way to a more rational and supportive process where the parents, kids and other important stakeholders can all create new lives with dignity and the perception of winning."

—Dr. Peter Gregg, Negotiation Expert, and Founder & CEO of Success Lab

"When you start a court case, you are starting a war. Alternatives allow you to and your ex-partner to retain the decision making powers rather then giving them up to a judge. This increases your chances of being satisfied with the results"

—Mr. Justice Harvey Brownstone Family Court Judge and Author of "Tug of War"

"The journey through divorce shared so personally by the writer makes this book very difficult to put down. Karen Stewart exposes the abuse and manipulation of adverse practices of divorce law that, as a senior divorce lawyer, I too find frustrating. Her solution is the answer for many couples seeking divorce."

—Gordon Ball, Divorce Lawyer

"I have just finished reading *Clean Break* and want to say 'thank you.' It's an amazing document that will surely become required reading for anyone going through the qualms and traumas of divorce. Congratulations to you for rising above such a difficult divorce. Your strength, tenacity and vision will change the way people view divorce and its processes. Your experience has made a significant difference in many lives, and the best is yet to come."

—Barry Tuff, CityTV and Access Television

"The Independently Negotiated Resolution" (INR) mediation model of divorce offers a much less costly and stressful alternative to the legal system; the legal system is premised on the parties being 'adversaries' and 'battling it out.' As a practicing lawyer, I see the stress and turmoil families go through when dealing with divorce. Karen Stewart's mediation model offers those involved a lifeboat, a fair way to end their marriage and move on with their life, without becoming mired in the legal system."

—Brian Conway, Lawyer

"If you are even remotely contemplating divorce, then for sure read this life-changing book. *Clean Break* along with The INR Process will absolutely save you time, money, and energy, and months of unnecessary heartache. It is about time someone cleaned up the messy and costly divorce process."

—Dr. John F. Demartini, best-selling author of
*The Break-through Experience: A Revolutionary New Approach
to PersonalTransformation* —as seen in *The Secret*

"You guys are great—I would recommend you to anybody."

—Leslie D., An INR client

"INR is the first ray of sunshine I have had since the thing started."

—Brad L., An INR client

Acknowledgments

Creating this book was an unforgettable journey for me, one I could never have completed had I not surrounded myself with supporters whose guidance, wisdom, encouragement, and unconditional caring gave me the strength and the courage to persevere.

The family friends and associates to whom I own debts of gratitude are far too many to list.

Author's Note

Clean Break is a cautionary tale that begins with a narrative about my own journey through divorce—a narrative that is broken into three parts and which is intended to illustrate why I came to the decision to find a different solution to divorce and to contrast traditional divorce proceedings with a new model I call the Independently Negotiated Resolution Process™ (INR Process).

To achieve my goal of providing an object lesson, events described and opinions expressed are loosely based on my own experience, in part on the experiences of others who have shared with me the details of their divorce, and in part from my own imagination in order to complete the narrative. Dates, place names, personal names (with the exception of my own), and personal details are fiction. The words and actions of the fictional characters in the story do not directly reflect the words or actions of any particular person or persons.

The objective in writing the book is not recrimination, but to create a parable through which I hope to steer readers to a less painful, less expensive approach to resolving their divorce, and one that is humane and caring as best as can be managed in the circumstances.

Prologue

A FOOL'S MISTAKES

Crisis. To describe divorce and all its outcomes, there really is no better word.

The process of divorce as we know it is brutal—nothing less. Many professionals within the system profit handsomely from this brutality. Many others do little to alleviate or even minimize the insanity of it all.

On one level, this book is about learning whom to trust and how to empower yourself in a system that shows little mercy – especially to the naïve and unsuspecting. On another, much more practical level, it's about being proactive. If you or someone you love must face the much dreaded, much maligned but often unavoidable prospect of divorce, you'll discover so many reasons for proactively embracing a new and better approach— one that accelerates the process and reduces the costs while it protects children, preserves assets, and minimizes emotional fallout.

Finally, it's about moving graciously and gracefully through the inevitability of change rather than getting bogged down in the chaos it fosters and the fear that surrounds it.

I'm educated and intelligent, esteemed among peers as a purveyor of common sense. Yet for all my pragmatism and business acumen, I made some profoundly poor decisions during my divorce—decisions endorsed and encouraged by people with no accountability for the outcomes.

I have no desire to be a martyr or don the victim's mantle and finger-point in blame. For my poor choices and my misplaced trust, I humbly accept due responsibility.

I believe strongly in the time-honored adage, "The wise man learns from the fool's mistakes." My story is rife with learnings for the taking. I invite you to help yourself.

Of all the lessons I'll endeavor to share, I'll begin with this: Before you put your life into other people's hands, make sure appropriate consequences are attached to any outcomes. In the system as it is, very few people are accountable.

Wisely place your trust in people and processes with a vested interest in your financial and your emotional survival—your family, your friends, your children, and others whose unselfish motives and intuitive wisdom will help you reach the light at the end of a dark and terrifying tunnel.

Introduction

THE PERILS AND THE PITFALLS OF THE SYSTEM AS WE KNOW IT

Is it possible? Can divorce *really* cause . . .

- Complete financial destruction?

- Hopelessness and despair?

- Loss of significant time with your children?

- Paralysis by fear?

- Crazy thinking that leads to crazy-making behavior?

- Damning affidavits filled with perceptions and labeled with fear?

- Years of legal battles?

- Vicious accusations and demands to appear in court?

- Destruction of any possibility to co-parent effectively?

- Fear, pain, and feelings of powerlessness in your children?

- An inability to focus or direct life in positive ways due to exhausting legal battles?

- Utter exhaustion and complete defeat, with nothing left but resentments and painful memories?

- The answer is *yes*, all these outcomes are possible. And to prove the point, I will share a real-life story based on the events surrounding my own divorce.

- By contrast, is *this* possible? Can divorce really involve . . .

- A strategic, step-by-step process that brings win-win resolution regarding both children and money?

- Empowered decision making that leads to consensus and an outcome you know is fair?

- Empowered children who, even in the face of your divorce, remain grounded and well balanced and feel unconditional love from both parents?

- Controlled costs that keep assets in your pockets?

- Feelings of empowerment rather than victimization, no matter who pulled the plug on the marriage?

- Movement through the emotional journey as it unfolds without those ups and downs that interfere with your ability to make educated decisions?

- Focus on the future and letting go of the past graciously?

- Confidence about your new beginnings because you have a well-thought-out plan for both finances and parenting?

Again, the answer is *yes*. And to prove these points, I will share with you the many advantages of using mediation and a fair, measured and effective process like Independently Negotiated Resolution.

First, though, let's put divorce and the system in which it has traditionally unfolded into context.

HEADACHES, HEARTACHE, AND THE LEGAL BEAGLES

Divorce has become lucrative for the legal community. Spurred on by ambitious legal beagles, spouses now routinely seek major pieces of the assets regardless of whose name they are in. Commonly referred to as "the matrimonial property," this includes (but is certainly not limited to) stock options, retirement plans, and corporate earnings, even staking claim to potential future earnings. These days, couples contemplating divorce seek out valuation experts and forensic accountants almost as soon as they look for a lawyer. In turn, many divorce lawyers have escalated their fees to astronomical heights.

Family law lawyers have their own complaints about miserable, over-stressed clients demanding two pounds of flesh from their ex-partners and willing to concede none. But many of these same lawyers misconstrue their duty of zealous representation and act as hired guns, doing their clients' bidding using legal documents, relationship-destroying affidavits, and threatening letters as paper bullets.

Couples who go to court can expect to spend thousands or even hundreds of thousands of dollars in attorneys' fees and have no control over outcomes. A decree of divorce will generally not be granted until all questions regarding childcare and custody, division of property and assets, and ongoing financial support are resolved. In the end, a judge will tell them what to do with the house, bank account, pension, and children.

Family law litigants frequently complain about overworked judges; time-consuming, costly paperwork; lack of privacy and control over proceedings (and outcome); and legal constraints on their ability to tell their whole stories. In family court, judges never really know exactly what's going on in a case; they simply can't. The family court's job is to decide narrow legal issues based on limited permissible evidence.

Even when litigation is successful, in many cases the parties manage to settle only because they have waved big swords and doggedly prepared for a trial. By the time they settle, often on the courthouse steps, the process is extremely adversarial. They have spent a significant amount of money to prepare for trial, but they have polarized their positions and undercut their chances for a civil, ongoing relationship. For most couples, court is a blunt instrument unable to deal elegantly with resolving the intricate, personal, and emotional issues surrounding the dissolution of a relationship. It simply doesn't belong here.

And let's not forget the toll that traditional divorce takes on the children involved. For most children, their parents' divorce is an emotionally painful transition that can cause lingering feelings of sadness, longing, worry, and regret. Children of divorce may suffer from emotional disorders, exhibit behavioral problems, become young offenders, do less well in school, and have more relationship problems. But this has nothing to do with divorce and everything to do with how divorce is handled. As well, adults whose parents divorced during their childhood tend to have more marital problems and divorce more often.

When you look at a graphic representation of the traditional divorce process, it's easy to see its inherent flaws and to understand why it's slow, expensive, and divisive.

Interestingly, when you really get down to it, divorce involves only two issues: money and kids. Where in the traditional system of divorce is there a strategic approach to resolving these issues while weighing both the short- and long-term implications of the decisions? Try as you might to find it, it just isn't there.

THE PRESENT ALTERNATIVES

Alternatives to hiring a lawyer in the traditional system of divorce exist in collaborative law, mediation and arbitration. On close inspection, you'll find advantages and limitations to each.

Mediation is growing increasingly popular as a way to resolve divorce issues. It is less adversarial, it saves money, and it generally achieves similar outcomes.

In mediation, a neutral mediator helps facilitate decisions. Typically, mediation helps to identify the issues and choose the best solution. Once this is done and an agreement is reached, a formal legal document is prepared by a lawyer.

Mediation offers significant advantages over litigation. Couples make the decisions, not a lawyer or a judge. Although the couple may elect to have attorneys or financial planners present, ultimately they decide when to meet and for how long. The mediator is usually a psychologist, lawyer, or financial professional. Mediators work with both parties to resolve key issues, including but certainly not limited to visitation, child support, custody, spousal support, and property division. Unlike adversarial methods of reaching divorce settlements, mediation assumes the parties will cooperate to reach an agreement rather than compete to get the most for themselves. The goal of mediation is for the couple to reach a settlement that allows the marriage to be dissolved.

When their primary goals include protecting the well-being of the children and achieving a fair financial outcome, many couples are choosing mediation over litigation—especially when they're considering joint or shared custody. Mediation works best when each party wants to keep the process as civil and peaceful as possible. Generally, it is also cheaper, and because it is based on the premise that each person has legitimate concerns, it allows the couple to maintain some control and dignity during what can be an extremely difficult time.

In some way Mediation has got a bad wrap as it is often perceived that a couple "needs to get along" in order to use this method. In fact, that is not the case. A talented mediator can work with complex emotional and financial matters if they are well equipped and experienced.

While Mediators can get a couple to resolution on all issues, they will still need to go through some steps to get it legalized. This will include anything between full independent legal advice to online do-it-yourself methods.

Collaborative law is another form of alternative dispute resolution for divorcing couples who need strong legal representation but would like to avoid litigation. In a collaborative divorce, couples and their attorneys agree in advance not to litigate. If either party ignores the agreement and goes to court, both attorneys are required to resign from the case.

The major drawback is this: since the process still involves lawyers trained in position bargaining, you can spend a great deal of money on legal fees before you arrive at a settlement, and if you can't reach a satisfactory settlement and need to go to court after all, you have to start back at the beginning with a new lawyer. A strategic approach with an accountable, step-by-step process is not apparent within this model. Egos can still play a significant and devastating role in creating chaos rather than a fair outcome.

The problem with any approach to divorce is that the asset pie is usually up for grabs, with both parties claiming the biggest slice. The process of dividing up those assets often results in bitter acrimony, even when both parties start out with the best of intentions.

CLEARLY, IT'S TIME FOR A BETTER WAY

The foremost reason for this book is to help you see that there is a better way. An alternative that resolves issues in an efficient, strategic non destructive way is the answer. This answer falls within the boundaries of mediation or mediation like methods.

Several years ago, I endured a long journey through the dark and disheartening tunnel of traditional divorce. It was a financially and emotionally devastating journey that left me with little but an ardent desire to challenge the status quo and offer a true alternative to the way divorces are presently done.

Combining the hard-learned lessons of that journey with the financial acumen I've developed over the years as an MBA and president of a financial services company, I created a revolutionary new model for divorce mediation and launched Fairway Divorce Solutions—a company committed to using a practical, step-by-step process to dramatically reduce the time, costs, and emotional pain of traditional divorce and, most importantly, to spare the children.

I call this breakthrough process Independently Negotiated Resolution™"—INR for short. To assist people in using the process, I created a company called Fairway Divorce Solutions, which works with clients to reach consensus and win-win resolutions with respect to both money and children. Even without Fairway Divorce Solutions, you can hire another mediator and use the principles and tools presented in this book to transition peacefully and empowered through your divorce.

INR delivers mutually agreeable outcomes that empower both parties as well as their children to transition to new beginnings with assets, integrity, and self-esteem intact. The process focuses on three core areas:

- **Your dignity and self-worth:** Embracing INR will help you to be the best you can be in one of the worst times of your life (a true challenge for just about anyone during divorce!) Throughout *Clean Break*, I will share Key Insights and Key Actions to help you transition smoothly through divorce.

- **Your family:** INR was designed specifically to protect the emotional well-being of you and your children, and to preserve and reformulate a healthy parenting relationship so everyone can move forward feeling hopeful about the future. It will provide you with Key Insights and Key Actions to help you design your own parenting plan and road map to your future.

- **Your wealth:** INR takes you and your spouse through a step-by-step process of finding resolution on financial matters. It helps you identify the matrimonial assets and determine how they will be split. It also addresses such issues as child support and spousal support. Carefully designed to eliminate position bargaining and asset grabbing, it ensures that assets are valued properly regardless of who gets what. It brings you to a win-win outcome so that both parties can feel secure about the future while knowing they were treated fairly in the here and now. It provides Key Insights and Key Actions for you to keep your costs down and protect and preserve your assets as much as possible.

To illustrate just how well Independently Negotiated Resolution works,

Clean Break depicts a fictional but true-to-life couple's realistic journey through divorce using the process from beginning to end. Along the way, it will give you all the tools you need to bypass the traditional system and pursue a faster, less costly, less divisive divorce, and I will tell you how to pull together a team to help you through divorce and facilitate the process.

This much I know to be true: everything happens for a reason.

From my humbling personal experiences, from the exciting process of devising and refining INR and from working with thousands of divorcing couples who have chosen to use an alternative, I have gleaned significant Key Insights and Key Actions that I'll share with you to ensure that what happened to me and so many others doesn't happen to you.

To be receptive to those reasons and to discover within ourselves the courage to embrace them are our tasks in this lifetime. How else will we learn from life's lessons—lessons that, if we listen carefully, empower us to reach beyond ourselves and make a bigger difference?

Although they've cut deeply, I have embraced the lessons of my long and costly journey through divorce.

I have also embraced, with profound empathy, the experiences of clients and friends whose own caustic and convoluted divorces have borne striking similarities to my own.

I have set out to share those lessons with others who find themselves facing the daunting prospect of a marital breakup.

My sincere hope is that this book and my vision of an alternative divorce will help you avoid the financially depleting, emotionally devastating mistakes that I made. Perhaps you know people who have gone through divorce that too has cost them financial and emotional pain.

My aim as I challenge the present paradigm is to disarm the word "divorce" of its frightful power so that couples and families will no longer need to fear the process of divorce.

If I can help society as a whole redefine divorce, those who feed greedily off the vulnerability of others in the process will no longer be tolerated or sustained.

If I can help people see that mediation is a better way—one that is less costly, less time-consuming, less stressful; one that protects assets, children, parents, self-esteem, and love; one that people not only embrace but come to demand—then there is hope for happiness and serenity where in the past the outlook has been daunting and bleak.

If I can envision and introduce a new way, I can make a difference.

This book will reveal how the events of my journey through divorce empowered me to change my approach to life, relationships, and business.

It will lay bare the flaws of a system that no longer works, flaws that kindled my passion and inspired my vision for a business that redefines mediation and the divorce process and allows people to make a clean, quick, and cost-effective break.

By challenging traditional ways of thinking, it will show how you can turn a difficult, heart-wrenching experience into something personally empowering.

May you now begin to lay the foundation for bright new beginnings and to see that divorce is only a chapter in your life; it does not define your life.

Note to the reader: All names used in the book are fictional, except for my own.

Clean Break

✂

PART 1

---- ---- ---- ---- ---- ----

The Journey Before The Journey:

Navigating the Rocky Emotional Terrain

For many couples, divorce is a last resort—the only remaining option after many years of the slow erosion or the weathering of a stormy and turbulent marriage. For others, the marriage is just not meant to be any more, and while they cannot ever really put their finger on a reason, it is just time to end the relationship.

Whatever the cause, one thing is certain: the decision to divorce will be attended by emotional churning. The process will become even more charged, bringing turmoil into your life on a scale that's hard to imagine. Even those who have been through a divorce find it still hard to fathom.

During my divorce (and for many months before and afterward) I was an emotional wreck, blinded by denial, consumed by self-pity, staggering through each day feeling lost and alone and utterly hopeless. As a consequence, I made many imprudent decisions and missed out on many opportunities to hasten my journey toward new beginnings and the positive, rewarding future that awaited me.

The focus of this section is to share my journey and to reflect on all the learnings that could have made mine much less painful.

With this I hope you will have the foundation to minimize the emotional costs of your divorce through courageous acceptance and by staying relentlessly future-focused. I will also introduce you to the Cunninghams—Adam and Carolyn—whose example will illustrate, from beginning to end, a better way.

KAREN'S STORY

Divorces don't arise by spontaneous combustion. They are usually months or many years in the making, an emotional roller coaster ride that I call "the journey before the journey."

I am devoted to helping other people avoid the perils and pitfalls that beset me in my journey through divorce, I often find myself reflecting on the events that unfolded during that turbulent time of my life.

There is no ill will within these memories, no lingering resentment or nagging regrets. There are only reminders of why what I'm doing now— encouraging couples to explore alternatives—is so very important.

As I share my story, my heartfelt hope is that readers will learn from my mistakes (and believe me, I made some doozies) and be inspired to move gracefully through the turbulence in their own lives.

My mind wanders back to the day—so long ago now—that my journey began . . .

Chapter 1

FROM MARRIAGE TO MAYHEM

The sun came up as usual that morning, and the kids, as always, filled the morning stillness with their effervescent chaos just a little too early, especially since I'd been up twice in the night, once to feed Alexandra and again to assure Matthew the noise of the wind was not a bear outside his window.

Nothing about that day's beginning held so much as a hint of the nightmare about to unfold.

Tom and I had spent much of the previous evening bickering about this and that and nothing of consequence. Just the usual married couple stuff—too much to do and not enough time and wouldn't life be grand if I could be more understanding and he was a bit less demanding.

Yes, Tom and I could get the better of one another's nerves, but that, I believed, was just par for the course.

Our life to me seemed eerily normal, with a predictability that bordered on boring. Twice-a-week sex (before the baby came, at least); thrice-a-month arguments; and unruffled contentedness, or so it seemed, most of the rest of the time.

When there was friction in our relationship, I could usually trace it back to our mutual tendency to put our business and our children ahead of our relationship. The daily demands of running our business claimed, without apology, more than a fair share of our time and emotional energy. Whatever was left, we tended to spread among the kids. At the end of the day, we often found we had too little left for one another.

On the upside, two better-than-average incomes meant we could afford a live-in nanny—Camilla, who'd been with us since Matthew was a newborn. And in addition to our large city home, we owned a beautiful cottage in the mountains.

In fact, we had arrived at the cottage just three days before the fabric of my life began to unravel.

In some ways, the trip was a celebration; in others, a mourning. Alexandra was nearly five months old, and I, as I'd planned all along, would be returning to work at the end of the summer.

There were no more babies in Tom's and my future. I'd always dreamt I'd have three children and was lucky enough to have married someone who supported my dream.

So this was it: my last few weeks of maternity leave, and the end of a stage of my life that had been deeply satisfying on so many levels. With every ending, though, comes hope for new, often better beginnings.

On one level I was sad that my journey of bringing new lives into the world was over, but I scarcely had time to indulge such sentiments. Alexandra alone was a handful. Throw Matthew and Sarah into the mix, and nearly all of my waking moments were spoken for.

On the rare occasion that I found time for self-indulgence, I generally inclined toward a hot and restful bubble bath. And so when the opportunity presented itself later that morning after the breakfast mess had been tidied and the older kids had embarked on adventures of their own out in the yard, I decided to steal some time for a soak.

On my way to the bathroom, I thought about the cottage, the kids and the place my life had brought me to. I felt peaceful and proud.

As I disrobed, I was shaken from my reverie by a glimpse of a stranger in the mirror. I shook my head, slowly and sadly. "Alexandra," I said, squeezing and poking at my postpartum flab, "what have you done with Karen?"

I looked down at Alexandra, who was gurgling happily in her bouncy seat, and my fleeting regrets left me at once. Why was I worried? In time I'd get my petite body back, even if it meant some hard time at the gym. In the meantime, I'd cherish these irretrievable early days with Alexandra.

I picked her up and began to undress her. "I've got everything I've ever dreamt of, don't I, baby?" I cooed. "I've got everything I need."

With Alexandra on my chest, I slipped into the water's soothing warmth. While the baby nursed, I drifted again into dreamy reflections. The feeling of the baby's naked skin against mine was comforting and calming, and I felt content and secure and certain that all of life's trials and decisions had led me to the very place I was meant to be.

Then suddenly, startlingly, I saw something move in my peripheral vision. I pulled myself upright, clasping Alexandra close to my chest.

With instant relief, I saw that it was Tom. But the look on his face quickly dissolved my initial rush of giddiness.

He stood rigid and unsmiling, his arms crossed tightly across his chest. Even before he spoke, I knew something was up.

"We need to talk, Karen."

He spoke with icy detachment, which usually foreshadowed a fight or an exhausting talk about something I'd said or done to upset him.

My body tensed, and my mind raced to preempt the attack. For the life of me, though, I couldn't think of anything I'd done that might have set him off, so I just sat quietly, apprehensively, and waited.

I could never, ever have expected the words that followed.

"I'm not happy, Karen. You just don't do it for me anymore. I've lost myself in all of this, and until I find myself, I'll never be happy.

"I'm thinking about moving out."

Vulnerability and shame overtook me at once. The jagged edge of his pronouncement—"You just don't do it for me anymore"—slashed through my dignity and left me feeling ugly and exposed. I pulled Alexandra close to cover my sagging stomach and my bare breasts.

Intense and cold, void of anything resembling affection, Tom's words coursed through me like iced water. In that very instant I felt my happiness slew abruptly off track, like the needle skidding across an old 78 after someone lurches recklessly into the record player.

"Excuse me?" That was the only response I could muster, though in my mind I was spewing a disbelieving diatribe.

Excuse me, Tom? Did you just say "not happy"? Did you just say that I don't do it for you anymore? What the hell are you talking about? You have a family, Tom— three young children and a wife who loves you. I thought you adored me. I thought we were best friends. After you left your first wife, you told me I was the one—your soul mate. Now all of a sudden I don't do it for you anymore?

Yet for all the bravado of my inner dialog, all I could do, on the outside, was stammer.

"Tom . . . please . . . let's talk about this. . . ."

"No, Karen, no talk. I'm done with talking. I've given this a lot of thought. Moving out is the only answer.

"But don't worry: I'll still come 'round and pick the kids up for school in the morning. And we can still spend time together as a family at the cottage."

Don't worry? Son of a bitch. He had everything mapped out. Seems he felt a bombshell was the best way to share his plan with his wife.

In my panic-stricken mind, a million monkeys at a million type-writers were hammering away at the keys, but not one of them could crank out an explanation that made even a fragment of sense.

This wasn't a joke. And that droning in my ears was the sound of my life about to implode.

THE DIZZYING DAYS THAT FOLLOWED

I scoured my memory, desperate to recall the clues that must have been obvious. Why hadn't I seen this coming? Or if I had, how had I so convincingly repressed any conscious awareness of what had been going on?

Days passed. And while the passage of time helped ease the blunt force of my initial shock, it did little to illuminate what had happened. As if anesthetized by the spire of pain that had earlier pierced me, I spent the intervening days in a daze, staring at walls and feeling lost in memories that no longer made any sense.

A scene from our seventh anniversary swam to the surface: Tom and I sitting together in a quiet restaurant, a flickering candle floating on water in a crystal bowl casting wineglass shadows across our plates.

"Something sweet to finish off your meal?" the waiter asked as he cleared away the remnants of our dinner.

"Why not?" I thought. This was a celebration—a great excuse for some shameless self-indulgence.

"What do you recommend?" I asked.

"Normally," the waiter replied, "the white chocolate-amaretto crème brûlée. But tonight, the pastry chef has prepared a decadent Boston cream pie that's to die for."

I needed no more convincing. "Boston cream pie it is then." "Ditto," said Tom, with somewhat less sparkle.

A few minutes later, the waiter brought our desserts. I was about to sink my fork into mine when I noticed Tom staring at it, fork in hand.

"What is it, honey?" I asked. "Mine bigger than yours?" His reply was starkly emotionless: "I want your piece."

Seeing no reason to protest, I cheerfully swapped his plate and mine. But again, instead of eating, he simply stared.

We traded plates twice more until finally, perplexed and exasperated, I plunged my fork into my pie and started to eat, a show of defiance, according to Tom, that spawned an evening of me defending myself against Tom's allegations that "spoiled little Karen always gets her way."

It was perhaps my first clue that Tom wasn't telling me every-thing—that he harbored resentments, justified or otherwise, that had the potential to become explosively divisive.

And as I see so clearly now, it was a farcical foreshadowing of the legal battle yet to come: If I had it, Tom fought me for it whether he really wanted it or not.

Another flashback took me back just six days—our drive to the cottage: Tom sitting tall in the driver's seat; my mother sitting next to him, quietly enjoying the mid-summer scenery; me and the kids in the Suburban's back seats; and happiness, pervasive and pure, enveloping everything.

Since moving to our city half a dozen years earlier, my mom—Bram, as the kids and Tom called her—had become an important part of my life and our family. She and Tom always got along well, and the kids loved her dearly.

She and my father had divorced about 15 years earlier. Now, Mom devoted herself to her children and her grandchildren. She also helped out at the office, working there as a receptionist and office assistant a few days each week.

Bram came to the cottage with us quite often, which was a true blessing when it came to childcare, especially if we were joined by Emma and Jack, the children from Tom's first marriage. Yes, Tom had been married before. But now he was mine, and after almost eight years of marriage I figured we'd worked out most of the kinks.

So there we were, the six of us, rambling happily along through life at its sunshiniest on the way to the cottage.

I was sitting in the back seat so I could tend to Alexandra, though she rarely made much of a fuss. I closed my eyes against the late afternoon sun, which was flashing through the trees like a ceaseless strobe light.

And at that very moment, I realized how completely in love I was with everything about my life. "I've got it all," I whispered to myself, eyes still closed—"lovely children, a wonderful marriage, a successful business, financial security. . . . What more could I possibly ask for?"

We packed it in and returned to the city on the fourth day after Tom's declaration.

He'd said very little since the scene in the bathroom, and I was simply too scared to bring it up. A part of me, I think, hoped he'd forget the whole thing if only I didn't mention it. The rest of me just kept wondering when Tom would tell me he'd just been having a bad day and that he didn't really mean what he'd said.

Instead, Tom kept his distance.

The return trip was shrilly silent until the lights of the city came into view half an hour from home. Mom and the kids were asleep in the back, and I spoke up cautiously in the darkness.

"Tom," I said in barely more than a whisper, "I really need to know what's going on. I just don't understand where all this is coming from." I paused. "Are you seeing someone else?"

His knee-jerk reply was laced with spite. "I shouldn't even dignify that with a response. But no, there's no one else."

"Then why—"

"Dammit, Karen, don't you get it? I just can't do this anymore. You, the kids—I love you, but I'm forty-five years old and I deserve to have my needs met. I don't know who I am anymore. I feel life is passing me by."

I wanted to understand, but I simply couldn't. How could he feel his life was so empty when I felt exactly the opposite—that he and I had everything we could possibly want? We'd worked for eight years to get to this very place in our lives, and all of a sudden it wasn't what he wanted or needed. I was completely bewildered.

"But do you really have to leave?" I pleaded. "The kids and I—we can give you more space. As much as you need. Just tell me what you need from me, Tom."

With caustic finality he snapped, "I need you to can the sales pitch and listen to what I'm saying."

We drove the rest of the way in silence. In the fleeting spotlight cast by each oncoming vehicle, I scanned Tom's emotionless face.

"Listen to what I'm saying" kept playing over and over in my mile-a-minute thoughts.

My intuition had gone complete haywire.

In the past, it had always been my compass, reliable and true. But this thing with Tom so disrupted my balance that I had no idea which way was up. How could my intuition have let me down so completely?

The two weeks that followed are blurry at best, though I know I spent an inordinate amount of time staring out windows and at walls.

Thank goodness I had Camilla and my mother to help out at home. Except to nurse Alexandra and give hugs and kisses to Matthew and Sarah, I could scarcely function.

Tom, during those two weeks, kept a low profile, busying himself with work and who knows what else.

Work! With the date of my return coming up quickly, I should have been getting my mind back to the business. But how could I possibly think about work? I could hardly even dress myself in the morning, let alone focus on the needs of our clients.

Tom and I had started The Wealth Management Corporation eight years earlier, mere months after we were married. It was, and remains, an accomplishment of which I'm immensely proud.

With doctors and lawyers and a pop musician to round out the brood, I was the lone businessperson in my family. I started my career with one of the big accounting firms, but soon realized the only way for me to succeed as both mother and businesswoman was to venture into the world of the entrepreneur, where I could set my own rules.

For Tom and me, the old saying that "Success comes when luck meets preparedness" bore itself out. The economic climate was sunny, and we proved to be perfect partners with just the right mix of my business savvy and Tom's salesmanship.

Yet self-employment wasn't without drawbacks. The system doesn't step eagerly up to the plate with maternity benefits, so I took less time off than I would have liked with my first two babies. I managed to nurse both children past their first birthdays, but it often meant taking the nanny along to work or popping home throughout the day, which was a small price to pay, I felt, for those all-important bonding opportunities.

When I became pregnant the third time round, I promised myself I'd take at least six months off to spend with the newborn and the two older kids. And after those six months, who knows? Maybe I'd slow things down and work a lot less, especially since we had a new cottage and a good measure of financial security. I would bond with the baby, get back into shape, and just enjoy life with my perfect family.

How had everything gone so suddenly and terribly wrong? And how much worse could things possibly get?

I simply had no idea.

MY HEAD-ON CRASH WITH
MARRIAGE COUNSELING

I'm a strong advocate of seeking outside help with the issues that accompany the breakdown of a marriage, but only if there's a good philosophical fit between the counselor and the people he or she is trying to help. Otherwise marriage counseling may do little but delay the inevitable while protracting the misery of those who use it.

Soon after my marriage began to disintegrate, my decision to seek some professional help led me to Dr. Renée Goldsmith*. Well decorated with degrees and clearly committed to helping couples salvage their failing marriages, Dr. Goldsmith looked great on paper.

Looking back, I have little doubt she tried her best to help me and that her advice was well intended. I had to learn the hard way, though,

* a fictional name

that credentials alone cannot guarantee a fit between counselor and client. During our first session together, during which I described all that transpired at the cottage and in the days that followed, Dr. Goldsmith announced, "Don't you worry. We're going to land this plane smoothly. We certainly don't want to see it explode in midair!"

A soft crash landing! Even at the time, it resonated with absurdity. With retrospect on my side, it's utterly laughable.

At that moment, I should have heeded my intuition, which said "She's not the right fit" over and over and over like a 1950s ad jingle stuck in my head. But I was so blinded by my emotional mayhem that I just couldn't see that I had other choices.

Dr. Goldsmith framed the turmoil within my marriage to Tom as a mere symptom of deeper, more divisive problems from our pasts. "If we can just ferret out the *real* problems," she asserted, "we can fix whatever's derailing your marriage and get your relationship back on track."

These early days of counseling did shed a little light on the baggage I took away from growing up in a semi-dysfunctional household. But of startling revelations they were notably void, and they did nothing whatsoever to strengthen my relationship with Tom.

They simply wrapped our life together in a kind of artificial contentedness, a deceptive lull before the fast-approaching storm.

THE CELL TELLS ALL

The thought of returning to the cottage—to the scene of Tom's brutal and devastating revelation—brought a surge of dread into my throat, but it was a fear I'd soon have to face. Tom and I had promised the kids we'd spend the following weekend at the cottage, from Thursday the ninth of August through to the following Monday, and even in my emotional crisis, I fully understood how important it was for me as a parent to follow through on promises.

Part of me—the naïvely optimistic part—looked at the getaway as a chance to reconnect with Tom and win him back into the family fold. Intuition, meanwhile, screamed at me to wake up and smell the coffee.

The eighth of August, the day before our planned departure, rolled slowly around. I was in the garage packing jackets, tennis shoes, and assorted toys into the back of the Suburban when I heard something move behind me.

Startled, I turned, and there in the basement doorway stood Tom.

"I'm not coming with you," he announced abruptly. His eyes, glassy and distant, stared right through me.

"But Tom," I said pleadingly, "you promised. You promised the kids. They'll be crushed."

"Ken Calvert called. He wants to meet on Friday afternoon. I asked if it could wait till next week, but he said no. I couldn't say no to him, Karen. He's one of our biggest clients."

My mind was scrambling to find a solution. "Okay. No problem. We'll all leave on Friday then after your meeting. The kids'll just have to understand."

"No, you take the kids. I'll drive out by myself on Friday." "It's okay, Tom. We can wait—"

"I said I'll drive out by myself."

I could tell the matter was closed to discussion. I had no choice but to relent. "Okay, Tom. We'll go ahead. But do you think you could bring Bram out with you? She wasn't going to come because she's working Friday morning, but if you're coming later she'd probably love to tag along. I could really use her help out there for the weekend."

"Tell her I'll pick her up at five," he muttered as he retreated broodingly back into the house.

According to plan, I drove with the kids to the cottage the next morning. I can only imagine what my nervous energy must have felt like to my children!

All the next day, I waited anxiously for Tom to arrive with my mother. This weekend, I'd decided, would be my chance to prove to him he was making a huge mistake.

Eight o'clock rolled around. Then nine o'clock. Then ten. I grew increasingly fretful with each excruciating movement of the minute hand. Where could they be? Even when the traffic was slow, the cottage was never more than three hours from the city.

When at last they arrived—long after the kids had gone to bed, and far later than I'd been expecting them—relief washed over me. I greeted Tom with hugs and smiles. But he, distant and detached, pushed me away indelicately.

"I've got to get something from the truck," he said brusquely, and he trotted off into the darkness. I started to follow, but my mother held me back with a gentle hand on my shoulder.

We stepped inside, and I let loose with a barrage of questions.

"What's going on, Mother? It's ten-thirty. Where have you been? Did something happen?"

"Tom was late, Karen. He didn't pick me up till seven-thirty."

"What did you talk about? Did he say anything about—about us?"

"We really didn't chat, honey. He slept most of the way while I drove. He said he'd been up most of the night preparing for his meeting. Didn't he tell you that when you phoned?"

I didn't follow. "Phoned? When? I haven't talked to Tom since before I left the city."

"Oh." She appeared unsure about whether to continue. "What's going on, Mother? Who called Tom?"

"I—I don't know. I figured it was you—that you were wondering why we were late. Tom's cell phone rang at around eight and again at eight-thirty, right around the time you'd have been expecting us."

I knew beyond a doubt that something was up, but the most important piece was still missing from the puzzle.

I found it on the kitchen counter early the next morning.

Tom had leapt out of bed just before six to go for an early morning walk, leaving in his wake a heavy feeling in the air.

I followed him downstairs, though too late to see him off. As I was up so early, I decided to make a hot breakfast for him and my mom and the kids. That plan took a spot on the back burner, though, when I spied Tom's cell phone on the kitchen counter.

I picked it up and turned it over in my hand. This was odd. Tom never went anywhere without his cell phone. Never. Not to the grocery store. Not to the gym. Not to the bathroom. And certainly not for a morning walk.

I flipped the phone open and thumbed through Tom's call records. I recognized a few numbers—mine, Mom's, the office, and the nanny. The rest were foreign to me, but not for long.

With a sudden surge of self-empowerment, I decided to call every number Tom had called, just to see who or what turned up. And if I embarrassed him somehow, well, so be it. He had it coming for thinking about abandoning me and his children.

Be careful what you wish for. You might just get it. How rife with wisdom those words seem now!

As I dialed the first number on Tom's cell phone, my wildest imaginings couldn't have prepared me for what happened next.

Voicemail picked up during the first ring. Whoever the number belonged to must have been talking on the line.

I listened to the message—a man's voice in tones lilting and soft, as though speaking to a woman he'd resolved to seduce:

"Hey, Dee. How are you, babydoll? Gawd, I miss you *so much*. You're my everything—you know that, don't you? I honestly can't stand it here, being away from you. Can't wait till we chat again. I'll try you at six Saturday morning. And if I can't get away, I'll try again at seven. Okay, baby, talk to you then."

I hung up and called again, incredulous. It was Tom's voice. The bastard! He'd got himself a second cell phone, with a voicemail message just for Dee, whoever the hell Dee was!

I kept calling the number, knowing Tom would eventually pick up. And every time I listened to his message, I felt as though my soul was being viciously ripped out of my body.

I heard my mother come downstairs, and I called her to listen to the message to make sure I wasn't just losing my mind. As she held the phone reluctantly to her ear, the look on her face said it all.

At long last the phone rang through. Tom picked up on the second ring. "Hey, Dee, miss me already?"

I spat venom into the handset. "Get your ass home, get your things, and get the hell out of my life!"

In the time it took to pick up Tom's cell phone and dial seven simple numbers, I'd been reduced to one of "them"—one of the millions of people each year who find themselves amid a marital breakdown because of a spouse's infidelity.

Another statistic.

My discovery of Tom's affair spawned a period of painful imbalance.

In the state of shock that ensued, I moved through the days in suspended animation. I couldn't sleep. I couldn't eat. I could scarcely even formulate a coherent thought.

Thank goodness I had Mom. And thank goodness I had the wherewithal, before I shut down completely, to call a few other important people in my life—my dad, my sister, my brother, my best friend Serena—all of whom rallied about me and did more for me than I would ever have asked or could ever have expected.

A CONSPIRACY OF SILENCE

With unfettered zeal, Dr. Goldsmith applied herself to preserving "the marriage" even if it wasn't the best thing for me.

She'd seen me on several occasions and had even had a session with Tom, a session he reluctantly and grudgingly attended. Now, she was clear and unbending in her single-minded mission: to keep Tom and me together.

As for me, I naively trusted that she knew best, so I followed her lead with blind faith. That was my mistake.

(I understand now that it was up to me to ensure I was getting the right advice and that the counselor with whom I aligned myself shared my values and understood my needs.)

Nearly hysterical with panic, I called Dr. Goldsmith the day after Tom's affair came to light.

"Oh, no," she exclaimed, her voice infused with unaffected disappointment. "I knew nothing good could come of that."

I honestly didn't think I had heard her correctly. "I'm sorry, what did you say?"

"I said I knew nothing good could come of his affair. How could it? And now look at the mess it's put us in."

Us? What did she mean *us*? She wasn't in this mess, *I was!*

"You knew?" My cheeks burned as I asked the question. "You knew he was cheating and you didn't tell me?"

"I—no, I didn't. I couldn't, Karen. Tom asked me not to, and I owe it to him to keep his confidences."

What was she talking about? Was this the same woman who had told me and Tom during our first meeting there could be no secrets between us—that our lives needed to be open books?

I was utterly confused. I certainly couldn't recall any conversations about keeping this kind of thing confidential. But then again, I didn't ask.

It's easy now to accept my part in it all. I simply wasn't asking the right questions. ("So, what's your policy if my partner admits to you that he's having an affair?") Bloody hindsight!

This clarity came much later, of course. Right at the moment, I was madder than hell.

"And what about me?" I screamed. "Doesn't anybody owe it to me to tell me my husband's been screwing another woman?"

"I told him he should tell you—"

Bristling with rage, I slammed down the receiver. This was a conspiracy of silence, I decided, and I was being kept in the dark.

THE HOMECOMING

I arrived back in the city with Mom and the kids on the fourteenth of August.

I had wondered, during the drive home from the cottage, what it would feel like to come home, for the first time, to an empty house.

I needn't have wondered. As I stepped through the front door I spotted Tom hovering in the living room.

Matthew and Sarah crowded eagerly around him. His abrupt departure from the cottage had spawned a lot of questions and tears and fears about the future. Finding him at home must have come as a great relief to them.

For me, the effect was quite the opposite.

I turned to my mother. "Mom, can you take the kids upstairs and start getting them ready for bed?" I could see the concern in her eyes. "Don't worry, Mom, I can manage. Here." I handed her Alexandra's car seat, in which the baby was sleeping soundly.

"Sarah, Matthew, upstairs with Bram, please. Time to get ready for bed. I'll be up in a little while to tuck you in."

They hugged their father and then followed Bram upstairs.

Tom beckoned to me to sit beside him on the sofa, but I sat instead in an armchair opposite. I tried to appear collected, but my insides churned relentlessly, an unbalanced washing machine spinning off-kilter with a waterlogged load of dirty laundry.

After a long silence, Tom spoke up. "I don't want a divorce, Karen. I love you too much. I don't want to lose you and the kids. Please, let's try to work through this."

"It's too late, Tom. I mean, you're having an affair."

"I've ended it. As soon as I got back from the cottage, I called Deanna and told her it's over."

"Deanna. So that's her name, is it? I want you to tell me about her— what she looks like, where you met her, why you picked her over me."

Do I believe curiosity is the number one killer of cats? Absolutely. But for some reason, I needed to know all the details, however hurtful and unsavory they might be.

Tom, however, wouldn't play along. "Karen, please—none of that matters. I haven't picked her over you. I'm here, aren't I?"

"I don't think—"

"Then don't. Don't think. Don't torture yourself. And don't make any rash decisions. Promise me you won't make any decisions till we've had a chance to talk to Dr. Goldsmith."

"Dr. Goldsmith?" I became suddenly livid. "No bloody way, Tom. I'm done with her. If I go to a counselor, I need someone who's going to look out for *me*. She knew all along you were having an affair, and I ended up playing the fool."

"You can't blame her, Karen. I told her not to tell you what was going on. She couldn't tell you. It's that confidentiality thing."

"She never said there was a confidentiality thing. Quite the opposite, Tom: She said she wouldn't let us keep secrets from one another. She said it and you agreed to it—that's what I remember."

"And I am so, so sorry I lied to you." As he spoke, Tom looked piercingly into my eyes. And as he always managed to do, he eventually coaxed me back into his confidence. He was ready, he said, to come clean with the truth and do whatever was needed to save our marriage.

He even suggested that maybe, just maybe, this was exactly what our marriage needed to get it back on track—"a blessing in disguise."

At last I relented. "Okay, I'll hear what Dr. Goldsmith has to say. But no promises, Tom. Intuition tells me I should cut my losses right now."

What had I done wrong?

Ad nauseam, that question played over and over and over in my mind.

I was a devoted wife, a fastidious homemaker, a capable business partner. Where, then, had I fallen down? What had *I* done—or not done—to precipitate all this?

I was helplessly trapped in the insane kind of thinking that stems from an utter lack of healthy boundaries, and I desperately needed someone to step up and say, "Karen, you both played a part in the breakdown of your marriage, but Tom's decision to have an affair has *nothing* to do with you."

I simply wasn't in a place to see clearly, and I needed so badly for my counselor to slap the rose-colored glasses right off my face.

At the same time, Tom should have been impelled to accept the consequences of his actions, and his infidelity should have been held to the light and exposed for what it really is: one of the cruelest things you can do to a person you once loved.

Had we been counseled differently at this very tenuous time—had Tom's transgressions not been candy-coated and swept hastily under the rug—the outcome for me would have been very different.

But this is not a story of *if onlys*. It is a story of brutal *becauses*.

On Dr. Goldsmith's professional advice, Tom returned not only to our home but to our bed. Instead of condemnation, he received our marriage counselor's endorsement.

He could have his cake and eat it too!

FROM SOFT LANDING TO CRASH 'N' BURN

The whole ordeal soon began to take its toll on both of us.

In the two months since Tom dropped his bombshell at the cottage, I'd dropped 25 pounds. At 95 pounds, bedraggled by stress, I looked strung-out and seriously unwell. Tom claimed to be suffering too—so much so, in fact, that he decided he needed some time away.

We were at Dr. Goldsmith's office for a session together when he broached the idea.

"The stress of this whole thing is wearing me down, Karen. If we're gonna make this work, I really feel I need some time on my own—time to figure things out."

Dr. Goldsmith became instantly animated by the mention of making things work.

"Well, Karen," she chimed in, "Tom's idea is certainly worth consideration. People *do* need to get away sometimes. Sometimes they see things much more clearly after they've had some quiet time away from the situation."

Deep down inside, I felt the now-familiar stirrings of skepticism. I looked at Tom, who looked back at me with pleading eyes and a boyish half-smile.

Then I looked at Dr. Goldsmith. "Well," I thought, again silencing the doubts that nagged at the back of my mind, "she *is* the expert."

As I write this book and share my story, I truly cannot fathom how she could have endorsed Tom's suggestion. I had just returned to work, had three young kids, was nursing a baby, and was fading away to nothing. Yet here she was, giving the nod to Tom's outlandish suggestion.

"Would you like me to come with you?" I asked Tom, though I already knew what his answer would be.

"I would," he said (just a little too eagerly), "but I really think I need to be alone. I feel so horrible for what I've done to you, Karen. I just need to hide away and, you know, come to grips with the guilt."

Tom decided to stay at the Atlantis Hotel on Paradise Island, one of the most expensive resort hotels in the Bahamas. He'd attend a three-day conference there starting on September 8, and then he'd stay on for a few extra days to sort out (we all hoped) the mess inside his head.

"I'll do some diving, Karen," he told me on the way home from Dr. Goldsmith's office, as if he knew I needed further convincing. "You know how much I love diving—how it relaxes me and helps me really get in touch with my feelings.

"Once I'm out there on the reef, all alone with just the fish, the sea anemones, and my thoughts, I know I'll see everything clearly.

"This is going to be so good for both of us. You'll see."

Most people remember where they were and what they were doing the morning of September 11, 2001 as news of hijacked flights and terrorist attacks spread rapidly across the civilized world.

And most people, in the wake of that news, experienced a normal human response—a sudden and imperative urge to connect with the people most dear to them—to assure themselves that everyone they cared about was okay.

My telephone rang many times on the eleventh—my mother, my sister, and several dear friends needing to talk about what was happening and reassure themselves their own lives' security had not been breached.

Tom, at this time, was in the Bahamas, and I ached to hear his voice— to know how the attack on America was affecting him. I could scarcely imagine how alone he must have been feeling.

But Tom didn't call—not on the eleventh, nor on the twelfth. And when he called at last on September 13, it was only to inform me he was stuck where he was and had no idea for how long.

Again, though, I gave him the benefit of the doubt. I just wasn't ready to think there was anything wrong beyond an eight-year itch that a little time away would surely cure.

For so many people, the weeks and months following September 11 were filled with chaos, confusion, and indefinable dread—ripple effects of the horrors that had befallen lower Manhattan.

The upheaval in my life had a source much closer to home. After his sojourn in the Bahamas—a time-to-think getaway made eight days longer than planned by the post-9/11 air travel disruptions—Tom was back.

The days immediately following his return had been relatively placid, and I'd begun to hope anew that maybe, just maybe, my life would return to normal—that the nightmare of the past couple of months had finally come to an end.

There was my mistake—thinking that order had somehow been restored to my universe. My lessons were far from over; in fact, they had barely begun.

About a week after his return, Tom turned in his travel receipts to my mother, The Wealth Management Corporation's part-time receptionist who used her downtime to sort receipts for the bookkeeper. Amid the stack, she spotted a red flag billowing in the warm Bahamian wind: two beach towels and two lounge chairs charged to Tom's hotel room at the same time on the same day.

Unencumbered by the same blindness I experienced when it came to Tom, Mom immediately called the hotel. Through some trial and error, she was connected at last with the hotel's cleaning staff supervisor who told her, in broken English, that a man named Tom had stayed at the resort. With his wife.

I didn't believe her. I couldn't, for that would mean admitting my entire existence had become a sham.

"I wouldn't make something like this up, honey," my mother insisted.

I then decided to do a little investigating of my own. Maybe if I uncovered the truth myself, I'd have an easier time believing it.

Pretending to be Deanna, I called the travel agent through whom Tom booked his tickets. I explained that for business reasons, I needed her to fax me a copy of the receipt for my recent trip to the Bahamas. "Okey-dokey," she chirped. "What's your fax number, Deanna?"

As the facsimile of Deanna's itinerary inched its way out of my office fax machine, I felt numb with disbelief.

What more proof did I need?

Numbness soon gave way to a sudden sense of panic—a consuming urge to flee. I grabbed my handbag and dashed from the office. I just had to go somewhere, anywhere—but not home, nowhere familiar, nowhere that might remind me who I was or why my life was stretching at the seams with too much pain to endure.

So I walked. Aimlessly, I wandered up avenues and down side streets, through a maze of back alleyways, across parks and playgrounds. I tried desperately to get away from myself, but I couldn't outpace the anguish and fear and frustration any more than I could outrun the shadow of myself cast by the setting sun.

I would simply have to let it be—to sit in the pain and experience fully all the lessons it needed to teach me, no matter how uncomfortable it all became.

When you're desperate to hold on to someone you're dangerously close to losing, you bid farewell to your power to reason. Common sense and intuition get completely swept away, like thistledown on a warm summer's breeze.

After the travel agent had faxed me Deanna's travel information—after I had proof beyond any doubt that she'd been there in the Bahamas with him—I called him on his cell phone. And when he answered, I attacked with unrestrained ferocity.

"You liar!" I shouted. "How could you? How could you take *her*? Why are you doing this to us? It doesn't make any sense." I paused, trying to breathe, trying not to cry.

I wish I had known then what I know now: that he really wasn't doing *anything* to me. Instead, I was 100-percent responsible for how I let

Tom's actions affect me. I was playing the victim to a perfect tee. How incredibly disempowering!

"Karen, listen—you're wrong. It wasn't like that. I didn't take her with me. She found out where I was and just showed up. But I told her to leave me alone. I told her I was there to figure out how to make things work between you and me and that I wanted her to leave me alone."

He stopped, and for a few moments the line bristled with

ominous silence.

"Karen."

"What?"

"I love you, Karen. Only you."

Despite every effort, I sobbed into the handset.

"I'm coming home. Wait for me—we'll talk about this."

I wanted to be mad at Tom—I really did. But even more so, I wanted to believe him. Deep down, I still wanted to believe everything between us was going to be all right.

And when he allowed me into his energy field, I felt loved and adored and invincible, as if I were the center of his world—the only one who mattered to him.

In this fragile mental state, I was vulnerable to all manner of mind games and madness, and wholly incapable of setting healthy boundaries.

Every time I thought I'd caught Tom in a lie, he was able not only to convince me I was mistaken but to make me feel like a heel for accusing him in the first place.

Slowly, my self-worth was being eroded away, a fragile sandcastle smoothed to oblivion by the breaking waves' ceaseless assault.

When Tom got home, he pleaded innocence on his knees.

"I love *you*, Karen. You're my life! I didn't want her there. And I certainly didn't sleep with her. She showed up on her own, and she got stuck there when the airlines shut down."

"Why didn't you tell me she was there? Why did you lie to me?"

A mien of genuine compassion came over his face. "To protect you."

"Protect me? Protect me from what?"

"Karen, sweetheart, look at you. I can see what this is doing to you—this mess I've caused. You don't need any more stress in your life.

"The woman's nuts. She's hounding me nonstop, and I don't know what to do about it."

Even crazier than Tom's story is the fact that I swallowed it hook, line, and sinker. In my utterly illogical desperation to save my marriage, my intuition had completely shut down.

Feigned though it was, Tom's affection engulfed me and made me feel I was still, and would always be, his little princess.

After everything and over anyone else, he had, in the end, chosen me.

DROWNING IN DENIAL

From the 20/20 vantage point that hindsight offers, the power of my denial seems utterly impossible.

Tom's transgressions couldn't have been any more obvious. At some level I knew he wasn't being truthful, yet time and again I kept shutting down my intuition. It was as though I'd decided that without irrefutable, black-and-white, no-way-to-deny-it evidence, I was unwilling to convict the accused and sentence our marriage to death.

Quite the opposite, in fact. Apart from the bare necessities of functioning as a mother, my focus shifted entirely toward saving my marriage. It became an all-consuming obsession, the only thing I could think about every second of every minute of every day.

In October 2001, my resolve would be tested yet again. We were together once again in a session with Dr. Goldsmith when Tom admitted that he struggled with addiction. I knew he indulged in a few vices now and then, but it turns out I had no idea just how bad it really was.

"Pardon me?" I managed. I genuinely hoped I'd been hearing things because I really didn't think I could take another of Tom's out-of-the-blue pronouncements.

Affairs and addictions. I knew that these were the two most effective enders of marriages, and now I was up against them both!

Looking back from where I now stand, I have to admire Tom for his honesty that day. Admitting that addiction has a stranglehold on your life is a noble act, and one that takes a tremendous measure of courage, I am sure.

Yes, they create chaos and havoc while active in their addictions. But addiction is no less a disease than cancer or diabetes, and an addict trapped in his mind's obsessions and his body's cravings deserves our censure no more than the cancer patient whose brain tumor triggers a seizure or the diabetic whose hypoglycemia causes dizziness and sweats.

Addicts are often good people whose lives have become plagued by a horrible affliction. They are gifted in ways non-addicts are not because their diseases have taken them places and given them understandings the rest of us can only guess at. I have profound admiration for those who find recovery and exert the commitment it takes to pursue (and never give up on) a lifetime of sobriety. An alarmingly small percentage of addicts find a way to overcome their addictions, and those who do deserve to be celebrated.

"I feel like I'm losing control," Tom explained quietly and with unprecedented honesty. "My work, my life, everything—it's all spinning out of control."

"That's addiction, Tom," said Dr. Goldsmith. "And you're right: You are no longer in control. You've become a slave to your cravings and your obsessions. And as long as you're stuck in your addiction, you're going to continue to make poor choices.

"With ongoing therapy, we can certainly help get you over these hurdles. But I'd like to get you into a 12-Step program as well."

"12 Step? You mean like AA?"

"Yes, the principles of the program are the same."

"Forget it," said Tom matter-of-factly. "I'm not sitting around with a bunch of addicts hell-bent on cramming God down my throat."

"It's not like that, Tom," said Dr. Goldsmith. "It's not a religious program. Nobody's going to try to indoctrinate you. It's less about drinking or drugging and more about living a more manageable life. It's saved millions of lives, Tom, and millions of marriages."

Tom had backed himself into a corner, and now he was groping for an escape hatch. "Look, things may be tough right now, but my life really isn't as unmanageable as you two are making it out to be."

"I'm going to challenge you on that, Tom. If your life's so manageable, why are you here? Why are you here trying to save a marriage that's failing because of your ongoing infidelity and telling us your life is out of control?

"Listen, I'd like you to try at least one 12-Step meeting. Please. You might just find what you're looking for there."

* * *

I thought at the time it was just his addictive personality, but before long Tom was attending three or four meetings a week.

"You were right, Dr. Goldsmith," Tom told her at our next appointment, "it's not all God-talk. And it's pretty easy at every meeting to find a reason to keep coming back."

Also at Dr. Goldsmith's bidding, I joined a support group for families and friends of addicts. Dr. Goldsmith felt it would help me understand my role as a codependent.

I attended faithfully for almost nine months, and it was a wonderfully humbling experience, one I will always treasure and whose lessons I'll never forget.

Everyone in the group was so different, from a 30-something single mother struggling to make ends meet to a silver-haired retiree with a wife of 26 years to me, a well-off professional whose marriage was in shambles, yet we were united by a common denominator that made all our differences irrelevant. We were united by the power of addiction.

As I and the others shared our experience, strength, and hope—as we cried and laughed and shook our heads with out-and-out exasperation, and as we looked into ourselves and sought to understand our roles in our dysfunctional relationships—through it all, I gained life-altering insights not only into myself and my relationships, but into society as a whole.

We talked a lot about healthy boundaries, and it became pretty clear pretty fast that with Tom, I didn't have any.

When someone gets caught up in the cycle of codependence, there's a tendency to project his or her own values and beliefs onto the other codependent. I wouldn't cheat on Tom, so surely Tom wouldn't cheat on me. I just couldn't seem to get beyond the idea.

Looking back on my meetings, I find it fascinating that I could see so clearly in others what I simply couldn't see in myself. I remember one woman in particular: Anny, whose husband was active in his addiction more often than he wasn't. He'd lost his job as a middle manager and now spent countless hours locked in an office at home, consumed by his addiction, no longer able to cope or to function in the real world. It made her crazy, yet still she stayed with him, unable to break free.

So often, I would think to myself, "What's wrong with her? Is she nuts?

How can she stay with someone like that? Can't she see what he's done to her—that she's lost herself in her husband's addiction?"

We were kindred spirits, Anny and I, convinced we could eventually bring our men around if only we tried a little harder.

What we really needed to do was accept our powerlessness, to surrender to the simple fact that, try as we might, we could not and could never control our partners' actions or attitudes or intentions or anything else. Until we admitted we were powerless, life was going to be a painful and arduous journey.

ANOTHER FLIGHT OF FANCY

Women's intuition got its reputation for good reason. If only I'd had the wherewithal to tune in to mine—and to trust it!

From our first meeting, I knew—*knew*—that Renée Goldsmith wasn't the right counselor for me. But I gave her something with which I was becoming far too generous: my trust.

During a particularly prickly session in late October—three weeks into Tom's supposed program of recovery—Dr. Goldsmith proclaimed, "I have a great idea: Why don't we invite Deanna to join us for a three-way dialog?

"That way, Karen, you can ask some of the questions that seem to be gnawing away at your sanity. And you, Tom, can *show* Karen that whatever was once going on between you and Deanna is completely over and done with. It's true what they say, you know: Actions do speak louder than words."

Tom responded with a ferocity that was unusual even for him.

"That's the stupidest idea I've ever heard," he snapped. "It's over. It's been over for a long time. Dragging her in here is just going to dredge up dredge up the past. Karen doesn't need that and neither do I."

Dr. Goldsmith looked shell-shocked. Tom had never really disagreed with her before, and certainly never so vehemently. He generally accepted her recommendations without debate.

If only I'd listened to his words—if only I'd been attuned to the moment instead of being lost in resentment and self-pity—I'd have clued in to what is now so painfully obvious to me. *The gentleman doth protest too much, methinks*. And why? Because the bastard was still seeing her!

But it wasn't yet my time to see the truth of the matter. And, as it turned out, it wasn't Dr. Goldsmith's time either.

"That's great, Tom," she exclaimed, recovering her balance quickly after his attack. "I'm so glad to hear that any extramarital ties have been completely severed. That shows me you're ready to focus your energy on your relationship with Karen."

Still promoting her "soft landing" idea as vigorously as ever, she seized the opportunity to recommend a course she was certain would set Tom and me back on the path toward unruffled marital bliss.

It was called LoveWorks, a workshop and step-by-step program that promised to create "a revitalized, honeymoon-forever partnership."

In a rare show of unity, Tom and I both balked at the price tag—$6,000 plus the cost of travel to Orlando, where the three-day workshop was staged—but Dr. Goldsmith insisted it was a small price to pay.

"It's certainly less expensive than a divorce!" she chirped, offering up the greatest example of understatement I've ever heard.

Immediately after our indoctrination in Florida, Dr. Goldsmith demanded that we surrender to the terms of the course.

"Divorce is the easy way out," she lectured. "You're both worth more than that. You've got something worth saving. But rebuilding takes time. It's going to require a real commitment.

"So that's what I'm asking for: a commitment from both of you. I need you both to promise you'll stay together and work on saving your marriage at least until the end of the year. Three months, just like LoveWorks prescribes."

"Shit," said Tom with unveiled indifference, "that seems like an awfully long time!"

Conventional wisdom maintains that actions speak louder than words—that the true measure of a man's intent is not what he says but what he does.

Not necessarily true. A person's words speak volumes, and in Tom's words was everything Dr. Goldsmith and I needed to know. They were our cue to say, "Clearly, Tom, this isn't going to work. The willingness on your part just isn't there. You need to pack up your things and clear out of this marriage *right now*."

Sadly, we both missed our cue.

Thus were the shackles fastened: For at least three more months, I would stick it out and try to work it out with Tom, and he with me.

In the Toltec teachings of *The Four Agreements*, Don Miguel Ruiz tells us, "Everything we do is based on agreements we have made—agreements with ourselves, with other people, with God, with life. But the most important agreements are the ones we make with ourselves. In these agreements we tell ourselves who we are, how to behave, what is possible, what is impossible.

"One single agreement is not such a problem, but we have many agreements that come from fear, deplete our energy, and diminish our self-worth."

Yes, Don Miguel, we do have many such agreements, among them the one I had just struck with Dr. Goldsmith. And for the two months to come, you really couldn't have penned a better epitaph.

* * *

"Cut your losses" is the best advice anyone could have given me during the entire ordeal of my divorce.

At the first indication of Tom's refusal to change his unfaithful behavior, I should have slammed the door shut on our marriage instead of wallowing pathetically in hopes of reconciliation.

That isn't to say no marriage can survive infidelity: some can, and many do. But because Tom was wholly unwilling to own up to his transgressions and to change, the total dissolution of our marriage was just a matter of time. Only a fool blinded by false hope goes through the same pain over and over and over again, somehow expecting that sooner or later, the outcome will be different. The same thing goes for the legal battle that later ensued. In retrospect, I should have settled much, much earlier. I didn't need to give up, and I didn't need to give everything away. I just needed to know my own limits.

I could have and should have been proactive—a far cry better than the reactive mode I was stuck in from start to finish. But I was pitifully naive. I put my faith in a system I didn't understand, and I trusted the professionals whose very subsistence depends on the system's abysmal flaws. How was I to know the system sometimes protects the guilty and cannibalizes those most in need of its help?

Life coasted along relatively placidly for a little while after our sojourn in Florida.

A *very* little while.

As part of my commitment to following through on the Love-Works workshop's edict, I'd determined to work as hard as possible on our relationship, at least until the end of January.

In truth, I was just a tired and nerve-shaken basket case clinging so desperately to the unraveling threads of my marriage that I was ready and willing to try almost anything.

During November, Tom and I went away on two honeymoonish getaways. Fighting like hell to keep Tom happy, I transformed into a minx who'd do almost anything her husband desired.

I had to learn the hard way that pretending everything is back to normal doesn't make it so.

The busyness of the winter holidays became a welcome distraction, and Christmas came and went, thank goodness, without incident. And as 2002 dawned, I wondered what the New Year held in store for me. One thing was certain: It couldn't be worse than the last!

All the while, I continued to attend my support meetings every week. During the first week of January, I was chatting before the meeting with one of the men in my group, the spouse of an addict who just happened to be an addict himself.

"So you go to 12-Step meetings as well?" I asked.

"Yep. Tuesdays and Thursdays. Just over on Baker Street, in the Methodist church."

My face lit up. "That's Tom's home group. My husband. You must know him—he's been going to meetings at the Methodist church for almost two months now."

Jerry looked perplexed. "Tom? Nope, there aren't any Toms in our group."

"But there is. He goes on the same nights—every Tuesday and every Thursday, almost without fail."

"Maybe he's using a different name."

"Strange. I wouldn't think so. But I guess you never know, especially with Tom. You can't miss him—six-foot-three, wavy black hair, a very fit 45-year-old. . . ."

Jerry shook his head, shrugging apologetically. "Sorry," he said, genuinely sympathetic.

That's when I made my New Year's resolution.

Early in January 2002, while most people were already breaking theirs, I was busy keeping mine.

I told Tom to move out.

A LIGHT IN THE DARKNESS

In times of crisis, and it bears repeating—a divorce is one of the greatest crises any person is likely to endure in his or her lifetime—the people with whom you surround yourself are *so* important.

Jim Collins makes the same case for business in *Good to Great*. Before you drive it anywhere, you need to get the right people on your "bus" (and, by extension, you need to get the wrong people off).

With my counselor and, later, my lawyers, I thought I was placing my trust in the best people out there. When intuition told me I needed to get them off my bus, I simply didn't listen.

In *The Seven Spiritual Laws of Success*, Deepak Chopra illuminates how people like Dr. Goldsmith—people who, when I was at my lowest, unwittingly acted as forces whose only seeming purpose was to prolong my misery—are actually put on our paths for a crucial life purpose. "Whatever relationships you have attracted in your life at this moment are precisely the ones you need in your life at this moment. There is a hidden meaning behind all events, and this hidden meaning is serving your own evolution."

As to where my own evolution was taking me, I simply had no idea. Nor did I appreciate, as I do now, that the events involving Dr. Goldsmith were necessary parts of my journey.

Shortly after Tom moved out, I decided to stop seeing Dr. Goldsmith as I could finally see quite clearly that what she felt was best for me truly wasn't.

That's when I began to see Dr. Dennis Sinclair*. ("But I want you to call me Dennis," he'd insisted at the get-go.)

Dennis quickly proved to be exactly what I needed—a tell-it-like-it-is, pull-no-punches reality check.

"Karen," he said at the end of our very first meeting, "your marriage is over. As for divorce, it's not a question of if, it's a question of when. And the sooner the better."

"So I should just give up? I've invested eight years of my life into this relationship, Dennis. How can I just throw that all away?"

"You help people manage their assets, right? Well, if a client sunk $80,000 into a company whose stock suddenly plummeted and you knew it had zero chance of recovering, would you encourage that client to invest even one more cent?"

"No, of course not, but—"

"It's time to cut your losses, Karen," Dennis said solemnly.

During our sessions together, Dennis and I talked a lot about lessons.

"Life," he said, "has certainly put you on a path well lined with lessons. If someone had placed you in a room with 10,000 potential relationships to choose from, I don't think you could have picked a better disaster."

I had lessons to learn, and I found someone who did an impeccable job of helping me learn them. Now, as I strive to pass along some of those lessons through this book, I finally understand why.

Dennis pointed out to me the painfully obvious: "For your marriage to work, certain things must happen immediately, and certain others must stop happening. Tom must choose to be honest, always. He'll need to end an affair that's been going on for who knows how long. He'll need to

* a fictional name

commit to a lifelong program of recovery. And he'll need, above all, to regain your trust.

"For that to happen, his life will need to become an open book. He'll need to make himself 100 percent accountable to you. That's really the only way trust can be rebuilt.

"Now, how likely is it that any of these things will come to pass, let alone all of them?"

I knew he was right: There wasn't a chance in the world. Once I started seeing Dennis, my rational side began slowly to resurface. I began the arduous journey back to clarity and sanity and realistic boundaries, but it was still slow going, even at the best of times.

Two mutually exclusive things had started to take place. In my mind, I was beginning to prepare for a new life, a life as a single mother, a life without Tom. At the same time, though, I was gripped by an unwillingness to let go, by a relentless fantasy that my family could still, somehow, come out of all this okay.

That's what happens when our lives begin to crumble under the weight of an emotional crisis: We become fragmented. Our thoughts and our emotions and our actions become disconnected.

"After the emotional devastation of a partner's affair and a marital breakdown," Dennis told me, "getting back into step with the normal pace of life takes baby steps. First you start with the head: You need to see and understand at the head level what your new life is going to look like. Then you start to put it into practice. It'll seem strange at first—everything will still seem off-balance—but you have to fake it till you make it.

"It's just like learning to walk again after a debilitating accident. Physiotherapists begin with visualization activities: You imagine yourself putting one foot in front of the other—right, left, right, left. Then, with plenty of support systems in place, you try it for real. You'll stumble a lot; you'll fall a few times; and no doubt you'll want, especially at first, to crawl back into your wheelchair where you feel comfortable and safe. But after a lot of practice, the act of walking becomes integrated again into who you are. It becomes natural, effortless, painless."

This was my journey. I needed to learn to walk on my own and be accountable for all that had happened, even my husband's infidelity.

(I certainly wasn't responsible for it, but it was time for me to become accountable for how I dealt with it.)

And in the early going, when the walk was still largely an intellectual exercise, I found myself matching every one step forward with two steps back.

In my head, I was done with Tom, but in my heart he was still causing arrhythmia and palpitations.

THE GIFT OF REALITY

They were crazy-making, those first few months after Tom moved out.

Although Tom had moved in with his friend Garrett, he remained a very prominent figure in the lives of the kids and, as much as he could manage it, me.

At the office, we continued to work together under the terms of a Unanimous Shareholders' Agreement (USA), which simply stated that we remained 50/50 partners and were jointly responsible for the smooth operation of The Wealth Management Corporation.

The USA was part of my ongoing attempt to settle our issues amicably, to resolve our personal, financial, and business matters with as little hurly-burly as possible. But the system eventually sucked us in like dirty bathwater down an open drain, and my hopes spiraled rapidly into disillusionment.

While Tom was all in favor of retaining his 50 percent share of the company, his presence in the office was hit 'n' miss at best (with a lot more miss than hit). Still, we crossed paths just enough for my life at the office to be tinged with a constant wariness and nagging discomfort.

Tom also came to the house a great deal, ostensibly to spend time with the children. And often when he'd drop by, he'd bring expensive gifts, not only for the kids but for me too.

It wasn't long before the take-me-back talk began.

"This is silly, Karen. I should be living here with you. You know we were meant to be together. That's what soul mates do, isn't it?"

"Tom, don't. Please. It's too late. We're done. Just accept it."

"I won't accept it. I'm gonna fight for you—for us. You'll see."

"Save your energy, Tom. Maybe you should save it for Deanna. I believe *she's* your everything, is she not?" I tried to sound matter-of-fact, but I just couldn't contain my cynicism. Although I knew such jabs accomplished nothing positive and just created more chaos, I couldn't help myself sometimes.

"Please don't say her name, Karen. That's over. She was a mistake—a stupid mistake I'll always regret."

A couple days later—it was Good Friday and the kids had the day off school—Tom showed up at the house to take Matthew and Sarah to a matinee showing of *Shrek*. Afterwards, they'd go to Tom's apartment for a sleepover.

After lots of hugs and *I love yous* in the front foyer, I walked the kids out to Tom's car. While they got settled into their seats, I spoke to Tom through his open front window.

"Sarah's going to a birthday party tomorrow, so you might want to put her to bed a little earlier tonight. And make sure Matthew has plenty to drink. He's been having more migraines than usual, and Dr. Dunham said he needs to stay hydrated."

"Relax, Karen. I'm not totally irresponsible, you know."

I was about to say, "No, actually, I don't know," but stopped myself. Even when we were still together, I tried never to challenge or contradict Tom about his parenting in front of the children. When parents bicker endlessly because they don't see eye to eye, children's sense of security is always the first thing to suffer.

"Pop the trunk," I said instead. "I'll put their backpacks in the back."

When I lifted the lid of the trunk, I discovered two beautifully gift-wrapped boxes, identical in every way except for the tags. One was for me, the other for—

"Tom, could you come back here for a moment, please?"

I'm guessing that as he stepped out of the car, Tom suddenly re-membered what was in his trunk. As he reached the back of the car, he quickly slammed the trunk shut, narrowly missing the fingers of my hand that used to wear a wedding ring.

"Karen, I—"

"Don't even bother, Tom. I've truly come to expect nothing less from you. Just do me a favor: Give both gifts to Deanna. There's absolutely nothing I want from you. Except my freedom."

Tom lay pretty low for a couple months following my Easter weekend discovery. His visits with the kids became shorter, and I only saw him at the office when he needed to come in and sign cheques.

I filled the time with very pragmatic, forward-looking decisions and actions both at home and at work, solidifying plans for the business, negotiating child-care schedules, making sure the kids had plenty of opportunities for healthy social interaction. In short, I was laying the groundwork for a life without Tom.

Even though Tom was almost entirely absent from the office, I kept my mom on high alert when she was helping out as receptionist. "If Tom gets a call from a woman who isn't one of our clients, put her through to my office. And don't tell Tom."

The call came in one afternoon while I was eating lunch in my office. "There's a woman on line two, asking for Tom," my mother informed me. "She actually told me her name: Deanna."

How brazen, I thought at first. But then again, who knows what Tom had told her? For all Deanna knew, I was completely out of the picture, which was true in some respects, though it was far from being a clean break. Tom had, after all, moved out of our house.

I picked up line two and took a deep breath. The sudden rush of my adrenaline was intense, and a wave of anxiety swept over me as I spoke. "Deanna? This is Karen Stewart."

To the silence on the other end of the line, I said, "Listen, I need you to leave Tom alone. Surely you know he's got three young kids. They've been through enough. We all have.

"Tom has been trying to get his act together. He says he wants his family back. But you—you keep harassing him, begging him to come back to you. I need you to stop it."

At last she spoke. "Come back to me?" She sounded confused. "But he never left me, Karen. We've been together since you were pregnant with your youngest."

"But—"

"Tom said he was divorcing you so he could be with me." Despite my rising anger, I felt a sudden surge of empathy for Deanna. Like me, she'd been duped.

"There's no divorce, Deanna. Not yet, anyway. Tom and I are separated, but he tells me over and over he wants to work things out."

"I'm sorry," she said quietly, sadly. "I have to go."

Moments after she hung up, my mother appeared at my office doorway. "Do you want to talk about it, honey?" she said softly.

Despite myself, I felt so sorry for Deanna. "The poor thing," I said. "She's as tangled up in this web as I am."

The phone rang at the front desk and Mom excused herself to answer it. I began to wonder what to do next when the universe handed me my answer.

Mother buzzed me. "It's Deanna again. Want to take her call?"

I picked up the phone. "Hello, Deanna." There was no anger in my voice. In fact, there was no emotion at all, save for a slight twinge of pity—a little bit for each of us.

"I know I'm the last person you want to talk to," she said, "but I've got some things I need to tell you. And some things you should see."

"What kind of things?"

"I'd rather show you in person. Do you think we could meet?"

I tried to picture it: Tom's girlfriend and I, sitting together and sipping tea. The mental image actually made me smile. Perhaps I was beginning to appreciate the sad humor in all of this.

"Okay, Deanna. I'll meet with you."

We got together that weekend—our first and only meeting—at a crowded coffee shop in Willow Creek Shopping Center. When she walked in toting a shoebox, I was struck by the boldness of her looks—long and wavy red hair, stark cheekbones, a prominent nose and pouty lips painted brilliant pink. With broad shoulders and a full figure, she was nothing at all like me. But I guess that was the reason for Tom's attraction in the first place. Blonde, petite, and soft-featured added up to "wife." For "girlfriend," it stood to reason that Tom would gravitate toward opposites.

With the shoebox tucked under one arm, she walked up to the table with her other arm extended. "You're Karen. I recognize you from Tom's pictures. I'm Deanna." I took her hand and shook it with more warmth than I'd actually intended.

"Thank you for meeting me," she said in a soft voice that betrayed a whispered undertone of apology. Of embarrassment, though, I sensed nothing at all.

"I know how much you must be hurting. But you deserve to know the truth."

"But why—"

"Because I've had enough of the lies. And the empty promises. Every time he tells me he's over you, I find out he's still trying to win you back."

I nodded all too knowingly.

"Anyway, this is some stuff from my time with Tom. I don't want it anymore."

I opened the shoebox and sifted through its contents. Letters from Tom, with exactly the same lines he'd used to seduce me. Photos of Tom and Deanna on the beach in the Bahamas, including a few topless shots I didn't need to see. Greeting cards Tom had left for Deanna whenever he was away with me. A keychain from Orlando. The cell phone Tom bought her. And a ring.

I realized something at that moment—something very reassuring and reaffirming: every time I had denied my intuition, my intuition had been right!

Deanna and I didn't stay for coffee. We chatted a while longer and then went our separate ways.

Deanna was done with Tom, and I've come to admire her for having the inner strength to walk away from him, to recognize she'd be better off moving on. I never saw or heard from her again, and I doubt Tom did either.

On the way to my car I passed the restaurant's dumpster. I looked down at the shoebox in my hands. Then I drove home and placed it high on the bookshelf in my bedroom, a constant reminder of the power of intuition. And the importance of honoring it.

I call that day the Bringing Home Day, the day I received the gift of reality.

TRANSITIONS

The Bringing Home Day brought home with sudden clarity a reality that had been, for far too long, foggier than a Liverpool February: my marriage was over.

(I'm sure my readers are thinking, "Good grief! It took you that long to realize your marriage was over?" Sadly, yes. And that's one of the reasons I'm writing this book—so you can learn from the fool's mistakes and avoid the traps of denial and avoidance that beset me.)

My eight-year reign as Tom's bride—over. My often-desperate hopes of reconciliation—over. My rose-colored naiveté—over, over, over.

With that reality came a stark and alarming void, one I would need to fill fast lest I lapse again into self-piteous bouts of staring at the walls.

To help distract myself from the unsightly crater on the surface of my personal life, I immersed myself first in motherhood and secondly in the business.

Throughout my entire journey, my children remained my top priority and that, it turns out, is the greatest gift I could have given them—and myself. I have three happy and well-balanced children, successful in school, in sports, in social situations. The long-term payoff for keeping your children's needs in sharp focus is incalculable.

Knowing I was on the right track with my children—and that I was beginning to get The Wealth Management Corporation back on track too—did a lot to bolster my outward confidence, but not far below the surface, my self-esteem remained abraded and sore.

Scarcely a day went by that I didn't relive the mortification and shame of the day at the cottage when Tom announced his plan to exit stage left. Sitting there, naked under Tom's icy stare, Alexandra providing the only shield for my pregnancy-battered body, overwhelmed in an instant by the sadistic delusion that I could get my life back—and get Tom back—if only I could get my thin and pretty body back.

So I exercised. Every lunch hour, I pedaled and I pumped and I "pilated" my way back toward the body I left behind shortly after Alexandra began to show.

By June 2002, just one month shy of the anniversary of Tom's pronouncement, I was there. I was fit. I was attractive. I was 39 years old.

And I was eager to venture out and have fun.

I was really ready, then, for my "Princess Diana Times."

For three exhilarating months that summer, I pursued a mission to resuscitate feelings I'd left floating, face down, in the tub's tepid waters following Tom's fateful decree—feelings of attractiveness, self-worth, being needed, and desired.

Beyond rebuilding the business side of my identity, I needed to mend my shattered ego and reassert the power of my femininity. I got a tattoo (albeit a small one, in a very private place). I started dating. And flirting. And on a couple of occasions, I let promiscuous urges prevail.

Yes, I took some risks, but I would do it all again in an instant because it was, at the time, exactly what I needed.

While I was in my "phase," I thought a lot about a woman I really admired and about her journey through life in the face of infidelity—the Princess of Wales after her fairy-tale marriage to Prince Charles came to its media-frenzied end.

The Princess Diana Times were a crucial phase in my journey through change. I often feel some kindred spirit with her and her journey of self rediscovery after divorce, for I too discovered that there's no better way to rebuild a shattered self-image than by attracting the admiring eyes and the amorous attentions of handsome, well-to-do suitors.

Princess Diana was killed during her phase. Had a paparazzi mob not pursued her to an untimely death, I'm certain she would have come out of it, landed firmly on both feet, moved gracefully forward, and brought us many gifts from her journey. How terribly sad that we didn't get to see her worldly wisdom blossom!

In my phase, I started out as a woeful Rapunzel, locked up in the prison of self-flagellation and doubt. Salvation came when I let my hair down to a couple of dashing princes who came—rather unwittingly, I expect—to my long-awaited rescue.

By the time summer ended, I was coming out of my flirtatious phase ready for some grounding. In mid-October I met Todd Warner, who was destined, from day one, to be my transition man.

Todd was six years older than me and had achieved an enviable measure of financial success and status. And he was deeply empathetic to my plight as his own marriage had ended several years earlier.

Yes, Todd was a breath of fresh air, a sweet and sensitive man who, unfortunately, was at a stage in his life far removed from where I was at. He was ready to settle down for good, a need I simply couldn't fulfill. So while we dated for a couple of years, at some level we both knew (though neither of us would have admitted it at the time) that a future together as Mr. and Mrs. Warner just wasn't in our stars.

Although I couldn't, for the long term, offer Todd anything more than my steadfast friendship, he was truly a blessing in so many ways. While my marriage was unmistakably over, I was about to endure a long and far nastier journey through the labyrinth of matrimonial law. And Todd was there through it all, holding my hand and giving me strength.

While Todd helped me get grounded, he had exactly the opposite effect on Tom.

Tom caught wind of my relationship with Todd in early December. We'd been dating for about two months, so I decided to introduce him to my kids—not as Mommy's new boyfriend, just as a friend. I didn't ask the children to keep Todd a secret from their father, so naturally, they didn't.

Tom didn't take it well. Within a week, he'd hired a private investigator to look into Todd's life and his background. And on the rare occasions that Tom came to the office, he was accusatory and mean-spirited.

"What's the matter, Karen? Are you that desperate for love and attention that you need to shack up with the first guy who gives you a second look? He's a loser. Can't you see that?"

"You're one to talk, Tom. Do I need to remind you why we got separated in the first place?"

"You could at least wait for the sheets on my side of the bed to cool."

"You've been gone for almost a year, Tom, and our marriage ended long before that. It's over. You know that, or at least I hope you know it. I'm moving on now—without you."

REFLECTIONS:
YOUR DIGNITY AND SELF-WORTH

Several years have passed since the events I relate in this book trans-pired, and in those intervening years, I've had countless opportunities to reflect on what went wrong and why.

By objectively deconstructing my own divorce, I cultivated my vision and grew the conceptual framework for a new and better way to end a marriage.

The Reflections here and in parts II and III explore issues that can (and usually do) arise in any divorce.

The Reflections that follow here deal specifically with the emotional aspects of the journey toward and through a divorce. Those in parts II and III deal with financial matters and with ways to protect your children from undue emotional harm during your divorce.

Chapter 2

ACCEPTING THE TRUTH

— — — — — — — — — — —

Denial is fear-based reaction to adversity that prevents you from seeing, accepting, and moving beyond the truth of your situation.

Denial is the conscious or unconscious avoidance of reality. When the going gets tough, we put on the proverbial rose-colored glasses to soften the harshness of our reality. But when facing difficult circumstances like death or divorce, it is especially important to learn how to deal with *what is* rather than getting stuck in a *what was* frame of mind. We need to keep moving forward, with our eyes wide open.

Our journey here on earth is one of constant, lifelong learning. Those who embrace life and take risks may face adversity, but the potential returns include freedom, opportunity, and fulfillment.

We take a risk every time we enter a relationship, especially a relationship that leads to wedding vows. All but the blissfully naive understand there are no guarantees in life, so when we offer or accept an invitation to marry, we assume the risks. Life is always a balance between risk and reward, and with the wonderful reward of marriage comes the risk of divorce, a risk most of us are willing to take.

Often, though, when our best-laid plans go horribly awry—when our optimistic visions of "happily ever after" turn sour—we become resentful.

We let fear flood our lives. And we default to the most well-worn of all defense mechanisms: denial.

Denial's strategy is straightforward and insidious: what we do not allow ourselves to see, we do not have to deal with. Fear is its underpinning. Fear of the unknown.

"Everything points to the fact that my husband is having an affair? Nonsense! There's a logical, innocuous explanation for all of it. Now, let's take those silly suspicions and sweep them under the carpet."

Denial is difficult to move out of because doing so means seeing things you're desperately afraid to look at. But you may take it from someone who learned the hard way: denial is completely dis-empowering; it effectively prevents any kind of positive movement forward.

If, on the other hand, you open your eyes and allow yourself not only to see but to accept the truth, you can surely deal with it.

I floundered in denial about my partner's infidelity for more than a year, all that time enduring enormous emotional pain and allowing my self-esteem to suffer. I simply wouldn't allow myself to see the truth: that my husband's affections had moved elsewhere, and that our marriage was dead in the water. I was blinded by fear.

For a long time, I regarded the end of my marriage as a personal failure. It wasn't. The simple truth is that people change. My ex-husband and I just happened to have changed and were running away from each other in different directions.

Compounding the challenge is the fact that denial is systemic. We continue to live in denial at all levels—legal, governmental, political. We live in denial about world poverty, about war and conflict, about the health of Mother Earth. We also live in denial about our attitudes toward divorce and infidelity.

Breaking free from denial is by no means easy, and it's something you may not be able to do on your own. Usually, you must look to those you love and trust to help you see the reality of your situation.

In truth, though, most people *can* deal with reality, no matter how harsh it may be. Compared to the woes human beings through the centuries have proven themselves capable of enduring, a divorce, even a particularly messy one, seems but a trifling matter.

Trust in the old saying "We are never handed anything we cannot handle."

Humans are survivors by nature, and time really does heal most wounds, no matter how deep the cuts. Yes, many such wounds leave scars for life, but what doesn't kill us makes us stronger, and most people carry on after a divorce and find happiness in some context.

Freeing yourself from denial is the first important step in a healthy and fruitful transition through your divorce.

Chapter 3

TRUSTING YOUR INTUITION

— — — — — — — — — — —

During times of emotional crisis, we often shut down or lose touch with our intuition, which can have devastating consequences.

There are two types of intuition. The first—your "fight or flight" intuition—helps protect you from real danger. The other—your insight intuition—functions as your emotional navigation system and is the intuition of which I speak in this book.

Many commonplace phrases acknowledge the power of this type of intuition: "My spider senses told me to stay away." "My gut told me not to sign the deal." "I had a nagging suspicion something was up."

One of the greatest gifts I took away from my long and convoluted divorce was learning the power of my own intuition. When I retrace the steps of my turbulent journey, I can clearly see that every single time I denied my intuition, I made the wrong decision.

If you take nothing else from this book, please take this promise: if you learn to trust your intuition during a divorce (or any other challenging time in your life) and if you act on it, you will benefit in so many ways.

During my divorce, my inner voice nagged at me night and day, but all for naught. Smothered by chaos and drowning in denial, I lost touch with my intuition, and on the rare occasions that my intuition and I managed to connect, I chose not to trust it. My insecurities and feelings of low self-worth gained an absolute stranglehold over reason, forming an impenetrable barrier between me and common sense.

When reason did filter through, it was warped into a jumble of mixed messages, like a cell phone picking up several conversations at once. Even when I tried hard to listen to my intuition, nothing made sense.

I understand what it feels like to not be grounded in decision-making: it feels like hell. Making ego-based decisions from a place of fear erodes self-esteem and amplifies the chaos in which you are floundering. Tuning in to your intuition and getting crystal-clear reception takes time, but if you sharpen that skill one day at a time, you will be rewarded. You will have renewed confidence in your decisions. More importantly, you'll be able to make them, but only if you remain true to yourself at a soul level, not at the level of personal wounds and emotional distress.

Work to keep your intuition finely tuned, and let it be your guide at all times. It will never fail you.

Chapter 4

BREAKING FREE FROM
CRISIS AND CHAOS

— — — — — — — — — — —

*Crisis and chaos close the doors on positive change
and forward movement. A system that creates chaos
and perpetuates crisis simply cannot lead people to
healthy resolutions.*

Crisis is a state of elevated emotions and cognitive dissonance where
random reactions lead to random consequences. When crisis breeds
chaos, people get stuck in pain and despair. Making a healthy transition
from crisis to contentedness is most easily achieved by peacefully trusting
that everything in your life has purpose and is on purpose.

Make no mistake: divorce is a painful process, a breeding ground
for raw and abrading negative emotions. But here, as in everything else,
life presents us with a choice: de can wallow in our misery, or we can
accept the inevitability of pain and embrace its invaluable lessons. In
many respects, crisis is merely a matter of outlook and perception. As M.
Kathleen Casey wrote, "Pain is inevitable; suffering is optional."

After my husband announced his intention to leave me, and again
after I learned he was having an affair, I spent not only hours or even
days but weeks on end staring at walls. I could sit through a movie and
realize afterward that I couldn't recall a single scene. I became completely

preoccupied with my pain, and I obsessed relentlessly over the events that had precipitated it. I was stuck in it, like a terrified animal tangled up in a barbed-wire fence.

This is how many people respond in the face of serious emotional upset: they become paralyzed by their pain, and they can't see a way to move beyond it.

Pain degrades into crisis when we get stuck, when we find that the days and weeks we spend in bed or staring at the walls turn into months or even years.

The wellsprings of chaos and crisis are denial and deceit. People in faltering or failing relationships deny or lie about their feelings for any number of reasons. Perhaps they think they're protecting the other person; perhaps they're waiting for 100 percent certainty that their dissatisfaction is justified; perhaps they've subscribed to the notion of "better the devil you know."

No matter how reasonable or even noble these reasons may seem on the surface, they suffer unanimously from a major flaw: they force truth into the shadows. In order to be an authentic, unselfishly loving person, you must speak the truth at all times.

If honesty and integrity are in everyone's best interest, why, when it comes to divorce, is the truth so elusive?

The answer is clear in my mind: it has much to do with the label society applies to divorce. Until we can move away from stigmatizing divorce and labeling it as "bad," we will remain, as a culture, creators of chaos, mired in crisis.

So you've fallen out of love with your spouse and you've decided, for your own happiness's sake, that you don't want to spend the rest of your life with that person. Your feelings aren't wrong. Your desire to leave the relationship doesn't make you a bad person. The splitting up of your relationship isn't a crime, yet society—and the way the traditional system deals with divorce—would have you believe that it is.

To shift the paradigm, we need to start challenging conventional thinking. If people no longer feared the backlash and censure of falling out of love or wanting to leave a relationship, they'd feel freer to speak their truth. With that truth come freedom and enlightenment for everyone, especially for the parties who didn't want to end the relationship but who need to come to terms with reality and transition through it to new beginnings.

Imagine if divorce's connotations were neutral rather than negative. We will explore later what this would mean to our children, but you can begin to imagine it now.

It would be wonderful, of course, if marriage always meant forever and the idea of divorce passed quietly into history, but the statistics don't bode well for that likelihood. Why, then, should we persist in labeling 30–40 percent, more or less, of the population as "wrong"?

Acceptance opens up opportunities to grow and become a better person.

Chapter 5

BECOMING PROACTIVE

— — — — — — — — — — —

Every action or reaction has consequences, both short-term and long. Being reactive, which involves acting without due consideration of the consequence, diminishes your ability to influence outcomes.

Self-help author Brian Tracy writes, "You cannot control what happens to you, but you can control your attitude toward what happens to you, and in that, you will be mastering change rather than allowing it to master you."

For the most part, you're powerless over other people's attitudes, emotions, and behaviors. Of the factors that influence your future, all but a small fraction reside well beyond your sphere of influence.

The only things you can control with absolute certainty are *your own* attitudes, emotions, and behaviors, all of which directly impact your life tomorrow. Your response to every situation, even where seemingly minor matters are concerned, directly shapes your future.

If you want to change future outcomes, you need to change your attitudes, emotions, and behaviors today.

Isaac Newton's Law of Reciprocal Actions holds that in the physical world, every action has an equal but opposite reaction.

A similar precept holds true in the world of human relationships: Every reaction has an outcome, and every outcome spawns another reaction.

The cycle is endless: reaction, consequence, reaction, consequence, reaction, consequence, and so on.

Many respected authors and thought leaders have explored this notion of "re-action." In *The Four Agreements*, Don Miguel Ruiz dis-cusses the power of our words: every word we utter to another has impact—sometimes positive, often negative. To underestimate this power is a shame; to misuse or abuse it is a crime.

Unfortunately, the traditional system of divorce, where rival parties scramble to get the upper hand on one another in the legal proceedings, creates a climate of reactivity. Such a state renders us powerless as reactivity precludes the active shaping of a positive future.

When we are operating in reactive mode, we respond to people and situations without due consideration of the consequences of our responses. Our reactions are knee-jerk. Our decisions lack prudence. Our words are ill-considered.

You can typically tell when you're being reactive: it generally sets off a rush of adrenaline, a racing heartbeat, or some other symptom of panic. You experience a swell of second-guessing. And you feel completely out of control.

If you've been stuck in reactive mode and things turn out well, that's just dumb luck. They usually don't.

Reactivity breeds chaos, and chaos is a terrible place to spend your days. If we can be empowered in such a way that we understand the difference between being reactive and being active, we can enjoy a measure of control over our outcomes and, more importantly, be accountable to them. I try hard to instill this lesson in my children, so that they can dodge the dire mistakes their mother made.

> *Acting without anticipation of consequence is very different from anticipating and understanding the outcomes of your actions before you act. Being proactive during your divorce will minimize the emotional fallout and financial repercussions.*

Chapter 6

ESTABLISHING HEALTHY BOUNDARIES

— — — — — — — — — — —

Unhealthy boundaries hinder you from making prudent decisions that serve your own best interests.

Simply put, a lack of boundaries involves a failure to recognize or to respect where you end and others begin. People who lack healthy boundaries find themselves obsessed, often in futile ways, with trying to impose order on their own lives by controlling other people's attitudes and actions.

A symptom of codependence, poorly defined boundaries are common in relationships that involve addictions (not only to alcohol or drugs but to work, sex, cleanliness, control). The codependent believes that if only he or she tries hard enough or nags long enough or screams loud enough, the addict will reform. There is an utter lack of acceptance that we are, in the end, powerless over other people.

Part and parcel of unhealthy boundaries are the following beliefs and behaviors:

- A tendency to borrow and internalize other people's values and belief systems

- A tendency to take on other people's pain, and to take the blame for it

- Trusting others before you trust yourself

- Looking to others for approval

- Knowing something to be true (e.g., an affair), but allowing others to deny your intuition and convince you otherwise

- Low self-esteem

- Negative self-talk

- Internalizing your perceptions of other people's opinions toward you

- Saying yes when you want to say no.

On the flip side of the coin are people with healthy boundaries. They have the confidence to say no and to not feel guilty about it. They possess a self-understanding that allows them to trust themselves, even when their convictions fly in the face of what others (like a soon-to-be ex-spouse) are telling them. With healthy boundaries, you can discern what's in your own best interest and act on that knowledge.

If either or both of the parties in a relationship lack healthy boundaries, the relationship will be to some degree dysfunctional. The fewer the boundaries, the greater the dysfunction.

They're also prerequisite to individual happiness, self-actualization, and understanding (and fulfilling) your purpose in life. After all, how can you be truly happy if your sense of self-worth is externally defined?

I have had numerous conversations with experts about the ability of a marriage to survive one partner's infidelity. Most are strong in their view that if the offending partner is ready and willing to change and to do whatever it takes to reestablish a climate of trust, then yes, survival of the marriage is a possibility.

When you're rebuilding a relationship after an affair, especially one that's gone on for an extended period, it's entirely reasonable to expect the offending partner to be available by cell phone 24/7 (unless he or she is in a meeting with the boss or is having a fluoride treatment at the dentist), to be willing and able to account for every second of every day, and to humbly answer every question or concern, no matter how uncomfortable it is or how ridiculously suspicious it seems.

It's so clear to me now that the scenario above has two possible outcomes:

1. The offending spouse plays by the rules. The cell phone stays on and slowly, over time, trust is rebuilt.

2. The offending partner flouts the rulebook. The suspicious partner calls the cell phone and gets a "This customer is currently unavailable" message with no prior warning or verifiable explanation. With clarity of mind comes the only healthy response: "This is a broken promise and a show of disrespect. To forgive or excuse this breaking of the rules would be to condone it. Clearly, my partner cannot commit to doing what needs to be done. It's time for me to follow through on the consequences we both agreed to."

There is, of course, a third possibility, but it comes from a place of fear and a sense of self-worthlessness: "What have I done to cause this? What am I doing wrong? I know I promised myself I'd leave if any of the rules were broken, but that seems so harsh. I'm only going to offer one last chance, though . . . ."

Failure to keep your promises to yourself quickly turns your messy life even messier. And by not holding others accountable to the rules and to their promises, you diminish your boundaries even further.

> *People with healthy boundaries have a clear internal locus of control that guides them in making loving decisions without the fear of losing someone or something. They understand and accept the limits of their influence.*

INTO ACTION

Since launching Fairway Divorce Solutions, I've helped thousands of divorcing couples reach resolution on their assets and their children using Independently Negotiated Resolution (INR).

Although this process cannot erase the sadness and pain that attends the dissolution of a once-loving relationship, it dramatically reduces the time, costs, and emotional toll on adults and children alike.

To show you exactly how it works, I'm about to introduce you to the Cunninghams, whom you'll follow through the INR process from beginning to end.

Although the Cunninghams are fictional, their characters, their situation, and the issues with which they're struggling are drawn from commonalities among the hundreds of clients I've worked with. They are, in every respect, a "typical" divorcing couple.

Here in Part I, the Cunninghams set off down the INR pathway and work through some of the emotional fallout from their breakup.

In Part II, you'll follow the Cunninghams as they work toward resolution on their financial issues, and in Part III, they'll contend with the question of the kids.

Chapter 7

MEET THE CUNNINGHAMS

— — — — — — — — — — —

I usually see people at the worst time of their lives. But that's okay because I know there is hope.

My assistant rings me in my office. The Cunninghams—Adam and Carolyn—are waiting in reception.

The new couple.

She tells me a bit about them. Married 20 years. Three kids. First marriage—and first divorce—for both.

Stepping from my office at the end of the hall, I see the Cunninghams before they see me.

Adam appears to be in his late forties—tall and reasonably fit, with dark hair just starting to gray around the temples. Carolyn, a few years his junior, has an air of vivacity about her. Sassy auburn hair frames fine features and large brown eyes, and her sporty outfit is a perfect fit on her slim frame. They make a very attractive couple—on the outside at least.

They are sitting apart, silently inspecting different parts of the wall. Fidgeting uneasily with his trouser legs, the husband looks plainly like he'd rather be anywhere else but here.

His wife, by contrast, looks like she simply can't wait to get started.

Breaking the toxic silence, I greet the Cunninghams, introduce myself, and walk them into Fairway's meeting room. We sit.

As always, I take a few moments to feel the energy in the room. This is an approach I've used in business for many years, one that saves many wasted words with no real meaning or impact. Talk less, listen more, and not just with your ears but with your intuition. With a newly divorcing couple, the energy in the room is very tangible, and it speaks volumes.

Adam, I sense, is caustically angry, while Carolyn is trying hard (and generally succeeding) to appear confident and together.

Having worked with countless couples, my intuition is usually spot on with respect to where people are at emotionally. Almost invariably, one of the parties in a divorcing couple is far ahead of the other in coming to terms with the end of the marriage. One will be focused on moving forward and making transitions; the other will be stuck in the past, seething with resentments and wallowing in self-pity, unable to consider any transition.

I can tell right away: Adam's the one having a hard time coming to terms with the ending of the marriage.

KEY INSIGHTS

One thing that makes divorce difficult, apart from the millions of more obvious other things, is the need to find one outcome with two people whose perceptions and emotions are worlds apart.

However, I like couples to know that this is perfectly normal. It's important to just be where you are and not get distracted by where your soon-to-be ex is at.

That said, after the decision to divorce has been made, there's zero profit in dwelling on the past and what went wrong (the very thing the traditional system does so well). It is far more sensible to become future-focused, asking yourself "What can I do to create the future I want?" (Easier said than done, I know, but this book will give you tools to make it happen.)

To stay stuck in what was is to play the victim. What is and what will be are the only things you have any control over. Right now, choose to trust that a beautiful future is waiting for you. The journey ahead is filled with great lessons. If you embrace them openly and even with gratitude (as difficult as that may seem right now), your future will begin to unfold gracefully, free from anger, pain, and sorrow.

After a short exchange of pleasantries, I lead with my usual first question: "So, apart from the obvious, what brings you to mediation?"

Carolyn answers for both of them. "We've both talked to lawyers, but we're really reluctant to go down that road. We've seen a lot of friends spend a lot of money on lawyers, usually for outcomes that neither one of them was happy with."

"We'd like to work with a mediator who'll act in our best interests," adds Adam, "someone who's striving for a fair outcome instead of a fat paycheque. Carolyn got your name from a colleague who worked with you a few months back. Claire McQueen."

I nod knowingly. Several months ago, I brought Claire and her husband to a quick and mutually agreeable resolution of their divorce. The McQueens appeared satisfied with the outcomes of their divorce process, which took a little over three months.

Carolyn continues. "Claire said you've developed a different approach to divorce—a system that keeps lawyers and judges and courtrooms out of the negotiating process."

"That's correct," I say. "The entire negotiating process proceeds can work with or without lawyers. For most legal advice is desired but when and how that is obtained can set the stage for ongoing conflict or resolution." "We really just want to get this over and done with," says Carolyn. "And we don't want to hurt the kids or lose everything in the process."

In an effort to keep Adam Cunningham distracted from his anger and engaged in the process, I direct my next question to him.

"Why don't you tell me a little bit about your situation, Adam. Do you have any children?"

"Yes, three. Our eldest, Cameron, is 15. He'll be starting high school in September. We also have twin daughters, Sarah and Christina. They're 11. All three attend a private school."

Carolyn Cunningham interjects. "Our greatest concern in all this is the kids. You hear so many stories about children from broken homes—how it messes them up emotionally."

"Yes," I say, "divorce can be messy, and its impact on children can be profound—something I can certainly attest to. But children are stronger than we often give them credit for. Through the new approach I've developed, children learn to accept the inevitability of change and to move through it with their self-esteem intact, just like their parents do. "How are Cameron, Sarah, and Christina handling the situation so far?" I ask.

"We haven't told them about the divorce," Carolyn answers, "but they can probably sense that something's up, especially Cameron. He's been more distracted from his schoolwork than usual, and he's really been keeping to himself."

KEY INSIGHTS

Children are hyper-intuitive. Try as we might to hide the truth from them, they generally know exactly what's going on.

Your children will sense something's wrong and may ask you about it. To think you're protecting their emotional well-being by assuring them nothing's wrong is to stumble into a trap laid with irony. In an effort to avoid burdening children with the problems of their parents, we deny their own intuition, which is an even greater burden that becomes more difficult to shed the older they get.

It's little wonder so many adult children of divorce are out of touch with their intuition: their parents failed repeatedly to validate their children's suspicions, and they repeatedly denied their children's right to know what was going on.

Mind you, it's just as important not to tell children too much. Simply answer their questions honestly, letting them know that what they believe to be true really is true. But you don't need to "fill in the blanks."

To this point, the Cunninghams have been in perfect alignment. Both want to get quickly through their divorce; they want it to have the least possible impact on their children; and they don't want to lose their shirts in the process.

It's with my next question that this unanimity begins to unravel. "Can you tell me briefly why you're seeking a divorce?"

"Why don't you ask Carolyn?" Adam snaps quickly, his tone and his angry eyes laced with spite.

"Very well," says Carolyn. "I will." With an almost detached calmness, Carolyn tells me a story I've heard so many times before: "We just grew apart. Adam's work consumes so much of him, there's nothing left for me. I've been telling him for years—"

Adam cuts her off abruptly. "Let's get real, Carolyn. Tell Karen the real reason we're here—that you're having an affair with your tennis pro!"

"I wouldn't have had a goddamn affair if my husband wasn't addicted to his work," Carolyn retorts icily.

"Sorry if I was providing for our family and building for our future. Apparently that gave you the right to go screwing around with another guy."

In an effort to steer the conversation away from blaming and to assess each party's readiness to forge ahead with the INR process, I ask a crucial question.

"Whatever the reasons, do you both agree that your marriage is over?"

KEY INSIGHTS

Traditionally, the signing of the so-called "divorce papers" has signified the end of a marriage, so that the entire divorce process, whether it takes a few months or many years, is seen as a gradual winding down or, perhaps more aptly, a gradual falling to pieces.

From my perspective—a perspective that I believe is necessary if people wish to get through the process quickly and with a minimum of emotional pain—a marriage is over the moment they decide to divorce. Both parties in a divorcing couple need to become now- and future-focused.

The question seems to take both of them by surprise. They hesitate, look at each other, then look back at me. "Um, I don't think we have any other choice," says Adam. "Too much damage has been done.

"Which is really sad," he continues, "because we'd just gotten to a point in life where we have everything we've always wanted. I was devastated initially when I found out about the affair. It felt like someone was sliding a knife up and down my gut. I spent a lot of sleepless nights and prayed for Carolyn to wake up and stop this nonsense. I was willing to put the pieces back together considering all the good we once had and how much we had to lose. But Carolyn was not at that place. I think her decision to step outside our marriage was her final decision to leave. I get that now and while this causes great pain, I at least get it and I have had enough—I am tired and ready to get on with it."

How often have I heard this? A couple spends their lives working toward certain targets—a big house, a Mercedes-Benz, a summer cottage, and buckets of cash in the bank—and then *BOOM*, their marriage implodes. With no goals left to hold them together, their relationship falls quickly to pieces.

"I agree," says Carolyn, with considerably less composure than when she first came in, "it is sad. I understand that Adam was hurt about the affair but I had a lot of pain too and I am still angry so while he makes it like I was the bad guy that is not fair. I did what I did because I felt at my wit's end. So can we please just get on with it."

With genuine empathy, I continue. "Adam, Carolyn, I know this isn't pleasant. And I know that the door marked DIVORCE is a nasty portal to pass through. But having acknowledged that your divorce is a *fait accompli*, there are really only two matters that need your full attention: the money and the kids.

"With INR, we keep these two important matters completely separate. Nothing's worse than seeing children used as pawns in a couple's disputes over houses and cars. While no one ever intends for that to happen, the lack of structure within the traditional system makes it all but impossible to keep the two issues separate. The kids typically find themselves in the middle of a vicious tug-of-war.

KEY INSIGHTS

Emotions play havoc with the decision-making process, which is a key reason the traditional system of divorce (where negative emotions are allowed to run rampant and unchecked) is so profoundly ineffective. Decisions concerning money and children need to stand the test of time, yet emotion-driven decisions tend to be impulsive and shortsighted.

This does not mean you should deny or repress your emotions. Rather, manage your emotions outside of the decision-making process with the help of counselors, coaches, spiritual advisors, self-help books, or any other system of support that works for you.

"With respect to the money, then, what do you suppose needs to happen?"

"That's simple," says Adam, totally engaged now. "We need to decide who gets what."

"That's right," I say. "Everything you own—your home, your business, your vehicles, your jewelry—they're all pieces of the asset pie that needs to be divided. The real beauty of INR is that the asset pie is divided only between Adam and Carolyn Cunningham, fairly and equitably, without big fees. Let's face it: divorce costs and it hurts financially. But splitting up what the two of you had together takes enough of a financial toll. You certainly want to split your assets in half, not thirds or fourths."

Carolyn nods understandingly. So does Adam. Suddenly, they're back to agreeing.

I ask the Cunninghams for a run-down of their major assets, which Adam summarizes for me: "A large home, recently valued at $625,000. A summer cottage. Two vehicles. A time-share. A membership at the Hillside Club. Roughly half a million in retirement funds. My pension. And Carolyn's catering business."

"Which doesn't make a lot of money," Carolyn adds quickly, which is my first clue that she's likely going to undervalue her ability to make money or be territorial over the matter of her business.

"The hell it doesn't," Adam shoots back. "You netted nearly 100 grand last year, and you'd do a heck of a lot better if you put more hours into it."

I cut in quickly, knowing I've got as much information as I need for now. "Let's not worry about that right now. Let's talk instead about Independently Negotiated Resolution and how it deals with exactly the thing we've been seeing here today—emotions that are running high, and perceptions that are very, very different.

"If you're like most, your divorce will be one of the most difficult times of your life. Emotions can get the better of you: it's as if you can go from fear to anger to love to hate to sorrow to resentment in the course of a single conversation. That is not a place for making grounded, intelligent decisions, and yet you have to make them.

"In fact, there are few times when you'll be making more important decisions than those you need to make during your divorce. Each decision needs to be based on a comprehensive understanding of the 'now' and consider every implication for the future. For this to happen, you need to be in a place where you feel safe and somewhat secure and where you can make educated, empowered decisions. There is no room in this strategic process for firing accusatory affidavits back and forth, or threats of any nature, for that matter.

"Take me, for instance. I pride myself on being financially savvy and having lots of common sense. But barrage me with affidavits accusing me of everything under the sun and you create a four-year, $500,000 legal battle. And those were just my fees. Who knows how much my ex spent.

"INR ensures that what happened to me and so many others will not happen to you."

KEY INSIGHTS

Very rarely do two people start out saying, "We want a divorce. And in the process, we want to destroy everything we've worked for—our net worth, our home, our children, our businesses, each other, and any chance of co-parenting or even being civil toward one another ever again. Yes, that sounds empowering and a whole lot of fun. Sign us up!" Yet that is exactly what you sign up for when you hire a lawyer and start pouring emotionally charged perceptions into affidavits.

As a judge once said to me, once words are put into an affidavit and filed with the courts, there's no taking them back, and there's little hope of rebuilding the relationship, even for co-parenting. Not only is this sad, it's simply unnecessary, even if you think your spouse is totally in the wrong. You are both human and you both make human mistakes.

Both Adam and Carolyn nod. "We've heard lots of stories like that," says Carolyn. "So many of our divorced friends will no longer speak to one another and neither one started out thinking that would be the outcome."

I now begin to share with the Cunninghams the specifics of Independently Negotiated Resolution.

"With Independently Negotiated Resolution, you'll each work through much of the process independently of one another.."

Adam and Carolyn glance at one another and share a look I've seen many times before—a look of relief shot through with sadness.

I continue, "This helps eliminate bias and remove emotion from important decision making.

"INR promises four key outcomes, which are appropriately represented by the word SANE:

S = Save money

A = Accelerate time lines

N = Nurture the children

E = Eliminate emotional chaos and empower you

"With your permission, I'd like to conclude this meeting by telling you a bit about each of these four cornerstones. May I?"

"Absolutely," says Carolyn, and Adam nods his assent. "Very well," I say. "Let's begin with *S*."

S = SAVE MONEY

"As I expressed earlier, there's simply no way around the simple fact that divorce costs money. Whenever you split one household into two, there are significant costs. Whether you have hundreds, thousands, or millions, it still stings. But the process itself should not take an even larger bite out of your wealth. Holding tight to what you've worked so hard to acquire isn't being greedy. It's being sensible.

"You'll recall that in most divorces there are only two important issues: money and children. So you're probably wondering if there are so few issues to resolve, why has divorce traditionally been such a time-consuming, costly, and vicious ordeal?

"I'll tell you why: emotion.

"The emotions that arise when a husband and wife are in the throes of divorce make mountains of molehills and turn simple matters into impossible obstacles, especially when it comes to division of assets. Rarely, in divorce, does a dollar on one side equal a dollar on the other.

"To illustrate what I mean, consider a house. Given the ease of obtaining a realtor's appraisal, you'd think it would be pretty easy to settle on the value of a house. Yet of all the couples I've worked with—thousands of them—fewer than five percent have ever agreed on the value of their house. Here's why:

"Let's say the wife in a crumbling marriage decides she wants the house. 'I raised my children in this house,' she says. 'It's filled to the brim with happy memories. I simply won't give it up.'

"'Fine,' say her husband and his lawyer. 'It's worth $475,000. Now we want an equal allotment of assets in return.'

"'Actually,' say the wife and her lawyer by way of a letter several days later, 'you can have the house. We've decided we want the cottage and the retirement savings instead.'

"'Very well,' reply the husband and his lawyer, who had put a premium on the house because they knew how much the wife wanted it. 'But upon closer inspection, the house is clearly worth no more than $350,000. It needs a new roof, the kitchen has never been updated, and the neighbors are letting their property run down.' And so begins another round of fruitless bickering."

KEY INSIGHTS

The traditional system of divorce revolves around (and around and around) the process of "position bargaining." In this reactive, defensive posturing, the opposing parties take positions on the value of particular assets and then maneuver to ensure they get what they want. The process amounts to little more than asset grabbing, which looks a lot like children fighting for the same toy out on the playground.

The problem with position bargaining is easy to see: values that have no business being anything but fixed become totally fluid. It's remarkable how fast the value of an asset can change depending on whose side of the balance sheet it's sitting in!

In the end, position bargaining pays—but only if you're a lawyer. For the rest of us, it's a terrible drain of money and time. The arguments that ensue over the value of each asset devour fees faster than a Minotaur devours sacrificial virgins. What's worse, position bargaining typically prevents participants from seeing other, often better solutions that could, over the long term, put more money in their pockets.

"The solution is to apply a system that ensures issues are addressed and assets are divided in a practical, irrefutable, mutually agreeable way.

"Because Independently Negotiated Resolution follows a pragmatic, step-by-step approach to resolution, it is possible to charge a reasonable flat fee that keeps most of your money in your own pockets. That's a stark contrast to the traditional system, whose lawyers will tell you there are no guarantees and no way to know how much your divorce will cost or how long it will take."

KEY ACTIONS

Whatever service or expertise you use, insist on either a flat fee or a reasonable prediction of cost. Determine at the outset what the deliverables will be and who is accountable for what. Do not leave your future in the hands of anyone who is not attached to the outcome.

"There is one best outcome for both of you. Using Independently Negotiated Resolution, we'll get you to that fair, win-win outcome.

I remind them that with Independently Negotiated Resolution, each member of a divorcing couple works through much of the process independently of his or her partner.

At this point, Adam Cunningham chimes in. "What you're saying about asset division and position bargaining makes sense, but I'm not clear why we have to be separated through much of the negotiating process. Wouldn't things proceed more quickly if we came together for the negotiations, like in mediation?"

"INR *is* mediation," I tell him. "It's a specialized system that offers all the benefits of traditional mediation, yet it has more structure and process. It's more 'holistic', and it often proves more effective for dealing with matters of the heart.

"Think of all the things that cause marriages to break down. Communication problems. Power struggles. A growing tendency to push one another's buttons.

"Now bring that together in a room with a mediator who may know next to nothing about the couple's financial details or parenting plans. How likely are they to arrive at a quick and equitable resolution?

"Ever since I started negotiating divorces, and for 15 years before that as a family financial advisor, I have clearly seen that married couples—even happily married ones—rarely see eye to eye on matters, and one party almost always has more power in a given area than the other. When they're divorcing, these imbalances of power get magnified many times over. It becomes a game of control, manipulation, and mistrust.

"How, then, can you expect two people who are getting a divorce, who are pushing each other's buttons, who don't share an equal understanding of the numbers, and who no longer trust one another to reasonably address major issues and settle on outcomes that serve the best interests of both? Except in rare situations, it simply doesn't work.

"Independently Negotiated Resolution overcomes all the problems that make mediation so impractical. A single negotiator takes each party through the process, and they arrive at a consensus independently of each other. Although both parties come to one final outcome, the paths they take to get there will be entirely different. Think of two roads that lead to the same destination. One may be a straight highway with one or two rest stops along the way, the other a winding gravel road with hairpin turns that need to be taken nice and slow. Though each journey is very different, they both lead the travelers to the same destination—a happy and comfortable outcome."

KEY INSIGHTS

An effective divorce process makes allowances for individual differ-ences, and it recognizes that in the journey toward divorce, each person follows a different path.

With Independently Negotiated Resolution, you can follow the path that suits you best, confident that a trusted negotiator will be with you along the way to ensure you never stop making forward progress toward your destination.

And when you get there, you'll rest easy in knowing you chose the desti-nation and did not have it imposed upon you by a busy family-court judge.

A = ACCELERATE TIMELINES

"Some experts in the field of psychology suggest that divorce is more difficult than dealing with a spouse's death because it comes with so many endings and beginnings and with so much turmoil that it seems to go on and on forever.

"This is the reason for INR's way of thinking," I explain to the Cunninghams.

KEY INSIGHTS

Move through your divorce as quickly as you can. Make smart, well-informed decisions and plan for your future without delay. Do not procras-tinate, and avoid the temptation to hold out for better deals. Remember, "A bird in the hand. ..."

And again, keep emotions out of the decision-making process. If you find that emotions are infringing on your ability to stay focused, seek outside help.

Do whatever you can to get things and keep things moving forward. Work only with a team ready to tell you what you need to hear (not necessarily what you want to hear) and willing to commit to a time line and a process.

"Hold on," says Adam. "Isn't there any truth in the old adage, 'Haste makes waste'?"

"In other matters, yes," I tell him. "But you can't apply everyday logic to matters of divorce. As the traditional system so deftly proves, the longer you spend in the process, the greater the waste.

"I've seen it over and over again: if people aren't focused on resolution—if they're not being taken step by step through a process that addresses key issues in a timely fashion—they'll stray into anger, resentment, and financial stress. Even if you manage to stay focused, your divorce is going to preoccupy your mind and drain your energy until all is said and done. It's going to interfere with your career, your relationships, your health, everything. It really is best to resolve the issues quickly.

"I like to see all key decisions made within a few months. It may take longer if there's a need for business valuations and the like, but in any case, it's best to get things done before the process gets derailed. And trust me, there are plenty of things that try to sneak in and derail the process—new relationships, financial hardships, fear, procrastination.

"That said, you do need to make sure all the important questions are posed and answered. We need not only to take a snapshot of the present and determine how to handle the money and the kids, but we need to plan for your future. 'Failing to plan is a plan to fail.'

"You're going to become single parents, and you'll both be managing a newly altered family on your own. Carolyn, you probably have fear about money and are wondering if you can make it on your own. Adam, you're likely wondering if you'll have to work until you drop to support everyone. You're wondering if you'll be 'taken to the cleaners' and Carolyn, you're wondering if you'll even be able to afford the cleaners."

I can see by their faces that I've hit the nail on the head. "I'm not psychic," I tell them. "I've just worked with so many couples, and while the details are always different, the issues tend to be very similar."

I remind them that many have walked this path before them. "You are not alone."

KEY INSIGHTS

Even while moving quickly through your divorce, it's crucial that you ask and find answers to all the relevant questions. Above all, you want to make sure that five or 10 years after your divorce, you won't find yourself saying, "If only I had known ..." or "If only I'd asked. ..."

Independently Negotiated Resolution makes sure all the necessary questions are asked so your plan can encompass all the answers and you can move through your divorce empowered in your own way.

"My divorce took over four years. Time destroyed assets, opportunities, relationships, feelings of self-worth. Ironically, in the end, the deal we ended up with was almost identical to a deal my ex and I agreed to in principle before we retained legal counsel. The only real difference was that we had far more assets the first time round. By the end of it all, a lot of what we owned had either been destroyed by the journey or found its way into our lawyers' pockets."

N = NURTURE THE CHILDREN

"We certainly don't want to lose everything we've worked so hard to build," says Carolyn Cunningham. "But even more than that, we want our children to get through our divorce emotionally intact."

"Then there's only one thing you need to do," I assure her. "Be the best parent you can be and your children will thrive. If you both choose right now to move through this divorce with honesty and integrity, your children will be fine. In fact, they may even be better for the experience.

"The fact that many troubled children come from divorced families prompts a lot of people to jump to conclusions. The divorce may not have been the problem at all. The dysfunctional family life that led to the divorce may be the reason for emotional or behavioral issues.

"It's time for society to stop stigmatizing divorce and accept that it's a fact of life. As long as people wag a shaming finger at couples who divorce, the children of those divorces will assume a share of that shame.

"I don't see divorce as a bad thing, so I don't treat my children or any children of divorce as if they are less fortunate or somehow missing something. I simply don't buy into that way of thinking. That's why one of my life's missions is to ensure that either we get rid of the word 'divorce' or we alter the connotations that go along with it.

"Children who find themselves in the path of their parents' divorce should not have to feel fear or shame, and they certainly shouldn't be treated like victims. Just as we need to empower ourselves to accept change as normal and healthy and frequently necessary, we need to empower children to do the same.

"Your new family will need a plan. I'm a huge advocate of well-articulated plans, and we will take you through the steps to create one. You may stray from it at times, but it will remain in place for the times when you really need it."

E = ELIMINATE EMOTIONAL CHAOS

"I admitted earlier that I'm not psychic, but assume for just a moment that I have a crystal ball and can look into your futures.

"If I told you your futures were full of joy, that you and your children were thriving and you had no financial worries, would you feel less stress over your divorce?"

"Of course," says Carolyn, and Adam echoes her answer.

"Then that is the future you need to envision because our thoughts and expectations help create our outcomes. You've probably heard about *The Secret?* This is exactly the same idea. Whatever we focus on—good or bad—is typically what we create.

"You're both scared. That's normal. But fear is merely the negative anticipation of something in the future that may or may not happen. If you can become now- and positive future-oriented, you can substantially reduce your stress and all the emotional chaos that comes with it. In this regard, nothing beats a well laid-out plan of where you are going and how you're going to get there.

"The past is in the past, and it needs to stay there. Debate the future, not the past. Starting right now, you are going to lay a positive foundation for the future, and the best way to do that is to follow a system that empowers you, shapes positive outcomes in your mind's eye, and moves you strategically through all the important decisions to make them come true."

KEY ACTIONS

Another key to managing stress and keeping negative emotions in check is to address any short-term issues that threaten to take you away from your future focus. If you need money in the short term, arrange a loan or borrow from a friend. Better yet, set up a plan with your spouse for dealing with parenting and money issues in the short term. This will ensure you don't get sidetracked by short-term stresses while focusing on long-term planning.

"The traditional system of divorce, with its 'may the most ruthless bully win' mentality, is all about exerting power to create stress. Few things are as emotionally upsetting as arriving home at the end of the day to find a demand to appear in court, a notice that deprives you of half your income, or an affidavit asserting you're addicted to Internet porn. Unless you are void of emotion, how can you possibly make good decisions in the face of these kinds of antics?

"INR promises to reduce stress and emotional upheaval by keeping you on task, committed to getting consensus, and focused on crafting prudent short- and long-term plans."

KEY INSIGHTS

Divorce is about an ending, but it's also about new beginnings. It's about two souls whose journey together as husband and wife has come to an end. Believe that you were brought together for a reason, maybe to have children, maybe to experience a certain kind of love or a certain kind of pain. Even if the reason seems unclear, trust that there was one. And trust, too, that a new journey awaits.

Every relationship offers opportunities to learn and to grow. If you are not emotionally ready to let go, try to remember that there are new beginnings, challenges, and opportunities to grow and learn awaiting you once you find closure.

KEY ACTIONS

Your children are on this path too, and for them you are encoding in their minds and their souls not only what relationships look like when you are in them, but how they look when it's time to move on. Show them that endings are okay and as much a part of life as beginnings. Show them how to leave a relationship with grace and integrity and be better for it. Show them how to treat others you once loved. Let's start laying new foundations for our children together.

"This is a difficult time for both of you," I say to the Cunninghams by way of wrapping things up, "but there's light at the end of the tunnel. If you stick with the process, I promise you'll be there before you know it.

"It's only fair to warn you, though: the road to resolution is rarely free of conflict, frustration, and anger. At the outset, you'll probably like your advisor and the INR process, but a time will possibly come when you begin to curse everyone and everything in your path. If you persist, though—if you push through the pain and stay focused on your goals—when you reach the end of the process, you'll feel empowered, you'll know you were treated fairly, and you'll probably find some new inner peace."

I escort the Cunninghams back to the front reception. I can sense the relief they both feel as they leave knowing there is a way to move through their divorce quickly and cost-effectively and with their integrity intact. They are definitely on the right path to resolution with respect to their money and their children, and I know the Cunninghams will come out of this process with a fair plan that will stand the test of time and allow them to co-parent with mutual respect. I know, too, the new family will thrive if only Adam and Carolyn can stay focused and avoid the pitfalls that lurk in the emotional shadows.

Chapter 8

ADAM'S EMOTIONAL PROCRASTINATION

With Independently Negotiated Resolution, the real key to success resides within the "Independently" part.

After my initial meeting with a divorcing couple—a meeting they attend together—they proceed through most of the remainder of the process independently, all the while working with a single unbiased negotiator.

This approach eliminates damaging and unproductive insults, sarcasm, and emotional outbursts of the type the Cunninghams exhibited in the preceding chapter.

In my first one-on-one meeting with each party, I take them through an exercise called the "painted picture conversation," a highly practical, highly focused, and profoundly important activity geared toward getting each person focused on his or her future.

The day after my meeting with Adam and Carolyn Cunningham together, I see them separately at my office. When Adam arrives, it's immediately clear that he's still stinging over the turn his life has taken. Beneath the furl of his brow, I can see the pain and dejection in his eyes. A look of utter defeat.

I begin softly. "It won't feel like this forever, Adam. You may not believe me—I probably wouldn't have believed it myself when it was happening to me—but this too shall pass.

"Something else you may not believe is that you can take control of how quickly it passes.

"Whether you want the divorce or not, it is what it is. The best thing you can do is let go of the past and become present- and future-focused."

KEY ACTIONS

If ever you feel you simply can't deal with reality, tell yourself you can, otherwise your path would not have led you to this point. Trust in the old saying, "We are never handed anything we cannot handle."

When the urge comes upon us to curse the cards we've been dealt, it may also help to remember that most of the cards in our hand are ones we ourselves have chosen. At some level, we create all of our own outcomes.

If you can train yourself to stop equating divorce with failure, you can apply the brakes to what will otherwise become an out-of-control emotional roller coaster. Accepting change and moving gracefully through it is so much healthier than beating yourself up, which will make you crazy.

To help ensure you stay the course, seek and accept help. Surround yourself with friends and family you can trust. Align yourself with good professionals.

And read. There is so much to learn from others.

"The best way to let go of the past, Adam, is to paint a picture for the future, a positive picture that fills you with hope."

"I don't feel very full of hope," says Adam, his eyes glassy with barely restrained tears. "My life before seemed almost perfect. I know I worked too hard, but I did it for our family. And for what? Carolyn dumps me for the tennis pro. What kind of payback is that?"

"I know it feels like a raw deal, Adam. But regardless of how you ended up here, INR will empower you to find and embrace a new beginning—as hard as that may seem right now.

"It's important that you address your emotional journey and get support, but it's even more important that you don't let your emotions play havoc with your ability to make sound decisions. INR must be grounded in prudent, forward-thinking decision making.

"Have you given much thought to what your future will look like?"

"The future? I hardly know what's going to happen five minutes from now. The rest is nothing but a blur."

"Don't worry. At this stage, some people have really clear pictures of their ideal futures, while others have difficulty imagining what might lie head. They're still trying to figure out how to get up in the morning."

"That's me, all right," says Adam, managing a faint smile. "I honestly feel like I have no future—like Carolyn took it from me, and from our kids too. I still don't understand why I'm here and why I'm getting divorced, but clearly I have no choice."

"That's true. Carolyn is entitled to a divorce if she wants one. So it really becomes your journey now, Adam, and we need to start formulating what that might look like.

"Of course, at this early stage of the process, it is only an imaginary picture—a wish list if you will. I call it your 'painted picture,' and it can be as specific or as vague as you like. After today's session, you'll take the painted picture home with you and continue to add to and refine it."

KEY ACTIONS

Create your own painted picture, your wish list for the future. It is absolutely crucial that you become future-focused—the past is in the past and needs to be left there.

Your painted picture can be a list or a story or a collage depicting what you want your future to look like. While this may seem flaky, it is arguably the most important of all the how-to instructions in this book as the exercise is crucial to creating an empowered outcome.

In words, pictures, or both, paint a detailed vision for your future as if you were in it right now. If you need to explore your emotions along the way, use supportive, empowering words.

Here's an example of a positive painted picture: "Although being single again isn't where I wanted to be at my age, I know I'll be okay and trust that I'll come through this a better person. Yes, there will be pain along the way, but eventually I'll move beyond the pain and find joy in my new beginnings."

Compare those empowering words to these disempowering sentiments: "I hate my ex. I can't believe he did this to me. My life is ruined. Single at my age? I'm going to die lonely. And broke!"

Avoid this kind of negative thinking at all costs. Even if it seems hard to believe right now, you do get to choose your outcome. Positive or negative, the future you envision is the future you will get.

Adam closes his eyes for a moment. When he opens them, I can see a glimmer of feistiness that wasn't there before.

"Okay," he says. "For starters, I want the cottage. *My* cottage. My parents gave it to me, and it's for me and my kids. There's no way she and her goddamn boy-toy are going to get it. No way in hell."

"Adam, I know you're upset—"

"Not upset. Enraged."

"Okay, enraged. And I understand that this is difficult. But the best thing you can do is stop yourself from playing the victim. I know as well as anyone how it feels to be dumped. But you will get through this, and if you stay focused on a bright future, the future will be bright. I promise. Moving on starts with visualizing life without Carolyn as your wife."

"Let's get back now to what you would like."

"Fine. My pension. It's mine and she can't have that. Oh—and I want her to move out. Right now.

"You know, I really just wish she'd been honest with me. It's bad enough she had the affair in the first place, but then she kept denying it. I knew something was wrong, but I just couldn't put my finger on it."

KEY INSIGHTS

Acceptance opens up opportunities to grow and become a better person, and truth turns crisis and chaos into a place where transition can begin. Consider this simple scenario:

With heartfelt sadness, Jack tells Jill his feelings have changed and he is feeling open to another's love. He realizes he must move on, but first, he must end his marriage to Jill.

For Jack and Jill both, the situation is rife with sadness and pain. At the moment of Jack's revelation, that is their reality. But except in rare cases, no reality is too overwhelming for a person to endure. Our humanness makes us resilient.

Yes, Jill is sad. She is shocked by the news, and her most likely reaction will be to cry and obsess and pass the days that follow in a tumult of emotion. But because Jack has been authentic in his disclosure and Jill now knows the truth—something she can come to terms with and act upon—she will be able to transition much more quickly into recovering her self-worth, reasserting her sexuality, and so on. Like all transitions through divorce, Jack and Jill's split-up will have ups and downs and tears and tribulations, but there will be movement to new beginnings in a way that is empowering and not destructive to self-esteem and to the entire family unit.

Consider how often the real story comes out long after the fact. ("Oh, and that new fellow she's been seeing, turns out there was something going on even before she and her husband separated!") How destructive and disrespectful to someone she used to love and who is, perhaps, the father of her children!

In my heart of hearts, I know the greatest gift someone can give his or her spouse is the truth. Yes, the truth about an affair is painful, but at least it allows you to start moving forward. Alternatively, if your intuition is continually stifled by denials and protestations, you can become mired in chaos.

Gloria Steinem said it best: "The truth will set you free. But first, it will piss you off."

This isn't to say we must deny our emotional pain. Allowing yourself to experience the sting of your divorce is an important part of coming to terms with your new reality. In *Rebuilding: When Your Relationship Ends*, Dr. Bruce Fisher delineates the stages people move through following the breakup of a marriage. According to Fisher, the "re-building blocks" of divorce recovery include grief, anger, self-worth, transition, love, sexuality, and more.

As a veteran of divorce and now working with so many couples, I can see, looking back, that I followed these stages to a tee. I only wish I'd lost much less time in grief and anger and segued more quickly and gracefully into self-worth, transition, and all the rest.

I didn't, but you can because the pace and the grace with which you move through divorce are entirely up to you.

Pain, emotional discomfort, sorrow, regret, anger—these are all facts of life—but so too are joy, hope and happiness. To be happy, we need to embrace the full spectrum of our feelings. Just as we cannot appreciate day without night or warmth without cold, we would not recognize happiness without grief or serenity without chaos. As Robert Gary Lee remarks, "Wisdom is nothing more than healed pain."

When we learn to accept the hardships in our life, we can move from a place of grudging cynicism and negativity to one of gratitude. Melody Beattie writes: "Gratitude unlocks the fullness of life. It turns what we have into enough, and more. It turns denial into acceptance, chaos to order, confusion to clarity. It can turn a meal into a feast, a house into a home, a stranger into a friend. Gratitude makes sense of our past, brings peace for today, and creates a vision for tomorrow."

Sometimes, though, getting there may take a while. During those times that you feel your life is flooded with chaos and crisis, allow yourself to "just be"—to sit with the pain without fighting it or feeling you need immediately to conquer it.

Just be. Allow yourself to grieve, to be angry, to scream, to cry—whatever it takes. You'll arrive at your new beginning not through avoidance but by transitioning over the terrain, however bumpy the going may get.

At all times, remember this: divorce is a transition, not a tragedy. Divorce does not define you, and it's certainly not an unforgivable sin. Dr. Joyce Brothers offers some illuminating reassurance: "For some reason, we see divorce as a signal of failure despite the fact that each of us has a right and an obligation to rectify any other mistake we make in life." Marriage is not a mistake. At some point it was the right decision or you would not have made it. That said, when marriage is no longer right for you, moving forward with a divorce is not a bad thing. In fact, it's just the opposite, especially if you're being authentic to yourself and those around you.

On a roll now, Adam continues: "I want to value her business so she can pay me out. Her business can be a real moneymaker, so no more gravy train. She's got the tennis pro. He can support her."

Sensing that Adam is slipping back into "poor me" mode, I change the subject to something I hope will be more positive. "What about the kids?" I ask.

"Oh, yeah, the kids. I want a 50/50 custody split, and on that I'm non-negotiable. She may think she can just dump me and get the kids and all my money, but she's wrong. The kids are going to live with me too."

"Fair enough. But what about the kids' emotional well-being while you and Carolyn work though your divorce?"

"Well, even though I'm angry with their mother, I certainly don't want the kids to suffer."

"With respect to your children, what do you think a positive outcome might look like?"

"Well, I guess Carolyn and I should try to get along. I'm really angry with her and wish she would just go away, but I know deep down that's not the best thing for the kids."

As he reflects on his future with his kids, Adam softens, even in his anger toward Carolyn. "I really would like to get over all these terrible feelings—this venomous anger. I guess I have to if I'm going to be able to co-parent with her.

"And while I feel sometimes like she deserves nothing, I'm intelligent enough to know that she'll get half. But I definitely want the cottage."

I can't help but notice that Adam is all over the map when it comes to his vision for the future. "Is there anything else?" I ask him.

"Yes, there is." He hesitates a moment as if fearful of articulating his thought. At last, though, he continues. "Lately, I've lost my ambition at work. There just seems no reason to bust my buns anymore. I'm thinking I'd like to cut back a bit, maybe even change jobs.

"I'd also like the kids to continue in their after-school activities." His eyes narrow and he stares upward, the look of a man deep in thought. After a few moments he shakes his head and continues. "Sorry, that's all I can think of for now."

"That's okay," I say, "but I want you to continue working on your painted picture at home. Keep it in your mind's eye, and keep adding details to your vision for the future.

"For example, what does your new bachelor pad look like? Who are you hanging out with? How much cash is in your bank account? What are you driving? What does your relationship with your kids look and feel like? How often are they around? What are you doing together?

"With every imaginable aspect of your future life, try to get really clear. The more future-focused you become, the closer you'll eventually come to creating the desired outcomes.

"I know, Adam, that you're struggling with a lot of emotions right now. Sometimes you may not know whether you're coming or going. But if you stick with INR, you'll get through your divorce with a practical plan for moving forward.

"Yes, there will be some bumpy roads along the way. Not even INR can change that, but there is a light at the end of the tunnel, even if you can't see it yet."

"I'm really just afraid of getting taken to the cleaners. I don't want to be pushed into any decision that doesn't sit well," Adam admits.

"Listening to your intuition is important, Adam, in INR and in everything else life throws your way. You really need to trust your gut."

KEY ACTIONS

Your intuition is always bang on, but to make sure it's there when you need it, you need constantly to hone your ability to tune in and trust it.

Like a healthy heart, healthy intuition benefits from exercise. When you let your heart idle too long, the arteries start to clog and the blood flow is compromised. Similarly, the flow of intuitive wisdom can get cut off if you let things get out of shape.

Here are a few exercises for tuning up your intuition:

As you go to sleep at night, ask yourself the question that's weighing heavily on your mind, and ask to be given the answer as you slumber. In the morning, you will see the answer beginning to unfold, even if you don't yet have complete clarity.

Another trick: make a decision one way or the other, and then sit with that decision for a few days. If it's the wrong decision, there will be signs—you just need to be receptive to them.

Deepak Chopra's *Synchronicity* is a great resource for helping you hone your intuition and open your eyes.

Once you tap into the innate gift of intuition, you will always know if you've made the right decision. Your gut will let you know. The right decision will just feel right.

Suddenly, Adam looks at me with a renewed seriousness. "You know, Karen, some of my friends say I should start to hide things—maybe move some stuff around so Carolyn can't get her hands on it."

"Yes, Adam, you could do that. A lot of divorcing people do. But INR has checks and balances built in, and the contract you sign at the end insists upon full disclosure. If concealing assets is something you're seriously considering, you're really just wasting your time here. At the end, the contract won't be worth the paper it's printed on if you've lied. But since I know you really want to avoid the War of the Roses. ..."

"Yeah, yeah, I know. I was just asking. Of course I want to be fair, and I know any misdealings catch up with you in the end. They always do. Just ask Carolyn," he adds with a wry smile.

Then he continues. "Carolyn was with me for a long time, and while I think I deserve more than her, I get it that she stayed with the kids so I could build my career. We've both made sacrifices."

I smile and nod, glad to see that Adam is finally coming around.

"I hate this feeling that my life is suddenly spinning out of control. I find I'm reacting to everyone and everything like I never did before."

"That's perfectly normal," I assure him. "This is a difficult time no matter how you slice it. But you can move through it, especially if you keep tackling the issues proactively. You're most definitely on the right track."

KEY ACTIONS

Being proactive during your divorce will minimize the emotional fallout and financial repercussions.

The best time to alter the pattern of reactivity is in the split-second before you react. Imagine: in one hand, with your arm outstretched, you hold a priceless crystal vase. With the other hand, you must catch it before it shatters to pieces on the tile floor below. What's the best tactic? To snatch it the moment you release it, or to try and catch it just before it hits the floor?

Neither, actually. Your best bet, of course, is to not let go of it in the first place. But if you do let it go, your best option is to catch it right away before it crashes on the floor.

So how does one hold tight to one's reactions? The first step is to recognize when you're in reactive mode. Then practice, practice, practice. Many methods can help stop you in your tracks.

One is a variation on the tried and true "count to 10" technique: take deep breaths, counting to six on each inhalation and on each exhalation. Do this six times to slow yourself down and give yourself time to think through your impulses.

Another tactic is to remove yourself from the situation (or if that's not possible, to close your eyes) and do some very positive self-talk: "I am strong—it's going to take more than this to get me riled—I'm not going to let this person (or situation) master my emotions. Everything is going to be okay."

Reactivity prevails when we feel threatened and we're full of fear. If you can put some positive thoughts into your head in moments of fear, you can often stifle the fear and circumvent a fear-based reaction.

I've heard many people's divorce stories, and they all confirm the conclusion I drew from my own experience: under the oppressive stresses of divorce, it is difficult to be the best you can be. Try as you might to rise above the negative emotions and not let them get the better of you, you will likely slip. Often.

That's normal. And it's okay. There's no such thing as a perfect parent, a perfect employee, a perfect person. Under stress, we all falter. To get through the tough times with your self-esteem intact, two things are crucial. Don't beat yourself up. And don't give up. When you find yourself raising your voice at your kids or snapping at your coworkers or thinking about doing things that will cause nothing but chaos (concealing assets from your spouse is a good example!), embrace the opportunity to tune in to the feelings that attend reactivity. See how it creates chaos (in contrast to self-disciplined proactivity, which restores order). Observe how profoundly your (re)actions impact others. And from that feeling of discomfort and pain, seek the strength to pull yourself back to a positive, proactive place.

When you switch modalities from reactive to proactive—in other words, when you clearly think through the consequences of your actions and make intelligent, forward-looking decisions—you can dwell in a place of peace. Proactive decisions and actions bring serenity, resolution, and light into your life.

Being proactive means being in tune with your intuition and letting it be your guide. And when your decisions and actions come from a place of proactive insight, everyone in your life will benefit.

Those around you will not suffer the consequences of your negative reactions. Proactivity's ripple effect is empowerment.

A proactive approach to divorce (yes, there is such a thing) doesn't sugarcoat reality. You accept that the journey will present countless, often unforeseeable trials and tribulations, but you're ready to receive life's lessons to empower your decision making and ensure that when you come out on the other side, your life will amount to more than just ashes and dust.

In any iteration, divorce is difficult and painful. But it need not be chaotic. Proactive divorce offers the promise of hope for a positive future full of hope and personal empowerment.

Chapter 9

CAROLYN'S "PAINTED PICTURE"

Carolyn arrives at my office a couple hours after Adam's appointment ends. (I always stagger appointments to avoid accidental meetings in the lobby or on the street out front.)

As with Adam, I introduce Carolyn to the concept of the painted picture conversation and explain how fundamental it is to the rest of the Independently Negotiated Resolution Process.

"Have you had a chance to think about what the future might look like for you and the kids?" I ask her.

"I certainly have," she beams. "In fact, I've written it all down. I'm very clear on what I want."

I smile, impressed by her focus and enthusiasm and rather awed (though hardly surprised) by the differing attitudes of Carolyn and Adam.

"That's great," I say. "Some people are very clear about their futures, while others have given it scarcely a thought. Please tell me about your thoughts and your wishes."

She pulls some paper-clipped sheets out of her handbag and places them on her lap. Then she looks at me seriously.

"Before we start, Karen, I want to set the record straight about a few matters—things I couldn't really discuss last time when Adam was here."

"Okay," I say. "Shoot."

"Frankly, life with Adam was hell. He was verbally abusive and emotionally bankrupt. He can pretend all he wants that we had a good marriage, but it was awful. Just awful. It's been at least six months since we last had sex, and for years before that, I was lucky if it was once a month.

"I really had to bite my tongue the first time we met. I just need you to know I'm not the villain here."

I listen patiently while Carolyn lambastes her ex, knowing it's a necessary part of almost every client's emotional process. It's important to divorcing individuals to tell their version of events. I don't let it go on too long, but I let it go on long enough that each person feels that he or she has been heard.

Carolyn continues. "Yes, I stepped out of the marriage, but who wouldn't have? All I wanted was a little of Adam's time and affection, but I got none of it, so what right does he have to be mad that I went and found it elsewhere? When a younger, more attractive man started paying attention to me, what else was I supposed to do? If only Adam had given me a little more attention, we probably wouldn't be here."

"Those doggone *If onlys*," I reply. "They can really trip us up and keep us dwelling on the past. Why don't we shift the focus now and start talking about your future? Tell me what you see for yourself in the coming years."

"Well, I definitely plan to continue with my business. It's so re-warding in so many ways. That said, it's really just a hobby, so I'm going to need lots of alimony and child support."

"It's actually called spousal support now," I inform her. "But it's the same thing."

"I also want to share the cottage. I know he thinks it's his, but I've put a lot of time and effort into it. Money too. We used money from my business to renovate the entire thing—almost $75,000. If it weren't for me, that beautiful cottage would be a broken-down shack.

"And I want my house. I am *not* moving. But Adam better be. I really need him out of the house. He's not giving me any space. He just seems to hang around all the time. One minute he says that he wants to get it over with and the next he's groveling for a reconciliation."

As is the case with many of the clients I've worked with, the Cunninghams have some real issues regarding boundaries. One of my first steps is to help divorcing couples establish boundaries by laying down some ground rules.

KEY INSIGHTS

Knowing exactly where you end and others begin—and then honoring those boundaries—is essential for a positive transition through your divorce.

Tripping into divorce without clear, firm boundaries is like starting a business without a business plan: failure and financial ruin are just a matter of time. Clear boundaries give you a reference point, something to focus on and swim toward when the waters get turbulent, and something to cling to when the swirling undercurrent of emotional chaos threatens to pull you under and sweep you away to oblivion.

In short, clear and healthy boundaries allow you to deal with otherwise overwhelming situations, trusting always that intuition will be your guide. Recognizing your own role and accepting the limitations of your influence can foster a peaceful transition through divorce.

"What about your tennis pro?" I ask. The question catches Carolyn off guard.

"Timmy? What about him?"

"Is he a part of your painted picture?" I ask the question without any hint of judgment.

"Oh, no," Carolyn laughs. "We still get together, but the kids know nothing about him, and I'm certainly planning to keep it that way."

"Tell me about the kids then. How do they fit into your painted picture?"

"I know Adam is demanding a 50-percent share of the kids, but I'm not comfortable with that. They're used to having me around, and Adam doesn't really have the time anyway. I mean, he travels all the time. I think the kids sometimes go weeks without seeing him. He acts like it'll be such a big loss for him, but he's honestly never around."

"So you envision that you'll have the kids most the time?" "Definitely. And as far as the kids' daily routines go, well, I don't

see why anything needs to change. They have expensive lives, what with private school tuitions and so many after-school activities, but Adam can afford to keep paying for those."

"You and Adam have differing views about the children, but that's something we'll work out later on. For now, you needn't worry about the matter. I promise we'll negotiate a resolution that works for both of you.

"The good news, though, is that you and Adam are both looking for many of the same things. If I recall correctly from our first meeting together, you want to remain civil to each other, and you want a co-parenting relationship that works for everyone and puts the kids first.

"You want to minimize financial loss and move through the process as quickly as possible.

"You both want to feel you were treated fairly through the process, and you want a sense of security moving forward.

"Although you may have different ideas about how certain goals might be achieved, your visions for the future are similar at a high level. Indeed, this is the case for most couples we work with.

"How we help fulfill these visions for both of you is what makes INR so extraordinary.

"You have both started to become future-focused. While the ups and downs of the emotional journey will likely cause you to fall back into old habits occasionally, you are now on a path that will get you through your divorce as quickly and painlessly as possible."

KEY ACTIONS

Whomever you choose to work with, it's crucial that the lead negotiator/mediator has a balance between negotiation skills, intuition, empathy, and wisdom.

I now know that good people make bad decisions. While a small percentage of our population are bent on destruction, most people are just trying to find their way in life and be happy.

Listening to the Cunninghams, I could easily have gotten caught up in the surface issues—the affair, the abuse, the neglect. I could have pegged them good guy/bad guy (the very thing lawyers do when they hear only one side of the story), but I know better. In almost all divorces, I hear words like "abuse," "addiction," "cheater," "liar," "lazy," "workaholic." But good people usually lurk behind these bad labels, so I read between the lines and find common ground on which to ultimately achieve a win-win resolution.

Ensure that whomever you use as lead mediator has the wisdom to do the same. Your friends can agree with you on what a jerk or a bitch your ex is, but the person or people you're entrusting to get you through the process need to be unbiased and nonjudgmental.

I end my session with Carolyn as I did with Adam, instructing her to continue fleshing out the details of her painted picture.

After she leaves, I pop into the staff kitchen to discuss the Cunninghams with Lori, another mediator.

Lori too went through a nasty divorce and, like me, wants to ensure that what happened to her doesn't happen to anyone else. She and her husband now get along well, but it took many years after the animosity that was created during their legal battle.

I say to Lori, "It's so great that couples like the Cunninghams get to avoid the legal battle you and I had to go through. They'll simply never know how bad it could have been."

PART 2

SAVE YOUR ASS(ETS)

Divorce is divisive, and in its traditional form, it is a terrific destroyer of wealth. According to a study by Jay Zagorsky, a research scientist at Ohio State University's Center for Human Resource Research, traditional divorce diminishes a person's wealth by an average of 77 percent.

Seventy-seven percent. That's more than three-quarters of your wealth—your retirement savings, the equity in your home, your cash, your household assets, the value of the business you've worked so hard to build—gone, divided in some fashion, swallowed up in lawyers' fees and all the other outrageous costs that lay in wait if you choose the traditional legal system.

In this section, I vividly illustrate the potentially astronomical costs of divorce by sharing another segment from my own story. I then share my learnings from that very costly journey (remember: the wise person learns from the fool's mistakes!) and demonstrate, through my story of the Cunninghams, how you can end your marriage while still preserving the vast majority of your hard-earned assets.

KAREN'S STORY

If, in the early days of my journey through divorce, someone had suggested that I'd end up retaining over five lawyers and incurring well over
$500,000 in divorce-related costs before all was said and done, I fully
expect I would have laughed in their face.

Unfortunately, they would have had the last laugh, because that's
exactly what happened!

Like so many divorcing couples, my ex-husband and I began with a
plan to end things quickly—to determine amongst ourselves who'd get
what and minimize the need for legal wrangling and wrestling. But you
know what they say about the best-laid plans o' mice and men.

As you read my story, you may catch yourself shaking your head and
saying to yourself, "Impossible!" I urge you to suspend your disbelief as I
have learned since then that it is shockingly repre-sentative, and if perhaps
you are a skeptic of my blunt opinions, ask around.

Chapter 10

LOSING MY WAY...AND LOSING IT ALL

The problem was trust. Tom's jealousy about my burgeoning rela-tionship with Todd simply precluded any possibility of running and growing a business together.

He came into my office the morning after the office Christmas party, the morning after he'd called my cell phone over and over because I didn't go straight home from the party like I'd said I was going to.

"I can't work with you anymore, Karen. I can't trust you anymore, and I can't work with someone I don't trust, so it's over. I want out of the business."

"Fine," I fired back, taken by surprise but nevertheless relieved.

When it comes to business, I've always been a realist, and the reality of our situation had been clear to me long before Tom's latest pronounce-ment. After all that had happened on a personal level, there was no way I could maintain a healthy business relationship with Tom through the long term.

Tom said it perfectly: "I can't work with someone I don't trust."

Also because I was a realist, I knew that moving ahead without the company's top salesman would be a monumental challenge.

Since we started the business together in 1993, Tom had always been the company's top producer. He was a masterful salesman, a man whose infectious charm and obvious intelligence won the wholehearted trust of many a client.

I, meanwhile, applied my business orientation in a behind-the-scenes role, formulating a vision for the company and implementing initiatives that moved the business forward.

Some of my concern was probably unfounded. After all, Tom's heart really hadn't been in the business for at least the past two years. (Thank goodness we were big enough and had the team to take up the slack.)

Tom's waning involvement was really no surprise as a person's efforts in everything he or she does always gravitate toward the lowest common denominator. What's happening in one area tends to be mirrored in every other area, and Tom's commitment to our business was sadly on a par with the lack of commitment he had shown in our marriage.

A few days after he voiced his intent to take leave of our business, I asked Tom if he was still of the same mind.

"Of course," he said brusquely. "I don't make these decisions lightly. Why would I suddenly change my mind?"

"Okay, then," I replied, "I guess we need to get a lawyer."

As our intentions seemed to align, we decided to enlist a corporate lawyer to lay out terms of the sale of Tom's share of the business to me.

In the Term Sheet, the trigger date for the transaction was set for three months later: March 1, 2003.

After all the horror stories I'd heard about divorce proceedings and the lawyers whose business it is to muck them up and mire them down, I couldn't believe that everything was moving along so smoothly.

From Tom, I required only one inflexible agreement: until the transaction date, he would have to bust his ass at the office, helping in every way he could to transition the staff and our clients to what would be a very different business than it had been in the past.

I really needed Tom in-house for the first few months of the year, especially since I'd moved the company to a new brokerage platform on January 1.

Tom agreed, and in early January he came back to work. And much to his surprise, he began to see the new business platform's significant potential. The future of The Wealth Management Corporation boded well.

Even in the midst of the chaos that had crept into every aspect of my life, we had managed to hold the business together. Sure, it was hanging on by barely a thread, but thanks largely to the efforts of a young and motivated staff, the company had a lot of renewed energy, both potential and kinetic.

On the fourth of March, three days after the sale of the business was supposed to have been finalized, Tom burst into my office, bellowing out-of-the-blue demands.

"I'm not going anywhere, understand? You are. I want you out of my business, Karen. Right now!"

The next day, I arrived at work to find that Tom had locked himself in my office. Through the floor-to-ceiling panes, I could see him rifling through my files, listening to my voice-mail messages, poring over my computer.

When he spotted me watching him, he glowered at me with a defiant smirk and then continued with what he was doing.

I realize, in retrospect, that I could have defused the situation. I could have walked away and gone for a cup of tea instead of letting Tom get me riled.

Instead, I exploded into a chain of reactions. I pounded on the glass. I yelled and cried. I called the police. And I rallied the exasperated staff to help me.

I played the role of the victim to a perfect tee.

I still have a lot of button-pushers in my life—people who know exactly how to get under my skin, and who seem to relish in doing just that. Now, though—difficult as it is at times—I make a focused effort not to let my frustration come out sideways, which just takes me to places of darkness and pain. Instead, I say to myself, "How can I turn this situation into something positive and enriching? How can I become a better person? How can I be proactive?" When I'm proactive, I feel more in control of my destiny, and life cruises along pretty smoothly. But back then, my transmission had seized in reactive gear, and Tom had a firm hold on my steering wheel.

After much ado, I managed to get Tom out of my office. Now I needed to get him out of my life.

I was growing terrified of Tom—not only his actions but the threat he now posed to my vision for the business. He was mucking about in matters that were sensitive and confidential, and he had the capacity to ruin everything.

There were two things I desperately wanted—two things I was relent-lessly unwilling to lose during my divorce—my business and my children. Yet I was fully unprepared for the fight, and in it, I nearly lost everything.

In hindsight (always in hindsight!), I'd have done many things differ-ently. If only I had known the inadequacies of the system, I could have prepared myself. If only I had known that "justice" has nothing to do with "fairness," I could have braced myself for the outcomes. If only I'd known of the need to be proactive, I could have dramatically cut my losses. But I didn't know. I put the trust in the system, and it failed me utterly. Naive idealism was my downfall.

I vividly recall my first meeting with Sandra Arsenault,* my matri-monial lawyer-to-be. She came by referral and was described to me as "tough and intelligent—definitely one of the best divorce lawyers around." She also had experience in business law, so I was entirely confident she'd be able to handle my complicated file.

I took an immediate liking to Sandra. She left me feeling that if I had to go down this road, she would be a valuable ally along the way.

I made it clear in that first meeting that my intent wasn't to stick it to Tom: I just wanted a quick and peaceful settlement that would spare me from the many horror stories I'd heard but would still allow me to hold my head up high.

"Amen to that," she said with a reassuring smile.

I had set the machine in motion. Now I wanted a drink.

After work on a Friday near the end of March, I met up with a couple of close friends at a downtown hotspot.

As always seemed to happen of late in conversations with my friends, the spotlight soon turned to me and my soap-opera story. I didn't mind telling it, really. Besides allowing me to release some steam, articulating my story gave me insight and perspective. It helped me distill answers to pressing questions and nagging doubts.

Over wine, I told Samuel and Anna all that had happened over the past couple months and how things with Tom had gone, once again, so sour.

"I was sure we could settle things without a fight. He was so willing to

*a fictional name

sell me his share of the business. Then all of sudden, he does a complete 180 and wants me out."

There was no question about it: something in my universe was terribly out of order.

In the days that followed, my antennae were on high alert. The craziness of Tom's energy was escalating, and his threats were becoming more frequent and more menacing.

"Get out of my company, Karen. It's mine, and if you don't get out, you'll live to regret it" was now a common refrain at the office.

Just a few months earlier, Tom had been entirely amenable to the idea of being bought out of the company. Now, he seemed ready and willing to do anything—anything—to hold on to it.

One day in early April, Tom's behavior descended to all-new lows. His attack became deeply personal and mercilessly cruel.

After most of the staff had left the office for lunch, Tom came and stood, as he tended to do, in my doorway, filling it with his intimidating presence. I looked up from my work with the customary measure of dread. I'd been conditioned to expect the worst every time he cornered me like this.

"You know what your problem is, Karen?" he said coolly. "You're a waste of a skirt. We both know I wouldn't have cheated on you if only you'd been a better lay.

"It's unbelievable, really. Unbelievable that I wasted eight long and unrewarding years with someone like you."

When he showed no signs of letting up, I stood up and pushed past him, still suffering his jeers. I ran to the bathroom, where I broke down in uncontrollable sobs. His words still held such power over me: I felt ugly and ashamed.

Without returning to my office, I drove home, shaken up beyond all comprehension.

Camilla was there when I came through the front door, tidying up toys in the family room while Alexandra napped.

"Karen! You poor dear—you look terrible," she exclaimed. "So I've been told," I replied, though with little humor.

INTO THE LABYRINTH

The mythology of the ancient Greeks tells of the Labyrinth at Knossos, a fiendishly intricate maze devised by Daedalus to house the insatiable Minotaur.

This notion of an impossibly complex series of corridors inhabited by a beast that devours all who lose their way is a perfect parallel to the current system of matrimonial law.

Once you get in, you get lost, and finding your way out before everything gets devoured—your assets, your dignity, your ability to trust—is all but impossible.

Many stumble into the perilous maze of matrimonial law believing they have no other options at their avail—that "taking the fight to court" is the only path open to them. But soon after they take the terrible leap of faith and hire lawyers, they get hopelessly lost in the labyrinth of the status quo, where bureaucracy bewilders at every turn.

Others get seduced into the labyrinth by the illusion of control, by the belief they're taking charge of their own destiny. The action comes from the attitude that "I need to take control of this situation!" But the moment you plunge yourself into the system and fetter yourself with a matrimonial lawyer, you run the risk of losing, paradoxically, any semblance of control, becoming little more than a billable pawn in each player's profit-driven agenda.

My own journey through the traditional divorce process was an exercise in accepting my powerlessness over other people, while my lawyers perfectly exemplified the notion of free will run riot. More often than not, the decisions they made on my behalf (and without my input) were imprudent, even reckless, and they spent my money on motions and counterclaims and valuations and assessments as if my resources were limitless. In fact, they spent and billed until I had nothing left.

Instead of moving you toward resolution (amicable or, much more likely, otherwise), the traditional divorce process mires you deeper and deeper in crisis and moves you closer and closer to financial and emotional destruction.

My own passage through the legal system was fraught with an endless string of defenses against false accusations and malicious affidavits from my husband and his lawyers. Instead of proactively preparing for my future, I was stuck helplessly and hopelessly in reactive mode.

* * *

Unless you've been through it, you simply can't fathom how destructive and costly the traditional divorce process really is. There are the costs of lost opportunities. The costs of assets whose value the process will often diminish. The costs to you as a human being—the loss of freedom, of dignity, of self-worth. The loss of hope.

And then, of course, there are the extortionate costs of the process itself: the fees for lawyers and assessments and valuations and disbursements and all the rest.

When you pause to consider the system's fundamental flaws—its lack of a standardized methodology, its reactive nature, and its utter absence of accountability—the outrageous monetary costs associated with traditional divorce come hardly as a surprise.

Things were out of hand with Tom, and by now it was clear—even to me—that we simply wouldn't be able to settle things on our own.

One of my friends, a successful litigator whose familiarity with the perils and the pitfalls of our legal system is intimate, offered me a solemn forewarning: "Just know, Karen, that once you and your lawyer start down that path, there's no turning back. And any notion that *you* are in control is simply an illusion."

At the time, I had no idea how much of an understatement that was.

THE LAWYERS' BATTLEGROUND

"I've got good news and bad news," Sandra announced in her office one Wednesday afternoon.

"The good news is that Tom has finally retained a lawyer with some matrimonial experience."

"Okay, if that's the good news, what's the bad?" I was pretty sure I didn't want to know, but I had to ask.

"The bad news is it's Rebecca Hartman*."

"I see," I said. But I didn't. The name meant nothing to me, and I told Sandra so. "Tell me, Sandra, why is Rebecca Hartman bad news?"

"Because you're not going to get that 'quick-finish, all smiles' outcome you were hoping for. We're in for a long and nasty battle. Long and nasty and expensive."

What Sandra failed to mention—something I didn't find out about until much later—is that she and Ms. Hartman had a vile distaste for one another. Now, unbeknownst to me, my battle with Tom provided a convenient arena for Sandra and Rebecca to continue their catfight.

I feel that much of the massive, financially devastating litigation, the countless court appearances, the application after application after application was perpetuated (unconsciously, I hope) to accommodate our lawyers' personal feud. Looking back at the monumental heap of correspondence Sandra amassed during her tenure as my matrimonial counsel, it's so obvious that she and Ms. Hartman were fueling the fire while I was pleading desperately to get things resolved.

Many of the lawyers with whom I aligned myself were among the many poor choices that plagued my journey through divorce, making it longer, more painful, and far more expensive than it needed to be.

Something I find interesting (and upsetting) is that in court, opposing lawyers address one another as "my friend." I came to hate this tradition as it seems to resonate with, "Remember, lawyers, we need to stick together. Unless we work together to perpetuate the madness, someone might catch on to just how ineffectual we actually are."

THE ATTEMPTED MUTINY

With respect to the business, Tom had been all over the map. He wanted out, he wanted back in, he reneged on his promise to sell, and now he seemed hell-bent on taking it all for himself. His moods and his mind seemed to change with the weather.

In mid-March, his lawyer (who seemed to share Tom's "win at any cost" approach and his "if you've got it, I want it" attitude) initiated

* a fictional name

efforts to oust me from the business by raising a mutiny among my crew. She rallied the staff and convinced them, one by one, to sign affidavits that they wanted me out of the business—that they'd rather have Tom at the helm, and if one of us had to go, it ought to be me. Tom was the company's top producer, a charismatic salesman, so Ms. Hartman's argument that "the business really needs Tom back" was pretty easy for the staff to swallow.

The truth was something else altogether. While Tom was indeed an effective front man, I supported him by toiling behind the scenes to provide the vision, planning, and stability that held the business together.

There were a few other things Rebecca Hartman overlooked (or simply chose to ignore): I was president of a private company; I was the board of directors' only member; and I alone had voting shares. Now I'm no lawyer, but I know enough about business to know the employees of a privately held company simply can't oust the sole voting shareholder from her presidency. That's Business Law 101—the very basics.

That didn't stop Ms. Hartman. She dragged me and Sandra into court with an application to remove me from the business and turn it over to Tom's care and protection, an unwinnable cause.

Still, I decided to play it safe and hire co-counsel, Dave Laidlaw,* a corporate lawyer who would represent me as the president of the company. (I realize now that my decision to "play it safe" was my in-tuition getting back into its groove. Obviously, I didn't trust Sandra enough to let her go it alone with my business on the line.)

We went to court, where Dave promptly proved himself a wise and business-minded lawyer. With a bare minimum of debate, he handily quashed Ms. Hartman's application by clearly establishing the obvious: that a private company cannot be taken over by its employees.

Tom's lawyer had led him down a path that led to nowhere but a dead end, a very expensive dead end.

As for me, I had to waste tens of thousands of increasingly precious dollars on lawyers of my own, defending a motion that spoke volumes about the other side's methodology.

I thanked Dave for his excellent efforts. He was a good lawyer, even

*a fictional name

though he was forced to operate in a tragically flawed system, and he left me with an observation that later proved an invaluable insight.

He said, "It's so obvious, Karen: whatever you have, Tom wants."

It was the Boston cream pie incident all over again.

I had one more thing to do before I moved on from the matter of this attempted mutiny. I had to round up the boys and slap some wrists.

"The boys" are the fellows from whom Tom and Ms. Hartman collected their fruitless affidavits, a few of the young gentlemen on my staff who back then made up for in youthful energy what they lacked in worldly wisdom.

They were called to the boardroom, and as they arrived one by one, expecting to see Tom but finding me instead, they looked unanimously shocked. And duly alarmed. Not one of them, I imagine, expected the mercy they were about to be shown.

Yet I was committed to taking the high road, and although abiding by my principles cost me dearly in most aspects of my divorce, I walked away at the end of it all with my soul intact.

"I really ought to fire each and every one of you right now," I said, trying hard not to sound too schoolmarmish. "But I'm not going to. I'm going to give you the benefit of the doubt. I'll assume that each of you was manipulated. What was asked of you was totally unfair. All I ask now is that you learn a very big lesson from this."

Sighs of relief. Smiles. Apologies. Assurances. And then they all slunk back to their offices, tails between their legs.

(I'm guessing the first thing each of them did was dust off his résumé. And who could blame them? Tom and I had failed miserably at keeping our personal issues out of the office, and morale among the staff had been on skid row for a long time already. Rebecca and Tom's attempted mutiny must've booted it all the way to the doorstep of the morgue. Interestingly, though, a couple of those boys are now shareholders and senior members of the company.)

I remained in the boardroom for a while, savoring a feeling that seemed distantly familiar. For the first time in a long, long while, I felt a rush of something like happiness. For now, at least, the business was mine.

ANOTHER GAFFE, ANOTHER 50 GRAND

I've always been drawn to intuitive wisdom.

Dave Laidlaw was a wise soul and good business lawyer with a knack for seeing things in a very straightforward, pragmatic way. He proved to be one of the many positive forces to cross my path during my divorce.

After the court proceedings that swiftly circumvented Tom's attempted mutiny, I met once more with Dave, seeking his advice on how to proceed. It was clear to both of us that Tom didn't know what he wanted. But what about me? Did I know what I wanted?

While I remained rigidly uncompromising in my determination to win primary custody of the kids, I was becoming less and less attached to the outcome of the business the more the legal battle dragged on.

Besides The Wealth Management Corporation, Tom and I had amassed a number of significant assets during our decade together: an investment property in Florida, our cottage in the mountains, and a tear-down home on one of the city's premier properties, with mountain views in one direction and a dazzling cityscape in the other.

This tear-down was one of our two most valuable assets; the other was our business. Both were very high in both innate and potential value.

Together, Dave and I took stock of all our assets and organized them into two groups, yielding a reasonably equitable distribution of our wealth.

Dave and I agreed that if I were to take my pick of the assets, my battle with Tom might never end, what with his tendency to covet anything I'd set my own sights on.

I thought about the rules of sharing my parents imposed upon my siblings and me when we were young: if one person cut up the treat, the other person got to choose the first piece.

With Tom, this seemed like the only viable approach.

It was time to settle things once and for all.

On May 6, we gathered with our lawyers for a day of negotiations.

In preparation for the meeting, I had jotted some rough numbers on a piece of notepaper. I had also divided our various assets under two columns to test the idea of splitting the pie and having Tom choose his half.

My plan was only to use these notes as a point of reference. I certainly hadn't done the due diligence to know whether or not my numbers were accurate, nor had I considered tax implications or a number of other material factors.

Truth be told, I was more concerned about who would get the business than anything else.

After a mere 10 minutes, Sandra returned from caucusing with Tom and his lawyer. She looked at me excitedly. "Tom wants the company, but he's going to let you have it."

I was thrilled, of course, but I was also cautious. I knew the numbers still needed to be crunched and that the process probably wouldn't be a smooth one. But at least Tom had relented and agreed to let me keep the business.

"At last," I thought, "the universe is unfolding as it should." Despite my delight, this victory was anticlimactic. By this time, I was so ready to lose yet again that winning came with a certain numbness.

In the days and weeks leading up to this moment, I'd been mentally preparing myself to let go of something I loved. And I'd convinced myself that if Tom chose the business, I'd get over the pain and life would go on.

"I've built a successful business once," I would say to myself. "I can certainly do it again. It's just a business, after all. It's not my kids. It's not my health. It's not my sanity. It's a thing, and things can be replaced."

Now, I felt it was safe to set those thoughts aside and start figuring out what I'd have to give Tom in exchange for the business . . . until the unthinkable happened.

For reasons I will never be able to fathom, Sandra provided Tom's lawyers with a copy of the rough notes I had made regarding a possible distribution of assets.

She called me at home shortly after I got home from the round-table meeting.

"Karen? It's me, Sandra."

"Sandra, hi. What is it? Did Tom change his mind about the business?" I felt an overwhelming rush of anxiety.

"No, nothing like that. I just wanted to tell you—I thought I should let you know that Tom's lawyer has a copy of the notes you made with Dave Laidlaw—your ideas for dividing your assets with Tom."

I couldn't contain my sarcasm. "That's just great, Sandra. How the heck did that happen?"

"They got sent to Rebecca's office." "By whom?"

"Well, by me, actually. I attached them to our offer to help Tom and Rebecca understand how we came up with the numbers. I thought it would help them see we were being fair. That way, they might be more inclined to accept."

"So what does this mean? They can't do anything with my rough notes, can they? It just means they know where my mind is at regarding the assets, right?"

"Don't worry," said Sandra. "It's just to help them see where we're at."

"But how can it, Sandra? Those numbers aren't even accurate. They're just approximations—guideposts for my eyes only."

"Relax, Karen," Sandra assured me, "there's truly not much they can do with those notes."

The next day brought a series of phone calls between the lawyers, with lots of talk about offers and counteroffers and acceptance. About a week later, I was served notice: Tom was suing for breach of contract, arguing that my asset-dividing doodles constituted a legally binding part of my offer, which his lawyers were willing to accept, but which I certainly wasn't.

Now I was going to have to prepare for a Trial of Issue, a mini-trial to determine whether or not there had been a contract and, if so, whether or not I had breached it.

I was dumbfounded. Who could possibly win in this ludicrous turn of events? I doubted very much if Tom would, and I knew with absolute certainty it wouldn't be me.

There was an issue, all right. I didn't need a trial to see that. The issue was this: my $400-an-hour matrimonial lawyer seemed completely oblivious to the chaos she was causing in my life. In the real world, people are held responsible for the outcomes of their actions, but in this strange world of traditional divorce, logical consequences didn't seem to exist.

I should have heeded the clues and my intuition much more carefully. And now I was being sued. But that's not all. Because of her role in the incident that precipitated the suit, Sandra would have to appear as a witness. As such, I was forced to hire yet another lawyer, Jordan Billings,* a litigator who added to my tally another

$50,000 in legal bills.

What must I have been thinking? My lawyer had made a monu-mental blunder that spawned a costly yet wholly unnecessary lawsuit, and I didn't fire her. Heck, I hardly even scolded her.

But from my perspective at the time, how could I? I was at sea in turbulent waters way, way over my head and holding on for dear life. To fire Sandra would have been to let go of my life preserver, even if it was doing a miserable job of keeping my head above water.

It was everything my friend had warned me about: once you dive in, you get overwhelmed and disoriented. You get swept away in a tidal wave of total confusion.

"Besides," Sandra had told me, "every lawyer in town knows about this case, and no one else will touch it."

Yes, I should have fired Sandra immediately. And I should have demanded justification of her bill—not just hours worked, but value delivered. Of the latter, there was very little that I could discern.

But I had become a codependent of the system, completely lacking in boundaries, caught up in the chaos and convinced I had nowhere else to turn. I felt paralyzed, like someone up to her neck in quicksand, incapable of anything but gasping for air and praying desperately that it would all be over with quickly.

The trial of issue was quick; the verdict was not. After the June trial, I had to spend the entire summer in excruciating limbo until a verdict was handed down on the first day of September.

To my delight, the judge who had presided over the matter handed

* a fictional name

down a judgment wherein Tom lost on every count and was ordered to pay costs—a paltry $12,000 of a bill that was over four times as much.

Even though the awarded costs were laughable (as is usually the case in matrimonial issues), the verdict represented a transitory moment of redemption for the almighty system until I remembered that there wouldn't have been a trial in the first place were it not for my lawyer's actions.

And where were we now? Right back at square one, without a deal.

And without any accountability. By this time, Sandra's bill was approaching the $100,000 mark. Six stressful months had passed since Tom had reneged on his deal, and we weren't so much as an inch closer to knowing who would get the company.

There had to be a better way. There simply had to be.

This is the thought that began to bubble to the surface of my mind and haunt me around this time, the thought that morphed, over time, into the impetus for this book and for my conception of Fairway Divorce Solutions.

My quest to bring about changes in the system began quite modestly, with a small handful of letters to Tom. Writing from my heart, I begged for his cooperation in coming to an amicable, reasonable, and mutually agreeable solution to matters that were snowballing rapidly into an avalanche I feared would lay waste to everything in its path.

What was wrong, I reasoned, with seeking a better way, a more efficient way that would keep at least some of our hard-earned assets out of our lawyers' pockets?

I knew I needed Tom on my side—that we could stop the train wreck only by getting off together. You see, once you're in the system, you're stuck there unless both parties agree to get out at the same time.

Sadly, though, all of my letters ended up in Tom's affidavits, and instead of change I spurred nothing but chastisement and admonition from the system I was holding up to criticism.

SWEETENING THE POT

I wanted so much to hold on, to preserve the business I had once nurtured and helped grow, like a child, into a thriving enterprise.

But all my thoughts had begun to revolve around one seeming inevitability: that the only way to gain complete freedom from Tom would be to liquidate everything. The business, the house, the cottage, the boat—we'd simply sell it all, split the proceeds, and go our separate ways. It would be an easy even-steven.

Though this wasn't my ideal outcome, it really wouldn't be the heartbreaker I once imagined it would be. As the divorce process wore on, all of the "things" in my life, including the business, really began to matter less. Keeping my soul intact and my children close to me were what really mattered.

I worked hard to resign myself to this outcome until the twenty-ninth of September. That's when Tom's lawyer made a casual remark that resonated through me like "Alleluia!" through a cathedral.

"Listen, Sandra," Ms. Hartman said to my lawyer, "why don't you and Karen put together an irresistible offer that includes the tear-down and the cottage? If you ask me, Tom is done with the business."

Dave Laidlaw had been bang on: Tom didn't really want the business, he was just yanking at anything I seemed determined to hang on to.

That was it, another turning point in this whirligig of legal chaos. I decided then that I would focus every last ounce of my energy and my passion on helping the business thrive and on making it my own.

The company, though still operational and modestly profitable, was suffering. It was so ironic. Because our legal wrangling consumed so much time and effort, the value of the asset we were fighting over was being compromised. Employee morale was in the toilet, and our clients, quite understandably, were growing restless and dissatisfied.

I knew that in order to rebuild the business, I'd have to show some real leadership. I'd need to bring all the employees together, inspire their trust, and help them really coalesce as a team.

With assurances to all that they could buy into the company if we reached our targets, my team and I launched Operation Phoenix, a two-year plan to resurrect the company, to bring it forth again out of the ashes.

I started by cleaning house. I downsized. I reorganized. I moved the office to a new location. I squeezed a guarantee of 100-percent commitment from every remaining member of the team.

And then I got busy.

THE SHOCKING VIEW FROM
THE HIGH ROAD

Taking the high road became a double-edged sword.

At the outset of this legal fiasco, Sandra had cautioned me against playing dirty. "Don't get sucked into doing anything unethical. Even if Tom and his lawyer start playing dirty," she said, "don't crawl into the gutter with them."

And I listened. I was honest; I was forthcoming; I didn't lie and I didn't cheat; I played by the rules.

And I got screwed, big time.

Don't get me wrong: I'm by no means advocating gutter-level tactics. Despite what it cost me, I will never regret taking the high road. To me, keeping your spirit and your integrity intact is always more admirable and honorable than winning at any cost.

Still, I can't help but think I wouldn't have been walked all over if only I'd known then what I know now: that the system *is* the gutter, where you need to fight tooth-and-nail for fairness and justice, and where those outcomes don't fall to you naturally just because you play nice.

But I didn't know then what I know now. So while I trudged along as best I could, I watched miserably as Tom's lawyer continued to create chaos.

To aggravate the matter—and, I might add, to aggravate the client who was paying her $400 an hour to fulfill her reputation as one of the city's most capable matrimonial lawyers—Sandra seemed never to find her legs in the courtroom.

In the face of the implausible, often insupportable allegations by Tom's lawyer, she rarely argued back, and when she did, her objections were weakly articulated and sadly unconvincing.

Perhaps she was underprepared. Or perhaps the intricacies and convolutions of the case baffled her. I simply don't know.

Whatever the case, I found myself standing by helplessly, going utterly berserk but completely powerless to do anything but ask myself, "Is this really the city's best?"

During the fall of 2003, Tom and his lawyer had me and Sandra in and out of court almost a dozen times, mostly for the sake of proving that I, as president of The Wealth Management Corporation, was utterly destroying the company in which Tom was still a 50-percent owner.

Rebecca Hartman filed affidavits as if they were postings on a sordid blog, a steady stream of accusations that I was mismanaging the business, eroding its client base, and lining my pockets from the company coffers. Nothing seemed too far-fetched.

For one of our court appearances, the presiding judge was the Honorable Madam Justice C.J. Molyneux*. As was typical, Sandra and I didn't find out who'd be presiding until shortly before the appearance. And on this particular day, the luck of the draw was definitely against me.

As much as the lawyers shattered any illusions that the legal system can be efficient, Madam Justice Molyneux destroyed any illusions that it is always fair.

I used to think the people appointed to judgeships had to be unbiased, but from the outset, Madam Justice Molyneux showed a thinly veiled distaste for me and my petitions.

This boded well for Tom and Rebecca Hartman in their efforts to prove I was mismanaging the business and compromising its profit potential when in fact the very opposite was true.

Although I had done much to solidify the company's foundation, revenue was down. Not only had we lost our top-producing salesman, but we were still adjusting to our new brokerage platform and the changes implemented under Operation Phoenix.

Tom's legal team seized this fact like hyenas on an injured gazelle. They presented a shocking misrepresentation of business facts, and Madam Justice Molyneux readily accepted as truth the web of decep-tions they so deftly spun—that I was pulling an annual income of close to a million dollars; that I stole money from the company; that I used my company

* a fictional name

credit card to fill my closet with shoes and fancy clothes—anything to cast doubt on my ability and my integrity.

"Your Honor," Ms. Hartman offered in sycophantic tones during one of our days in court, "I'd like to draw your attention to the second page of our brief.

"These numbers show the company's profits for the three months ending June 30, 2003, versus profits in the same three months in the previous three years. As you'll see, the profits under Ms. Stewart's leadership of the company have dwindled away to almost nothing." Of course they had! Reorganizing a company is a lot like reorganizing your house. Before it gets tidier, it tends to get a whole lot messier. As well, I was now paying others to replace Tom, and they didn't come cheap.

I looked pleadingly toward Sandra, hoping desperately for a vehement retort. But all she could offer up was a half-hearted coun-terattack, a vague argument devoid of the details I really needed the court to hear, which were the facts and numbers Sandra needed to articulate to quash Ms. Hartman's claims against me, but simply couldn't.

Madam Justice Molyneux was clearly unmoved. After a scant few moments' consideration, she looked up from the brief at which she'd been staring all the while Sandra had been speaking. Peering at me icily over the cat's-eye glasses that sat midway down the bridge of her nose, she said, "Clearly, Ms. Stewart, you're driving the company into the ground."

Ms. Hartman jumped in again. "I'd ask Your Honor to consider my client's application for a cash advance of $50,000. He'd like to make sure he gets fairly paid before there's nothing left of his business. As well, we'd like to commission a full comparative valuation of the company. After all, my client has a right to know exactly how much his assets are worth, and how much he's losing because of his wife's ineptitude.

"The cost of the valuation will be at least $45,000, a cost we feel Ms. Stewart should cover since she's the one whose mismanagement is compromising the company's value."

Madam Justice Molyneux smiled toward Tom. "I'm with you on the advance. Ms. Stewart, have your accountant advance your husband $50,000 lickety-split. And while you're at it, have him set aside an additional $45,000. The Wealth Management Corporation can foot the bill for

on their extracurricular activities—Sarah's horseback riding lessons and Matthew's hockey school. I even had to let Camilla go.

Nor did the repercussions end there. When the court cut my salary, it was "effective immediately." I had no time to renegotiate my mortgage or pay down my credit line or phase out certain expenditures. All I could do was cut back wherever I could while sinking further and further into debt.

MY LAWYER'S WHITE FLAG

The end of a full year in and out of court was coming up quickly, and still we were spinning our wheels on the slippery slopes of the legal system.

It was then, near the end of 2003, that Sandra came to two weighty realizations: "This case *really* needs to go to trial," she offered, and then added, "but I really don't feel I can continue as your counsel.

"Things between me and Tom's lawyer are getting too personal and too nasty. Her vendetta against me is holding us back from a resolution. It's probably in everyone's best interests for you to retain new counsel."

In other words, I helped create this mess, but I'd rather not stick around to help set things straight. I wish you luck. And oh, by the way, would you kindly tell me how you plan to settle my bill?

After a year of representation and over $150,000 in billings, Sandra had resolved *nothing*.

Along with her unceremonious goodbye, Sandra offered me the name of the only lawyer of any reputation who, to her knowledge, might be willing to take up my cause: Robert McWilliams.**

"He's with Peters McDermid McWilliams, a group of powerful lawyers with deep pockets," said Sandra, who knew full well that the past year had been as draining for me financially as it had been emotionally. "Who knows? Maybe they can carry you until you get your feet back on the ground."

Robert McWilliams was a well-polished pro, a McGill-trained smooth talker who wore Armani suits and had a reputation for getting things done.

*a fictional name

During our first meeting, he announced with irrefutable confidence, "What we need, Karen, is to get you in front of a judge so we can get this unsavory business over with."

That sounded great to me. My first impression said Robert was just what I needed: a lawyer who was going to really take charge.

Robert promptly got a trial date set for November 2004, nearly another full year of life in limbo down the road, but the best Robert could do given the backlog in the system. Then he got busy running up (and up) yet another bill.

We spoke seldom. During the entire year leading up to the trial, we probably met only 15 times, and never for very long. But he was working hard, he said, behind the scenes, and he always appeared exceptionally well organized.

Most of my interactions were with a junior lawyer Robert had assigned to help out with my case, someone whose attention to detail gave me an added measure of confidence in my new legal team. My only question was, did Robert know the ins and outs of my case as well as his assistant did?

In all, Robert's pretrial billings added up to a little over $200,000—a baffling sum toward which he expected a sizable payment before the start of the trial.

"$200,000? But how—"

"All the hard work happens long before you get into the courtroom, Karen. The one thing we must not do is walk into that courtroom unprepared. It's my job to make sure we don't get caught off guard."

"I'm sure you know best. But $200,000?"

"Just take a look at this," he said, plucking up a thick folder from his desktop and thrusting it toward me.

I leafed through the contents: letter after letter from Robert to Rebecca Hartman and back again. Petty bickering. Grandiose position-ing. And lots of piss 'n' vinegar.

This was supposed to impress me?

Robert was a talented litigator by anyone's standards, but he was equally talented at wooing me. And as with Sandra a year earlier, I was so far down the road with Robert, I simply couldn't see any other way. So I swallowed my misgivings and borrowed the money to pay my bill. What other choice did I have?

It was no longer a question of how much I'd have left at the end of my divorce; it was a question of how much I'd owe. Everything I'd worked for, everything I'd earned, everything I'd saved was gone, every last cent of it. But so long as I could beg or borrow enough to pay their bills, none of the lawyers really seemed to mind.

As troubling as Robert's bill was, there was something else that nagged at my intuition in the days that followed. Rattling about in my thoughts was a sentence that caught my eye in one of Rebecca Hartman's letters to Robert.

"You've obviously got better things to do with your time," she had written, "but maybe you should pay a little more attention to this case."

Here was yet another sign from the universe—another sign that took far too long to sink in!

Anxiety and dread were the only constants in my life all through the time leading up to the trial.

During that long and uncertain year, The Wealth Management Corporation was subjected to the second of two valuations.

It was part of a process insisted upon by Tom's lawyer early in the legal proceedings, a process that just happened to devour an additional $45,000 in fees.

The intent of these valuations: to prove beyond any doubt that my mismanagement was destroying the business.

The first valuation had been completed in the summer of 2003. Now, a full year later, it was time for the follow-up—the comparative figures— Tom's proof positive that I was, as Madam Justice Molyneux had so boldly asserted, "driving the business into the ground."

The results surprised everyone except me.

As a result of Operation Phoenix and the back-office change-over, the value of the business was up more than 25 percent.

I thought back to my meeting with Tom's girlfriend—to the box of evidence she'd set before me: her gift of reality.

I'd now received my second gift of reality: an affirmation that my devotion to the business was paying dividends, and that Tom's allegations of mismanagement were nothing more than the last-gasp protestations of a man consumed by the fear of losing control.

The only twist was this: because of the spike in the company's value, I was now going to have to pay more to buy Tom out!

THE "TRIVIAL" TRIAL

"You've obviously got better things to do."

As if I wasn't shaky enough in the weeks leading up to the trial, that statement rattled about in my obsessive thoughts like a silver dollar in the dryer.

It might explain why, during those same few weeks, Robert waved off two offers from Tom's side of the table as "not even worthy of our attention."

It might also explain why, during our pretrial preparations, he urged me to drop the matter of the costs I was awarded in the Trial of Issue—costs that, several months later, remained unpaid. "Let's not get distracted by trifling matters like that," Robert admonished. "I need you to stay focused on the bigger picture."

That's how Robert explained it: big-picture thinking, which seemed to be the mantra of all my matrimonial lawyers.

And now that I know the trial's outcome, I understand "big-picture thinking" for what it really is: a dangerous disregard of the all-important details.

At its excruciating pace, October crept at last to a close, and on the first day of November the property division trial began.

Robert, his junior helper, and I entered the courtroom together. Tom and his new litigator, a gray-flannelled, silver-haired courtroom vet by the name of Aldus Green,* were already seated at one of the tables near the front. I lingered for a moment and then ambled up the aisle behind Robert, who swung his briefcase onto our table and then turned to shake hands with Aldus Green.

"May the best man win," he said with a breezy laugh as he turned back to his briefcase and unloaded its contents.

"All rise." This was it, the signal to start. And the beginning of the end.

* a fictional name

"The Honorable Judge Parker* presiding."

The courtroom and the judge had been booked for an eight-day trial, though how it could possibly take eight days was well beyond me. I knew from our pretrial preparations that Robert would need about a day and a half to make our case. What could Tom's team possibly have up their sleeves that would take four times as long?

Robert had prepped me well on protocol and procedure. First, I would take the stand and present my case with the help of Robert's guiding questions. Then, after Tom's lawyer had had an opportunity to cross-examine me, Tom's team would present his case and then my team would cross-examine him. After all that was said and done, we would call our small handful of witnesses: the accounting firm that performed the comparative valuations of the company, and The Wealth Management Corporation's in-house accountant to help vindicate me from accusations of embezzlement from the company. Finally, Tom's team would have an opportunity to call their witnesses.

One question that played over and over in my mind was "Why are we here?" I wasn't a criminal. I'd committed no crime. Yet here I was in a court of law, about to be questioned and cross-examined like a common criminal. In my view (both then and now), divorce didn't belong in this place!

From the outset, the courtroom took on a carnival atmosphere as the lawyers for both sides jockeyed for position, brandished affidavits, objected loudly, and grandstanded as if a panel of figure-skating judges were rating their performances.

During my first day on the stand, my testimony was punctuated by incessant objections from Tom's table, and I had real difficulty maintaining a coherent train of thought. Although Robert tried his best to keep things on track, Mr. Green proved awfully adept at derailing the proceedings.

"Ms. Stewart," Robert prompted with a subtly reassuring smile, "please tell the court what Tom told you on the tenth of December, 2002."

"He said he wanted out. He said he was done with The Wealth Management Corporation and was ready to move on."

"And what were your plans for your company after Tom left?"

"Objection," Mr. Green clamored. "Your company? Please, Mr.

McWilliams, it wasn't her company then, and it isn't her company now. You set yourself up for disappointment when you get ahead of yourself like that."

Judge Parker peered down toward Aldus. "You may spare us your theatrics, Mr. Green. Mr. McWilliams, I think we'll let the court decide whose company it is."

"Your Honor." Robert nodded deferentially toward the judge and then turned back to me. "Now please tell the court what happened on March 1, 2003."

"Nothing happened," I said. "That was the trigger date for the transfer of Tom's shares to me. It was all laid out in a Term Sheet a lawyer had drafted for us, but it never happened. Tom reneged on his promise."

Robert continued his questioning. "What happened next, on the fourth of March?"

"Tom burst into my office and told me he wanted the company for himself. He said the company was his and I'd better get out or else."

"Objection! Your Honor—please. Didn't Ms. Stewart take an oath to tell the truth?"

"I think I said enough theatrics, Mr. Green," the judge replied.

I looked to Robert, wondering why he wasn't doing anything about these frivolous objections. He nodded reassuringly and put up his hand as if to say, "Patience. Remember: big picture."

And so, for the rest of the day and the lion's share of the next, the Carnival of Objections clamored dizzily on.

If only Aldus Green had shared Robert's big-picture view of the world! His tactic, it turned out, was all about the details. He would stone me to death with pebbles of trickery.

After I'd delivered my testimony regarding the status of the business—my original intention of buying Tom out, his reneging on the deal, Rebecca Hartman's futile efforts to oust me from my presidency, my commitment to rebuilding the company, Operation Phoenix, and finally the recent valuation that demonstrated my success—he launched into a cross-examination that seemed little more than a stalling tactic designed to try my patience.

And it worked.

For a full day and a half, Aldus Green went line by line through my business credit card statements, demanding that I explain every last expenditure.

Not only was this a monumental waste of everyone's time and my money, it was an insult to the court system. No wonder the courts are so backlogged that it can take a year, sometimes more, to get before a judge!

"July 27," Mr. Green probed. "You had an expensive dinner at Bon Appétit. That's just eight or nine blocks from your home, isn't it? Are you sure that was a business expense and not a night on the town with your boyfriend?"

I replied coolly. "It's also just four or five blocks from my office, which is why I often take clients there. Just like I did on July 27."

"You're sure of that?"

"Positive."

"And the client was . . . ?"

"Terry Batistella and his wife Brianne."

"Interesting. But wasn't July 27 a Sunday?"

"It was a Tuesday. Would you like me to lend you my day-timer so you can keep track?"

"Let's move on. July 29. ...."

Aldus Green's efforts to reveal some sort of misuse of company funds was failing dismally, but by the end of day three I felt beaten up and exhausted. And we still had most of a week to go. As the cross-examination plodded onward, things became more and more blurry to me. I consider myself financially astute—as president and managing director of a financial service company, I have to be. And I'd been feeling pretty proud of myself because I'd been able to cite, off the top of my head, the exact reason for every expenditure Aldus Green asked me about. For every one of his tedious questions, I had a legitimate and truthful answer.

But all of a sudden, there in the courtroom, I lost focus. Aldus Green was carrying on with restaurant names and dollar amounts, and it all washed over me like a silly tune from an organ-grinder's music box.

I tried to bring my mind back into focus. "Pardon me," I said, unsure of where we'd left off.

"Your trip to Los Angeles," Aldus repeated impatiently. "On April 7, 2004. Your boyfriend Todd had moved there three weeks earlier, had he not? So would you really have the court believe that was a legitimate business expense?"

For the life of me, I couldn't remember why I had flown to LA. It had to have been for business: my determination to take the high road extended to operations of the company, and I was always careful to keep personal expenses separate from business expenses. But why couldn't I remember this one?

I looked pleadingly toward Robert, who stepped in quickly and requested a recess.

Judge Parker acquiesced. "Let's take a 15-minute coffee break," he announced.

As I was still under cross, I wasn't allowed to talk to my legal team during our recess. Still, Robert's junior whispered to me under his breath, "Seems strange to Robert and me that you can remember everything but that one. What's going on, Karen?"

After expending so much energy to travel the high road, I felt beaten down, like a common criminal. And after all my efforts to be 100 percent honest, my lawyers were suddenly doubting me!

Of course I remembered later that evening why I had been in LA, but far too late to make a difference—the damage had already been done. I'd gone to a professional development conference for certified divorce financial analysts. How on earth could I have forgotten that one?

I called Robert. I needed him to know I was exhausted and doubted whether I could handle another day like this one. I guess, as well, I was expecting him to share some words of strength—to tell me to just hang in there and he'd make sure everything turned out fine. Instead, he handed the phone to his junior, who came up tragically short of the support and encouragement I needed.

What unfolded the next morning was a spectacle of shameless surrender that ended up costing me hundreds of thousands of dollars.

Why? Because Robert, I'm guessing, had better things to do than handhold his emotionally drained client.

THE COURT-STEP DEAL

Trust the universe. Trust intuition. But never, ever put blind trust in a lawyer.

When I got bogged down and caught up in the emotional turmoil of my divorce, everything changed. Try as I might, I just couldn't see clearly. So along with $550 an hour, I invested blind faith in Robert McWilliams, which was yet another mistake.

On the morning of the trial's fourth day—the day after a lapse of memory brought my legal team's spirits crashing to the courtroom floor—Robert began to talk about a settlement.

"Look, Karen," he said seriously, "it's pretty clear Tom's team has plans to drag this out as long as possible. If we don't wrap it up before our eight days are up, the judge will need to order a continuance. Then it could be six more months, maybe even a year, before we get another court date."

"So what's my other choice?" I asked.

"Let's settle this thing once and for all, Karen. Let's put an offer on the table."

Why? That's the word that pounded against my aching temples like a battering ram. Why now, after so much time and so much money? We had no more information now than we had before, so why wait till now? Why wait till the other side had squeezed some ammunition out of me before bringing up the possibility of settling? Once again, I was completely baffled.

Robert could see I was wavering. "You can take your chances, Karen, but I really think your ex is ready to deal."

Robert called me at home the next morning.

"Get a paper and pen," he said hurriedly. His mood was upbeat but urgent.

"Hang on." I rummaged through my desk drawer for a pencil, and I grabbed a paper napkin from the side table. "Okay," I said, "what's up?"

Robert ran through the terms of the latest offer on the table. I would get the company, and Tom would throw in the boat and the truck. Meanwhile, I would pay Tom $200,000 cash. He'd also get all our properties and the cash from the sale of our house.

"I don't know, Robert," I said, completely overwhelmed by the magnitude of the decision I was suddenly facing. "Is this a fair deal?"

"Based on the latest valuation of the business, it works out to a perfect 50/50," Robert said confidently. "I'd say take the company and run. You're not likely to get a better deal than this one out of Aldus Green. Come on down to my office and we'll put the deal to paper and ink."

I shook all the way to his office. What had just happened? Had two years of legal wrangling just come to an end on a napkin full of numbers?

As I sat across from Robert at his desk, my head was spinning. I was physically, mentally, and emotionally drained, and intuition was poking a stern finger into my chest, saying, "Don't rush into anything until you understand the outcome."

But Robert persisted. "Sure, he gets some properties plus 200 grand, but you get the business. The business, Karen. That's what you wanted, isn't it? Heck, you even get the boat."

"I guess it sounds reasonable, Robert. But I really need some time—"

"We don't have any more time, Karen. It just doesn't do to keep Judge Parker waiting, and we really can't afford to lose favor with the judge."

He handed me the contract.

"Are you sure you've covered everything?" I asked, my voice full of doubt and desperation.

"Every *i* and every *t*."

"Okay. I know you're in a hurry, Robert, but I really need you to go over the details of the deal with me. Just to reiterate: the company will pay Tom $200,000, and he'll turn his shares over to me at fair market value, right?"

"Not quite," Robert said impatiently. "The company isn't paying Tom. The way the deal is written, you'll be paying Tom the $200,000."

"Me? What?" I could barely speak. "You told me on the phone the business would be buying Tom out."

"You. The business. What's the difference, Karen? $200,000 is $200,000."

"I can't believe this." The room started swimming around me. "You really don't get it, do you? If the company pays Tom, it's pretax dollars. Paying Tom $200,000 from my own pocket is going to cost me an extra $70,000 at least! I—I can't do this, Robert," I stammered. "This just isn't right."

"Let me get this straight: you're prepared to pass up this sweet deal over $70,000? Need I remind you once again that there's a bigger picture you need to look at? For starters, consider the cost of another four days in the courtroom."

Even to this day I shake my head in disbelief: I relented. I brushed away the wagging finger of intuition and bowed to the pressure from my lawyer. "Okay, Robert," I said, "I'll sign." Against all reason, I decided to trust that he knew what he was doing. Lord knows I was paying him enough.

I okayed the offer without a clear understanding of the details, and in that I learned—for the umpteenth time—an invaluable lesson: when in doubt, the answer has to be *no*!

I walked with Robert and his junior to the courthouse to seal the deal. As Robert strode a few steps ahead of me, I remember saying, "This just doesn't feel right. I think we're making a huge mistake." Intuition was clawing and gouging at my thoughts.

"It's your decision, Karen," Robert said dismissively, "But if you ask me, it's too late for second guessing."

Wreathed in a cloud of confusion, I buckled under. I succumbed to the bullying and fear-mongering. I accepted the deal.

How could I have been so naïve? Where my mission was to get it done right, Robert McWilliams's was simply to get it done. And he got it over with, all right. But at what cost? In his wisdom and many years of litigation, he did know that dragging it on could amount to huge cost in both time and money, but to me right then, the cost was feeling like it could be high.

I had a feeling something was wrong. I just didn't yet know how wrong it really was.

After the deal was finalized, I took my lawyer and his junior to the pub.

Over drinks, I asked Robert if he felt we'd done the right thing in settling. He took a jovial swig of his scotch and soda and said, "Hey, never underestimate Aldus Green. He warned me during our negotiations that if we got back into the courtroom, he was ready to prove you're not the princess you come across as. What's that all about, Karen? You got a few secrets you haven't shared with me?"

Despite the hundreds of hours he'd billed me for, Robert didn't know me at all. If he did, he'd have known I'd been 100-percent honest with him—that I hadn't hidden *anything*, let alone a bombshell as Aldus had led him to believe. Perhaps if he'd taken the time to understand his client instead of constantly passing me off on his junior, he'd have said to Mr. Green, "My client is an honest person. I think I'll take my chances on her."

But this is not a story of *if onlys*. And it's certainly not a story of *good guys finish first*.

Sadly, I wasn't yet done with Robert. And Robert wasn't yet done with unpleasant surprises.

Still numb from the previous day's events, I called the offices of Peters McDermid McWilliams the morning after the deal was done. I needed Robert to fax my accountant a copy of the contract. I *really* just wanted to get things going and get things over with.

Sometime later, my accountant, Samir, rang me in my office. "Karen," he said, too seriously for comfort, "we've got ourselves a problem here."

"Great," I thought. "What else could possibly go wrong?" I simply had no idea.

"You said Tom's shares would be transferred at fair market value, correct?" Samir asked.

"Correct. Those were my instructions to Robert, and he assured me he'd taken care of it."

"Well, you'd better sit down, Karen, because that's not what he did."

Instead of fair market value, Robert had transferred Tom's shares at adjusted cost base—in other words, what the shares were worth when we started the company. In other words, zero (since we'd started the company from scratch).

Oh my God! Even before Samir told me, I knew exactly what this meant: a massive tax bill of well over $250,000.

I should have demanded accountability, but by this time I'd lost so much faith in the system, I really didn't believe anyone with the authority to mete out consequences would actually do so. And even if I found someone willing to challenge his peers and the status quo, it would have required money and hope, and I had nothing left of either.

I then decided to let it go—to quit fighting and move on with my life, my kids, and my business. In these matters, at least, I knew I could influence the outcome.

All in (including the $250,000-plus screw-up), the matrimonial legal system set me back nearly three quarters of a million dollars—an astronomical sum, but one that pales in comparison to what I really lost: faith, trust, and hope.

But I did get the business, and for that I will always be grateful. I also came away with my ever-growing passion to make a difference by challenging the present system of divorce and presenting a viable alternative.

As for the beautiful ski boat, we had paid over $35,000 for it three years earlier, but just before I took possession of it, the motor was completely destroyed. I simply couldn't afford the money to get it fixed, so my hopes of having a little fun with the kids on our boat went out the window along with everything else associated with my marriage to Tom.

How perfectly apt!

REFLECTIONS: YOUR WEALTH

For quite a while after it finally ended, I was pretty sure my divorce was one of a kind. I mean, who else needs to retain many different lawyers and incur costs of over one half of a million dollars just to move on from a dysfunctional marriage?

However, as I began to incubate my vision for true alternative to traditional divorce, I spoke to a lot of people who'd been through ordeals strikingly similar to my own. In the process, I became truly alarmed (and only slightly relieved) to learn that my case wasn't all that extraordinary. Over and over, I heard horror stories of the financial devastation wrought by divorce, often in cases where the couples entered into the divorce process determined to get through it quickly and amicably.

Something was (and is) terribly wrong with the system as we know it. In the chapters that follow, I expose the flaws of the tra-ditional system of divorce—and I establish a solid framework for overstepping its perils and its pitfalls.

Chapter 11

TAKING CONTROL—AND KEEPING IT

— — — — — — — — — — —

The notion that hiring a lawyer puts you in a position of control is a myth. Once you and your spouse retain lawyers, you're at the mercy of the system.

When the possibility of divorce looms large on the horizon, many people default to the conclusion-jumping tendency society has engendered in us: "I really don't want to waste my money on a lawyer, but I need to take some control. I feel like my life is spinning out of control and there's nothing I can do or say to stop it. If I hire a lawyer, I'll be heard, and I'll finally get the fair treatment I deserve."

Herein lies the lie.

Once you hire a lawyer and head down the path of traditional divorce, you surrender most (if not all) of the control you may have had over your destiny. You may, in the end, see justice, but in today's system of divorce, "justice" often bears little resemblance to "fairness."

It boggles my mind: how can society operate under such a startling misconception? It's time for people to start demanding accountability!

An outtake from the 1991 film *Other People's Money* seems apt. Danny DeVito, as Lawrence Garfield, says, "Lawyers are like nuclear warheads. I have them because the other guy has them, but the first time you use them, it fucks everything up."

Before I retained my first lawyer, a different lawyer (who is also a good friend) warned me I'd be surrendering control over my case. At the time, though, I just couldn't see a better alternative because there wasn't one.

There is actually very little in life over which we have control. But we have 100 percent control over our own decisions, including the decision about whether to hire a lawyer. We may not be able to take control in the truest sense of the words, but we can keep whatever control we have by not giving it away.

As I work with more and more couples, I become increasingly disheartened at the unfairness of the current system. I recently met with a couple in my office. Both are highly paid specialists, one in medicine and the other in business. They have three children under the age of eight. And they've fallen out of love. Neither is a bad person; they've simply grown apart and lost interest in one another.

Their case had been in the hands of two of the city's top matri-monial lawyers for six months before they came to me. Already, they had incurred over $75,000 in legal fees, and they'd gotten nowhere. What upsets me most and makes me so passionate about advocating for change is that their lawyers had instructed them to not talk to one another about anything!

This is exactly the problem. Here are two people who once loved each other and who had three children together. Neither has any desire to destroy their assets or their children's self-esteem or the other person's future. Yet the ensuing correspondence between the lawyers was threatening the remaining bonds of their relationship and creating a massive amount of fear. They were both at wits' end, but had nowhere to turn until they heard about Fairway Divorce Solutions.

I can well imagine what the outcome would have been. More than likely, their lawyers would have recommended property valuations, business appraisals, and parental assessments along with the ever-flowing stream of letters and affidavits that had already been wreaking havoc on both parties' happiness. Before it was all over, their fees would have been well into the six figures.

What's worse, their three children would have seen Mommy and Daddy (who had always had an open, healthy co-parenting relationship) stop communicating with one another and, in time, stop respecting and trusting and caring for one another. The children would be the real victims, and who would be left to clean up the mess? Two adults who had come to despise one another.

Is the current system flawed? You can decide for yourself, but I certainly know what I think. That's why I'm so committed to offering a fair alternative for divorce because every day I hear stories like this one. Except where there are extenuating circumstances (for example, spousal or child abuse or a party's refusal to divulge financial information), divorce simply doesn't belong in the current system.

The system as it is destroys people and relationships and money and self-esteem. It destroys trust. And hope. And it destroys without discrimination.

While the law is necessary to protect people's interests, lawyers are rarely needed to bring about a resolution. In fact, they tend to get in the way of resolutions rather than facilitating them, often making their exits only when little remains but ashes and animosity. As American author Jean Kerr humorously observes, "A lawyer is never entirely comfortable with a friendly divorce, any more than a good mortician wants to finish his job and then have the patient sit up on the table."

The current system is adversarial, not resolution based. And it destroys lives with no accountability. The entire model is profoundly flawed.

Unfortunately, the traditional system of divorce is occasionally unavoidable when, for example, one party refuses to consider an al-ternative course of action.

If you do end up in the traditional system during your journey through divorce, you may find yourself feeling an immediate and overwhelming loss of control. Like a common criminal, you become open to applications, affidavits, discoveries, expert witnesses, and assorted other legal assaults.

Furthermore, North American courts are busy and backlogged, and you may have to wait for months or even years to be heard in front of a judge. This long wait can be excruciating, but you're powerless to accelerate the process.

Nor do you or your lawyer have any say in who will hear your case, and while most judges are fair, you may end up with one whose personality or whose biases clash with your own. Let's not forget they are, after all, human.

Remember, too, that judges must operate within the constraints of an overloaded system. They have limited time to evaluate each case and must rely on evidence, including affidavits prepared and submitted by lawyers and presented in the courtroom.

An affidavit is, by definition, a sworn statement of truth. But when you factor in the emotions that go along with marriage and divorce and kids and money, truth has a tendency to unravel. Perception is often far removed from reality, yet your spouse's affidavits about what kind of parent you are or how you handled (or mishandled) the family finances or how many times in the past year you drove after drinking or smoked marijuana are mostly expressions of his or her perceptions packaged as truths.

All these uncontrollable factors make divorce court somewhat of a crap shoot. Justice may prevail, but fairness may not. Are you prepared to bet your future financial security and your children's emotional security on what may be a roll of the dice?

Committed as I was to taking the high road during my divorce, I endeavored at all times to be honest in my affidavits while recognizing, of course, that honesty is a function of grayish perception rather than black-and-white reality. I remember asking one of my lawyers, "What happens if my spouse submits a work of fiction that contradicts my affidavit? What will the judge do?"

Her reply: "The judge will accept both as statements of fact. He'll assume you're both attempting to tell the truth. The court assumes you are both honest citizens doing your best to reach a resolution."

I was perplexed. "But that's a faulty assumption. People lie, es-pecially people who are in the habit of lying, or perhaps people who are getting dragged through a divorce they never wanted. Surely the court understands that truth gets tainted by affairs, anger, jealousy, addictions, and spite?"

"Truth. Lies. In the eyes of the court, there's often no telling them apart. Unless there's evidence of abuse or some equally serious criminal-ity, a judge hears both sides of an argument and then has to decide what is truth and what is fiction. It makes sense then, with two affidavits in hand from two emotionally charged divorcing parties, that perhaps the truth lies somewhere in the middle. And if you really think about it, the approach is reasonably just."

"Maybe it is just, but is it fair?"

"Sorry, that's just the way it is. The judge has to assume that both parties enter the system in good faith and will put forth truthful information. No one ever said the system was perfect."

What an understatement.

My first mistake was trusting conventional wisdom, which says, "Hire a ruthless go-getter who'll really stick it to the other side."

Wrong, wrong, wrong: This proved to be a just-add-money recipe for extortionate lawyers' bills as my file became a battleground of legal egos.

If I had it to do all over again, I would use Fairway Divorce Solutions or a similar service, of course. But if that wasn't an option (as indeed it wasn't at the time) and I absolutely had to hire a lawyer, I'd have waited for Tom to choose his lawyer first. Then, to mitigate against a lengthy spectacle of one-upmanship, I'd have hired Tom's lawyer's best friend or the closest thing to it. (Remember, in any given city, many of the lawyers went to school together, attend the same conferences, sit on the same committees, and rub elbows with one another at social functions.)

If that wasn't an option, I'd certainly have done my research. Did my prospective lawyer have a personal vendetta against Tom's, or did his have one against mine? What sort of reputation did he or she have in the legal community? And among former clients?

Another important question: on average, how often do they go to court? The higher the number, the redder the flag that says, "I'm just no good at negotiating resolutions."

Current caseload is another important indicator. An overloaded briefcase screams, "Take a number. I'll get around to your concerns when I get around to them. And don't hold your breath." Of course, a lawyer with no other cases on the go may not be a safe bet either.

If you must hire a lawyer, learn from my mistake. The cost of my decision to "take control" is that I gave it up altogether.

A fair approach to divorce allows all parties to maintain control over their decisions and, ultimately, their destinies.

Chapter 12

FORMULATING A STRATEGIC
PROCESS AND PLAN

— — — — — — — — — —

A dizzying deluge of letters, affidavits, lawsuits, and demand court appearances is the hallmark of the traditional system of divorce. But when a process is reactive and seemingly random, there's no way to know whether the final outcome is fair.

Stumbling into your divorce and rushing to retain a lawyer without an ironclad plan is akin to setting sail across the North Atlantic Ocean without a nautical map, a GPS receiver, or a captain to steer the ship.

It's like ending up instead with a boatload of ego-inflated first mates clambering to get their hands on the wheel, with the loudest, most bullish lawyers setting the general direction. Eventually they get you to the opposite shore, but their haphazard zigzagging across the ocean consumes an alarming amount of unnecessary time and money.

A strategic plan not only straightens out the route toward resolu-tion, it clears the pathway of flotsam and jetsam while dramatically shortening the distance from point A to point B—from onset to resolution.

The backbone of INR is a strategic plan that begins with the final des-tination not only in mind but clearly in view.

It also rigorously defines each step that needs to be taken, and it effectively eliminates superfluous or counterproductive steps. It knows where it's coming from and where it is going.

For many people (myself included), the randomness of the legal experience follows seamlessly from the seemingly random events that got them there in the first place. During our year of slow marital disintegration, Tom's behavior was as wildly unpredictable as the string of correspondence that later followed from his lawyer.

Not only does random correspondence intensify an already stressful experience, it twists the pathway toward resolution into a dysfunctional, seemingly endless series of switchbacks and convolutions. It turns you into a frazzled, stressed-out rat in a maze, one who lives in constant fear of the next unpleasant shock.

The greatest tragedy, from my perspective, is that the lawyers' correspondence and affidavits make permanent and ineradicable the venom and spite that might otherwise have weakened or stopped stinging altogether after wounds began to heal. I know firsthand how hurtful divorce can be, and for even the kindest of souls it is fraught with the desire to hurt the other party, especially if you were wronged or betrayed. But there is a price to pay for this subtle revenge, and I can tell you the price is way too high. Once the words are put to paper and dropped in the mail, they can never be taken back.

Often, if there is any tenderness or mutual respect remaining when a couple begins their divorce proceedings, the ensuing correspondence quite effectively destroys it.

The lawyers might argue they're just doing their jobs. "C'mon, cut us some slack. We're not paid to manufacture happily ever afters. We're paid to fight for our clients. We're paid to secure the biggest slice of the pie. We're paid to be ruthless. We're paid to win."

And yes, lawyers do win sometimes, but at what cost?

Surely the divorcing couple doesn't win as any positives they might have taken away from their time together are decisively and permanently obscured by the mud their lawyers sling back and forth.

And surely their children don't win as they must stand helplessly by as their parents' relationship gets battered and beaten to an almighty pulp.

There's no question in my mind: lawyers' letters damage. Affidavits go one step further: they destroy.

I am firm in my conviction that unless one member poses a danger to the rest of the family (through abuse or other criminal acts), affidavits have no place within family law. They do little but destroy relationships, and for what? To prove that you're right and your spouse is wrong?

In divorce, the black and white of "right or wrong" seldom exists. Divorce is a world of gray areas, where everything is subjective and only perception exists. Remember, good people divorce, too.

When you pay a lawyer to draft an affidavit, the cost may far transcend dollars and cents. After the bill, you can tack on the un-foreseeable and immeasurable pain and suffering you'll bring upon others and yourself.

If I could press Rewind and rerecord my own divorce, I would not allow my lawyer to put on paper the words she put the first time round. To stop the train wreck that I now know was the outcome, I would have swept the debris from the rails.

But I was naive. I was full of fear and trusted my lawyers totally. I was unable to see as clearly, and for that I paid. The affidavits the lawyers sent back and forth destroyed so much, including any chance of co-parenting with my ex-husband.

While it was happening, this back-and-forth exchange of threats and invectives, I remember feeling utterly hopeless. Most of the people who've shared their stories with me felt exactly the same. Although my case was extreme, it was by no means atypical.

And after the damage was done, who was left trying to put the pieces back together? Not the lawyers, that's for sure. They'd been paid and were long gone.

The current system and its processes failed me utterly. And if you can't trust the process, it's extremely difficult to trust in the outcomes. It's extremely difficult to do anything but fear for the worst.

Illumination dissolves fear, and the INR approach to divorce illuminates. Through a logical, step-by-step process, it empowers wise decision making by imparting knowledge, insight, and foresight.

When you trust the process, you can trust the outcome.

When divorce involves a step-by-step, start-to-finish methodology, you can rest assured the resolution is fair.

Chapter 13

MOVING BEYOND FEAR OF
THE UNKNOWN

— — — — — — — — — —

*In a random, chaotic system like the traditional system
of divorce, you seldom know what's coming next. As a
result, making informed, forward-looking decisions is
all but impossible.*

Uncertainty resides at the core of many basic human fears.

A child's fear of the dark stems from uncertainty about what may be
lurking in the unlit corners. Fear of public speaking, one of the most
common and debilitating of all human fears, arises largely from uncertainty about how the audience will respond. ("Will they be able to see how
nervous I am? And will they listen, or will they just sit there, judging me
and tallying my inadequacies?") And those who fear death fear most of all
the uncertainty in which it is shrouded.

The current system of divorce is filled with fear, and rightly so, for
you simply never know what's coming next. Will it be a letter from your
spouse's attorney, suggesting you're an unfit parent? Will it be a court
order for a parental assessment? Will it be a motion to slash your living
allowance because your spouse alleges you squander money in casinos
and nightclubs?

Whatever it is, you can almost be certain it won't paint you in flattering brushstrokes, and after the picture gets framed in an affidavit, it gets filed in the court records forever.

When you make decisions from a place of fear, you give away all your power to your opponent, and I don't mean just your spouse. The system is your real opponent, for it is through fear creation that the lawyers position their clients to win, the same kind of "win" a general proclaims as the field is strewn with bodies from both sides of the battle.

"Win-win" is rarely the term that comes to mind when you're in the midst of a divorce, especially when you're aligned with a lawyer who stakes a position far, far away from "win-win" in hopes of ending up somewhere near the middle. The situation is made even worse when a client is on the path of revenge, determined to "win" at all costs.

Fairway Divorce Solutions takes a different view of victory: a "win-win" approach whose benefits extend not only to all involved in a divorce but to society as a whole. There is a better way to end things. It's not about "How can I lose the least?" It's about "How can we both win the most?"

The present system of divorce both creates and thrives on a climate of fear, the wellspring of which is uncertainty. As you move at a snail's pace through the divorce battle, with your spouse hunkered down in one camp and you hunkered down in another, you have no way to ascertain the other side's next move.

You remain, therefore, in a constant state of high alert, a position of perpetual defensiveness, ready to react (and we've already explored the dire negative consequences of operating in reactive mode).

So if you're not in control and your spouse isn't in control, who is? Some would say the lawyers, whose correspondence and maneuvering keep their clients constantly in the fear-inducing dark. But even they are not in control.

Never knowing what may come next from opposing counsel, the lawyers must remain forever ready in a defensive, reactive position.

Regrettably, this state of perpetual defensiveness precludes proactive problem solving.

Case in point: a recent client thought all was well—that things were moving slowly forward. Then out of the blue came a massive affidavit from her spouse. Her lawyer's comment: "Wow, I didn't see that coming.

They must have spent most of the summer preparing this attack." And what an attack it was, demanding full custody of the children and full control of the business—more than 100 pages of permanent relationship and co-parenting destruction.

You may very well land a lawyer who's a strategic thinker and pro-active problem solver by nature, but that nature simply cannot thrive in the current system because there's always another lawyer somewhere in the picture.

Another way to look at fear is as a negative anticipation of some-thing to come. In the divorce process as we know it, decisions are made, more often than not, from a place of such fear, a place plagued with *maybes* and *what ifs* and *I don't knows*.

"If I don't take forceful action right away, how do I know the other side won't try to take advantage of me?" "If I don't take this offer, maybe the next one will be even worse." "If I don't give in to my spouse's demands for the summer cottage, some of my unsavory secrets might come out during the custody hearings." "My spouse's lawyer said if I don't agree to my husband's conditions, they'll see me in court, and it won't be pleasant."

In each of these cases we may react, often with undue haste, in an effort to preempt the imagined negative outcomes.

We really need to heed Molière: "Unreasonable haste is the direct road to error." More simply, as the old saying goes, "Haste makes waste."

Another adage you've heard me use before promises "We are never handed anything we cannot handle." And like all enduring adages, this one arises from a timeless, universal truth. Sometimes to our great sur-prise, we find we can handle most of the curveballs, fastballs, knuckle-balls, and screwballs that life throws our way. Think about your past. In hindsight, was there anything you really couldn't handle? The answer must be *no* because you're still here to answer the question. In most cases, it is negative anticipation of what is to come that is our enemy, not what actually comes.

In this context, fear loses its legitimacy: it is reduced to a state of mind whose foundation is shaky at best. And if we can change our frame of reference, we can illuminate fear and chase it out of those dark places in which it resides.

For help, you can look to innovative thinkers who've expanded upon the "power of positive thinking" model and helped countless people tap the amazing power of their minds. For example, Brian Tracy's *Goals!* can help you use visualization to set in motion a positive future. When I started putting pen to paper and writing about my goals as you did in the painted picture—about what I wanted to create in my future—things started happening for me. Without setting my goals and steering in the direction of those goals, who knows where I would have ended up? Almost certainly it wouldn't have included writing this book or the clarity with which I now pursue my mission to change the way people move through divorce.

It is very difficult to make informed, "eyes wide open" decisions when feeling pressured or afraid. To ensure you're getting to the right outcome for you and your family, you need a step-by-step problem-solving process that facilitates decisions you can live with. After all, the division of assets and the other questions you'll face during your divorce will require some of the most important decisions of your life, and the impact of those decisions will extend far into your future.

As such, you need to be able to ask questions, get answers, and know you can trust those answers before you settle on any course of action, no matter how minor it may seem at the time. You need to trust that details will receive the attention they deserve—that all the *t*'s will be crossed and all the *i*'s dotted—because an error or omission can mean the difference between long-term security and financial ruin.

The only way to ensure you've made the right decisions and, in the end, arrived at a fair settlement, is to ensure you took smart steps along the way. Back-and-forth correspondence and position bargaining, the hallmarks of the traditional divorce process, are the very antitheses of methodical decision making. You need to know where you came from, where you're going, and exactly how you're going to get there. Only then you can trust that you've arrived in the right place.

Remembering that fear arises from lack of knowledge, giving people the knowledge they need empowers them to make enlightened decisions. Such empowerment springs from five main sources:

1. Knowing that a sound and intelligent process exists

2. Clearly understanding that process (not only what will happen, but why)

3. Trusting that each decision along the way will hold up and impact the final outcome exactly as it should (something I call "empowered decision making")

4. Having the information you need to make prudent, forward-looking decisions

5. Knowing full well the information that guides your decisions is based on fact, not on perception or fallacy or fear

A truly empowering approach like Independently Negotiated Resolution not only allows its participants to make informed, educated decisions, it ensures they do. To the participants, these decisions sound no intuitive alarm bells; they leave no lingering doubts about "what have I done?" They just feel right because they arise from a sound analytical process.

They feel right because they are right.

A fair approach to divorce empowers prudent decision making through knowledge, education, and removal of fear.

Chapter 14

DEMANDING ACCOUNTABILITY

— — — — — — — — — — —

In a system where those who profit by the proceedings can prolong them with impunity, quick and cost-effective resolutions are rare.

Michael Armstrong, AT&T's former chairman and CEO, relates the following anecdote from the annals of history:

> The ancient Romans had a tradition: whenever one of their engineers constructed an arch, as the capstone was hoisted into place, the engineer assumed accountability for his work in the most profound way possible: he stood under the arch.

Imagine if professionals today demonstrated that same kind of accountability, standing beneath (or behind) their work and their word! Instead, the traditional system of divorce engenders a "cover your ass" attitude. Deflecting blame and denying responsibility are commonplace techniques within the system of traditional divorce.

I said earlier that this isn't a story about *if onlys*. Now I take that back: when it comes to legal excuse-making, *if onlys* are epidemic!

"If only we'd ended up with a different judge."

"If only your spouse wasn't such a manipulator."

"If only the opposing lawyer could have convinced your spouse to see things more clearly."

"If only I'd seen that affidavit coming."

"If only I hadn't accidentally sent your private notes to opposing counsel."

If only.

If, during your divorce, you decide to hire a lawyer, don't do so with any illusions that the system will own its part when things go sideways. If a lawyer's advice has disastrous consequences or, as I experienced, a lawyer's gaffe spawns a whole new set of legal woes, the costs of cleanup will fall squarely on your bill.

My lawyer's misstep in providing opposing counsel with my rough notes concerning a possible settlement precipitated a breach of contract lawsuit from my ex-husband and his lawyer. Not only did this put me through yet another legal wringer, it inflated my already-astronomical legal fees.

In such cases, isn't it reasonable to expect a lawyer to step up and say, "Wow, did I ever blunder! I'm turning off the clock until I set things straight again." (Yes, I know there are many out there who would. If you are perhaps a matrimonial lawyer reading this book, would you?)

To ensure fair outcomes, I have created a system in which people are held accountable to their commitments and everyone's interests are aligned. In this system, hope is fostered by the setting of clear, achievable goals and the keeping of promises as all parties work toward their fulfillment.

In *Three Resolutions*, Stephen R. Covey, most noted for his *7 Habits of Highly Effective People*, explores the impact of bad habits and engrained ideas on positive change in organizations and individuals. Covey writes:

> Every organization—and individual—struggles to gain and main-tain alignment with core values, ethics and principles. Whatever our professed personal and organizational beliefs, we all face restraining forces, opposition

and challenges, and these sometimes cause us to do
things that are contrary to our stated missions, intentions and res-olutions. We may think that we can change
deeply embedded habits and patterns simply by making
new resolutions or goals—only to find that old habits
die hard and that in spite of good intentions and social
promises, familiar patterns carry over from year to year.

Much of what Covey says could be taken one step further to a discussion of the systemic change that's needed in the process of divorce.
There, old habits die hard indeed, and although many who operate within
the system recognize its deeply engrained flaws, the status quo barrels
stubbornly forward.

One of Covey's most powerful statements is "Accountability breeds
response-ability. Commitment and involvement produce change."

Independently Negotiated Resolution is truly responsive: it has pure
empathy for the emotional turbulence each of the parties is experiencing,
and it responds with a methodology that's kinder and quicker, and one
that turns despair into hope for the future.

*A fair approach to divorce is accountable for bringing people to a
mutually agreed-upon resolution as quickly as possible.*

Chapter 15

ACCELERATING THE PROCESS

— — — — — — — — — — —

*In divorce, a slow time line works in nobody's favor but
the lawyers'. It stands to reason: the longer your divorce
drags on, the more it costs.*

I've heard it said that all good things must come to an end, but bad things
seem to go on and on forever. How true these words ring in the context
of the traditional divorce process, where time is second only to money in
the list of things most recklessly consumed!

Movement through the traditional divorce process can be geologic in
its pace and astronomical in its costs. But time is rarely on your side when
it comes to the distribution of assets. Every now and then, a case will
benefit from being dragged on and on, perhaps because sheer exasperation finally motivates the two sides to agree to a mutually beneficial settlement. In most cases, though, more time means not only more money but
more pain.

The longer a divorce takes, the higher the costs (not only in dollars but
in lost opportunities). As long as you're stuck in divorce proceedings, it
remains very difficult to move forward—to turn your attention to healing
and creating a new life for yourself.

You will no doubt think a lot about the future and what it will be like
during this new stage in your life. You might even have the wherewithal

to piece together a plan, if not on paper, then at least in your dreams. But implementation is next to impossible until the assets have been conclusively divided and you can do with your part what you want.

So you wait. But as the old adage says, "In life there is no such thing as standing still; we are either moving forward or moving backwards." If you're not moving forward, well . . .

Time is reputed to heal all wounds, but time spent trudging through the matrimonial legal system actually makes wounds, already open and sore, much, much worse. In the interests of speeding up the healing of emotional wounds, you want to move through and beyond the financial issues as quickly as possible.

If you refer back to Part 1 of my personal story and take my emotional journey as an example, you'll appreciate that much of the rebuilding and emotional step work takes time spent focusing on yourself and your emotional needs. The all-consuming distraction of a legal battle unnecessarily delays your healing and growth.

A slow process wastes invaluable time that would be far better spent moving forward and building a new life. Remember, time is a finite resource. Once wasted, it is gone forever.

Divorce is an ending, but with every ending comes a new beginning. The time in between is no-man's-land, a place of limbo, and a tough place to be.

The ideal is to move through it as quickly as possible while still addressing all of the necessary issues. As painful as it is, that movement can be pragmatic. And while it can never pass by fast enough, the important thing is to create and sustain forward momentum.

As I've said before, divorce will be painful. An alternative approach to divorce isn't going to take away the sting. It will, however, move you through the pain much more quickly, bringing you to a place where you can deal effectively with the emotional fallout and then get on with your life. Because it's relentlessly focused on resolution and employs a strategically sound methodology for getting there, INR dramatically shortens the time line from the start of negotiations through to conclusion. Where the traditional divorce process can perpetuate itself over many months or even years, the alternative approach significantly abbreviates the time line.

That's time well saved.

A fair approach to divorce moves quickly toward a resolution that satisfies everyone's expectations of fairness.

Chapter 16

CONTROLLING COSTS

— — — — — — — — — — —

*Once you become entrenched in the traditional system
of divorce, you have absolutely no control over costs.*

During the Christmas holidays not long ago, I attended a function whose
attendees happened to include a large number of lawyers.

As I stood chatting with a circle of acquaintances, I couldn't help
but overhear an exchange between two of the city's senior matrimonial lawyers.

"I spent most of the day shopping for a new car," said one to the
other. "I've got my eye on a new Mercedes-Benz. The CLK is sporty, but
I'm leaning toward the S-Class."

"Top of the line, eh? Did you win the lottery, or is it a Christmas
present to yourself?"

"More like a Christmas present from a client. It's all thanks to that case
you and I have been battling over. What a doozie—nudge nudge!"

I was utterly appalled, so much so that I set aside my plate of hors
d'oeuvres, thanked the host, and left the gathering. I realized I had been in
a sea of strangers with whom I had little in common.

Sadly, though, I wasn't at all surprised.

Because the world in which I'm building my new model of divorce
is small, I later found out which case the lawyers were talking about.

What I can tell you is this: before their case was resolved, the couple's relationship was wholly destroyed. Not even a shred of respect or consideration remained.

But I imagine the new Mercedes-Benz made it all worthwhile.

In the traditional system of divorce, each side of the splitting couple typically hires one or more lawyers to represent his or her interests. These lawyers typically charge by the hour, with no guarantee (and rarely even an estimate) of how many hours it might take to reach a resolution.

In fact, there are no guarantees about anything, including an outcome. It's quite possible the lawyer you hire won't even see your case through to resolution, but that won't exempt you from paying his or her bill.

While variations in lawyers' billing structures exist, hourly fees are the norm in matrimonial law, ranging according to seniority and experience. Paying $450 or more per hour for one of the best (usually a senior partner in a large law firm) is commonplace.

The most important thing to bear in mind is this: unless they are working on a contingency basis, lawyers don't get paid well for fast and hassle-free settlements.

This is exactly what people need to understand: lawyers do not get paid well for cases that settle quickly, and the lawyers know it.

I certainly won't paint the entire legal profession in broad strokes of censure. I have encountered many family lawyers who care deeply about their clients and act in their clients' interests to the best of their ability. That's often difficult, though, within a system that no longer works except to move people further apart, deplete financial resources, and increase fear, pain, and anxiety.

If you plan on pursuing a legal course of action in your divorce, look very carefully before you board the train. Once the legal locomotive is in motion, there's no way to apply the brakes and prevent a train wreck without both parties' consent.

Knowing in advance approximately how much your divorce will cost—and seeing in advance that you'll be able to keep the vast majority of your family's assets within the family—reduces a great deal of the fear and apprehension that are common during a traditional divorce.

A truly fair approach to divorce—the alternative divorce I'm unveiling in this book—employs a step-by-step process with fixed, transparent costs and total accountability along the way.

Chapter 17

PUTTING AN END TO
POSITION BARGAINING

— — — — — — — — — — —

*Negotiating resolutions based on perceived values is a
long, costly, and highly frustrating endeavor.*

Underlying the problem of dividing assets is the assumption that each
asset up for grabs—each piece in a divorcing couple's asset pie—has a
specific value. As the lawyers prepare to squabble over these assets on
behalf of their clients, they try to establish a framework for the negotiations by taking a position on the value of each asset.

So far, so good, in theory at least. But the theory depends on unanimous agreement on the value of each asset: the house is worth X, the car
is worth Y, and the purebred Shih Tzu is worth Z.

Alas, such crystal-clear, indisputable facts simply can't exist in the midst
of a divisive and combative emotional crisis where there is no reality, only
perception. When matrimonial lawyers try to get resolution on perceptions, a case can drag on for years and years.

Emotions turn the asset pie into a muddy mess, and the ensuing debate
over values and equitable division is usually long, costly, and vicious.

Through Independently Negotiated Resolution, a true picture of
the asset pie—the sum of all assets and their agreed-upon values—is
established right up front. Input on the value of each asset is obtained

from both parties. Only when mutual agreement has been reached on the value of every asset in the pie do the "who gets what?" negotiations get underway.

Once fixed values have been assigned, dividing up the asset pie efficiently and equitably is usually a piece of cake!

This rock-solid process ensures a fair division of assets without the mudslinging, backstabbing, and lifelong resentments that often come with divorce in the traditional system.

For example, let's say the wife wants the dog. How much is a Shih Tzu really worth? Her lawyer will argue it's not even worth the $450 they paid for it; it is, after all, getting on in years, and it never fulfilled its promise as a prizewinner.

His lawyers, meanwhile (eager to acquire the largest possible trade-off), will position it as practically priceless: just think of all the training and grooming and veterinary costs invested on its behalf. Of course, they also know she loves that dog dearly and wouldn't part with it for anything in the world. (Well, almost anything.)

And so begins another round of fruitless bickering.

The traditional system of divorce revolves around (and around and around) what I refer to as "position bargaining." In this reactive, defensive posturing, the opposing parties take positions on the value of particular assets and then maneuver to ensure they get what they want. The process amounts to little more than asset grabbing, which looks a lot like preschool children fighting for the same toy in the toy box.

Position bargaining pays, but only if you're a lawyer. For the rest of us, it's a terrible drain of money and time.

What's worse, position bargaining typically prevents participants from seeing other, often better solutions that could, over the long term, put more money in their pockets.

Lawyers thrive on ambiguity, and ambiguity thrives in traditional divorce proceedings. Assets just simply seem to change value as they move from one person's column to the other's. Of course this does not make sense but that is exactly what happens.

An example will shed light on my meaning:

Sally says she wants the house. She puts a price on the house. Then, based on that price, she and her lawyer begin to bargain with her husband and his lawyer.

There are many problems with this approach, not the least of which is the possibility that Sally cannot even afford the house. All too often in divorce, people's actions (or reactions) spring from emotional attachments to an asset. ("But this house is where I raised my children," explains Sally. "It's filled to the brim with happy memories.") The problem here is easy to see: emotional attachment is driving a financial decision about an asset that will likely have an inflated price tag because the other party recognizes how important it is to Sally.

Herein lies the major flaw with position bargaining. Values, which have no business being anything but fixed, become dynamic.

When Sally announces she wants the house, her husband and his lawyer say, "Fine. It's worth $475,000. Now we want an equal allotment of assets in return."

"Actually," say the wife and her lawyer by way of a letter after several days of serious deliberation, "you can have the house. We've decided we want the cottage and the retirement savings instead."

"Very well," reply the men, who put a premium on the house for the purposes of negotiation because they knew perfectly well how much Sally wanted it, "but upon closer inspection, the house is clearly worth no more than $350,000. It's got a leaky bathroom tap, and the neighbors next door don't take care of their lawn."

I can anticipate your reaction: "That's ludicrous! An asset is an asset, and its value should be constant!" Exactly. But in the traditional system of divorce, such logic stands a slim chance of survival.

"Okay," you say, "then a third-party appraisal can solve the problem, right?" Wrong. Appraisals are largely subjective and, as a result, wildly inconsistent. If one side disagrees with the results of an appraisal, they can commission another. And another. This can go around and around in a flurry of legal correspondence and lawyers' fees, and still the value of the house may remain a mystery.

I know couples who (at the court's insistence) spent thousands of dollars for third-party valuations of their assets, yet as soon as ne-gotiations resumed, they were right back where they started: stuck in total disagreement over what their things were really worth.

Independently Negotiated Resolution puts first things first. Before negotiations about asset division begin, INR practitioners work with clients to describe the total financial pie. One by one, we come to a consensus on the value of each asset and each liability—each piece of the pie. Assets minus liabilities equals net worth—an easily divisible number. Only then do we begin putting assets and liabilities into the "His" and "Hers" columns.

Agreeing on values first and then dividing assets is the only way to ensure a fair outcome.

Chapter 18

DIVIDING ASSETS (INSTEAD OF DESTROYING THEM)

— — — — — — — — — — —

The traditional divorce process often diminishes or destroys the very assets the parties are vying for.

Let's face it: divorce is costly enough without the extortionate lawyers' fees. According to a study by an Ohio State University researcher, a person who marries (and stays married) accumulates nearly twice as much personal wealth as his or her single or divorced counterparts.

The same study found that divorce costs a lot more than giving up half of everything you own. During a divorce, people lose, on average, three-fourths of their personal net worth.

So the question is, how can you minimize the loss?

Be smart. Be pragmatic. And be greedy. Keeping your family's assets in the family is hardly a crime. The attitude Western society has cultivated—that we should expect third-party representatives to pocket a sizable portion of our divorce settlements—is warped and misguided.

The long and bitter battles engendered by the traditional system of divorce destroy wealth in three ways:

1. There are the hard costs associated with divorce: legal fees, property valuations, third-party assessments, and so on.

2. The devaluation of assets as they remain tied up until a final resolution is reached is a cost for which many people fail to account, yet it can be one of the most significant. Consider, for example, an investment portfolio that cannot divest itself of certain stocks in anticipation of a market decrease or a major drop in a particular stock. Or a business that cannot tap into its cash reserves to take advantage of a potentially lucrative, once-in-a-lifetime opportunity all because bank accounts have been frozen or other restrictions have limited the parties' ability to work with assets during the legal battle.

3. The value of assets may diminish through neglect as the re-sponsible party's attention is consumed by the legal chaos surrounding the divorce.

During my divorce, for example, my business suffered terribly. Our customer service was deteriorating, dissatisfied clients were taking their business elsewhere, and staff morale was in the toilet. With my attention focused almost solely on the breakdown of my marriage, I simply couldn't give the business the time and energy it required to prosper and thrive. Such distractedness is hardly conducive to increasing the value of assets. Even low-conflict divorce cases take the parties' efforts away from work and asset growth. In most cases, the very best to be hoped for is preservation of the value of assets.

I have spoken to so many people who underestimated the power of lawyers to restrict the positive continuance of a business, all under the pretense of protecting the assets for their clients. As I discovered firsthand, this can be one of the biggest costs a divorcing couple may face. And at the end of the day, even if the business is your spouse's, it usually forms part of the matrimonial pie.

A wise lawyer I know describes divorce as a zero-sum game. "It's not a win-win or even a win-lose. It's merely a matter of who loses most and who loses least."

What a scary arena to enter! Yet looking back, he was bang on. Tom and I both lost. It's impossible to say who lost the most, but I can say with 100-percent certainty that neither of us won.

Independently Negotiated Resolution is rooted in practices accepted by professional financial planners and certified divorce financial analysts (CDFAs), who can help people understand the financial implications of different settlement scenarios and make educated decisions regarding financial settlements, valuing and dividing property, alimony, child support, pensions, and tax issues.

If you feel you're financially savvy enough to dispense with such assistance, tread carefully. Even if you're well versed with numbers, don't underestimate the power of emotion to obliterate your objectivity and your common sense. Seeing your situation clearly can be difficult when you're bogged down in the emotional fallout of your own divorce.

For a perfect example, look at me. As an MBA and owner of a financial services company, I'm very astute when it comes to financial matters. Yet during my divorce I couldn't see the forest for the trees, and I made some surprisingly bad decisions. An objective perspective from someone with no emotional attachment to my case or its outcome would have been invaluable either to confirm what I already believed or to challenge me to look at things from an altogether different angle.

Independently Negotiated Resolution takes a long-term view of things, helping clients negotiate resolutions that will serve their financial best interests far into the future.

If you find yourself stuck in the traditional system because your spouse isn't open to alternatives, you'd be very prudent to seek the services of a well-qualified financial planner or an accredited CDFA. Either can help in the following ways:

- Providing forecasts and feedback about possible settlement scenarios

- Showing you how various settlements will translate into future financial positions

- Providing you with a measure of certainty and hope in an otherwise uncertain, sometimes hopeless situation

- Helping you define boundaries (what you're willing to accept and what you're prepared to fight for)

- Comparing the long-term differences between your and your spouse's financial pictures based on different settlement scenarios

This final point is very powerful. Often, distant-future projections reveal epic differences between the financial pictures for the two parties.

Generally speaking, North American women tend to receive less favorable financial outcomes than their ex-husbands for a couple of reasons.

First, the woman from a divorcing couple most often ends up with the children, which increases her daily living expenses.

Second, a woman who has sacrificed her career to raise a family often gets shortchanged by the system. Even if the courts account for the woman's indispensable role when dividing up the family's assets, the ex-husband will have had much more time and opportunity to advance his career. So as life after divorce begins, ex-wife and ex-husband will be starting from dramatically different footings. When the starting pistol sounds, the husband may have a 20-year head start, while the woman may still be tying her shoes in the locker room.

Staying home and raising children is a tough job, one that is still undervalued by society at large. As gender roles slowly evolve and men play increasingly prominent roles in raising children, the system may eventually arrive at a place of fairness, where the nurturing of children is worth as much as biweekly deposits into the family's bank accounts. Each party deserves credit for his or her unique contributions to the family unit.

I can also empathize with the other perspective: you spent many years busting your butt to build a business and now it becomes just another bargaining chip. Still, if the negotiating process is sound, a win-win is always possible. That is the art of achieving a good outcome.

Especially in cases like these, where disparity exists between a couple's relative financial contributions, projections of the financial future are a must. Traditionally, they have not been done nearly enough, though this is changing thanks to organizations like the Institute for Divorce Financial Analysts.

In divorce, division of assets is unavoidable, but they needn't be destroyed in the process. Fairway Divorce Solutions advocates a strategic approach to resolution that empowers people in the decision-making process and maximizes the assets each party receives. It achieves this through the following:

- Employing a clearly defined, step-by-step methodology

- Analyzing and assessing the short-term and long-term financial implications of a party's asset division options

- Accommodating the ability to create and choose a division of assets that satisfies the needs of all parties going forward

- Coming up with a plan that does not disempower the care provider (if one party was the primary breadwinner)

- Allowing both parties to be self-sufficient if at all possible (mutual personal empowerment)

- Ensuring children's lives can move forward in positive ways, with a bare minimum of loss

Importantly, in this approach, both parties accept the plan at the outset and agree to stick to it through to resolution, which is clearly in sight every step of the way.

Throughout this proactive process, both parties take part in the decision making without the malice and threats that permeate the traditional system of divorce. Yes, emotions will run high, people will yell, and greed will try its hardest to infiltrate the negotiations. But even with all the emotional baggage, it's possible to move quickly to a positive win-win outcome. You need to be relentless in your commitment to making it happen.

A fair approach to divorce keeps a whole lot of unnecessary (and unwelcome) fingers out of your family's asset pie.

Chapter 19

ATTENDING TO THE
ALL-IMPORTANT DETAILS

— — — — — — — — — — —

The current system is stuck in big-picture, "let's just get on with it" thinking. But there are few other times in your life when attention to detail is so crucial as the details can make or break your future.

Had I, during my divorce, heeded the words of William Feather, I might have fared far better than I did.

Said the American author and publisher, "Beware of the person who can't be bothered by details."

Beware, in other words, of high-priced lawyers who urge you to "stay focused on the big picture—don't get bogged down by the details—the details are just distractions."

This proved to be the worst advice I could have gotten. Lack of attention to details during my property division trial cost me a small fortune.

In his haste to get things done with a court-step deal, my trial lawyer transferred my husband's shares in our company to me at an adjusted cost base of zero instead of at fair market value. His lack of attention to details cost me hundreds of thousands of dollars.

I thought my story was unique. But as I speak to more and more people, I hear that they're getting the very same advice.

As someone who lives and breathes in the world of financial management—where every decision, however small it may seem, has profound repercussions—I simply can't fathom how anyone could suggest that when dividing assets attention to detail and the ruthless pursuit of accuracy aren't absolutely necessary. Yet every lawyer involved in my divorce counseled me to remain focused on the big picture.

I remember time and time again asking questions like "But what about the tax implications?" "But what about the adjusted cost base?" But, but, but. . . . In retrospect, I should have listened to my gut instincts and demanded detailed answers. Yet as the legal bills mounted and the months turned into years, I became burned out and beat-up by a system that continues to operate with reckless disregard for the details.

That's not to say the big picture isn't important. An encompassing understanding of your long-term financial future is crucial to making prudent financial decisions today.

Nor is it to say that every single detail matters. "I think it's outra-geous that my ex spent $200 on new running shoes for our son!" is really not important in the big scheme of things, and it's that type of detail that can bog down the process.

The details that do matter involve where the money is at, the tax implications of every asset, the wording on the transfer of property, the parenting decisions (who will decide what and when), the status of the stock portfolio, and what it would mean to liquidate rather than distribute without liquidation.

These are the very details that often get lost in the correspondence between lawyers, which often amounts to little more than accusations and criticisms without any real purpose except to hurt, grapple for position, and drag things out. If everyone's energy was spent instead on ensuring that the assets were protected and distributed in a way that maximized each party's share, then and only then would the system be doing a decent job.

Accuracy with numbers takes a great deal of diligence, but diligence is paramount. In the chaotic setting of most divorces, it's so easy for crucial facts and figures to get lost in the big picture.

Perhaps there's a method in the smoke-and-mirrors madness. After all, it's easier to pull a fast one if the other side doesn't understand the numbers. (To put a modern twist on a famous one-liner by W.C. Fields, "If you can't dazzle them with brilliance, baffle them with figures.")

Perhaps some matrimonial lawyers simply lack the necessary financial acumen to understand the numbers as much as their clients need them to.

Or perhaps lawyers simply prefer big-picture playoffs because delving into the details feels a little too much like hand-holding.

Whatever the reason, one thing is clear: there's got to be a better way.

When the word "divorce" rears its ugly head, a lot of people come to me for advice. Here's what I say:

"Now more than ever, you need to pay very close attention to details.

"You need to ask the right questions.

"You need to understand the complete financial picture, or find somebody who can help you understand it.

"You need to know the implications of any proposed resolution.

"Divorce needs to be about the details, and anyone who tells you different does not have your best interests at heart."

One approach that works wonderfully starts by first determining the true net worth of the couple—the combined total of their assets and liabilities. While on the surface this seems reasonably intuitive and straightforward, anyone who deals with numbers knows it's extremely complex. An in-depth look at these issues is beyond the scope of this book; suffice it to say that getting two people to agree on a balance sheet is rarely easy, but once the task is accomplished, the next step is to allocate the assets to each party. Even this task of putting the assets into two columns can be a challenge. The order of these steps—agree first on the size of the pie, and then split the pie into two equal pieces—is absolutely nonnegotiable to ensure a fair outcome for both sides.

Having a sound financial plan for your future (both short-term and long) is always important. This is especially true when it comes to divorce.

We've been hearing a lot lately about divorce planning. The term refers to the process of devising a financial plan for your future, one that ensures you've thought about the future and considered the impact of your decisions about asset division, spousal support, child support, and so on. All too often people going through divorce get so caught up with their lawyers, affidavits, court appearances, correspondence, and position bargaining that they neglect to consider the financial outcomes of their decisions.

I have worked with many clients who start out seeking a lump-sum settlement, but it's important to look beyond the lump sum of cash to what that cash will mean to your lifestyle. A financial advisor can produce projections that show you how your capital will translate into income and cash flow when you employ it in any number of ways, including short-term expenditures, investments, retirement savings, educational savings plans, and so on.

Whatever settlement you and your spouse arrive at will have to meet the law in your jurisdiction, but there's ample latitude to be creative. I've seen many creative ways to bring about win-win settlements that give both parties what they need to establish and maintain financial security. One example is a lump-sum payment in lieu of spousal support, or a combination of a lump sum followed by lower spousal support. Another example involves splitting an investment portfolio without liquidating any assets (and perhaps losing the upside in the market as a result). The party who is more market-savvy receives the stocks that require more vigilance, while the lower-risk investments go to the partner with less financial acumen. (Of course, the risk quotient of the portfolio may then need to be adjusted.)

Without professional assistance, opportunities such as these are easily missed. The result is serious grief.

Most people want certainty with divorce settlements. While some uncertainty cannot be avoided, much can be. A carefully considered financial plan gives people peace of mind going forward. As both a certified divorce financial analyst and someone who's been in traditional divorce's trenches, I would argue most adamantly that the big-picture approach is a recipe for disaster. Focusing on the minutiae will rarely be as important as when you're negotiating a divorce settlement.

Taking the time to understand the numbers can be crucial to your future financial security. CDFAs, financial planners, and accountants can be focused and resourceful at a time when resources are precious. The value in using their services is simply inestimable.

If there are assets and if you have to use a lawyer, in my view seeking the advice of a financial advisor is a must.

INTO ACTION

Like most couples entering into a divorce, Adam and Carolyn Cunningham have two key priorities: to preserve the collective sum of their assets as much as possible, and to win for himself or herself the greatest portion of the total asset pie.

Unfortunately, in the traditional system of divorce, these two priorities are mutually exclusive. In the battle to prevail as winner of the greatest share of assets, husband and wife usually watch in dismay as the very assets up for grabs get rapidly devoured by the fees of the lawyers locked in battle.

Independently Negotiated Resolution offers a new and better way to end your marriage—one that helps preserve the vast majority of your precious matrimonial assets. As you'll see from our example of Adam and Carolyn, division of assets using INR is by no means free of differences of opinion, but the outcome is mutually agreeable and fair.

Chapter 20

HE SAYS, SHE SAYS...

Independently Negotiated Resolution asks participants to keep a steady focus on two important areas: now and the future.

What's in the past is over and done with, over and immutable. No amount of sorrow or regret or paralyzing bitterness will alter a single thing that's already happened.

It's time to move forward.

This is my key message to Adam and Carolyn Cunningham the next time I meet with each of them. And to get them moving forward, I engage them in establishing a plan to carry them through the next few months. A short-term plan regarding money and kids is necessary as it allows you to focus on the long term. I find that if couples have an immediate game plan for the near future, stress is reduced and they are better able to make well-grounded decisions.

At first, both Adam and Carolyn are adamant about remaining in the house.

Adam: "We built and we bought the house with my hard-earned money. There's no way I'm just going to pack up and leave."

Carolyn: "I've kept that house running for so many years while my workaholic husband flitted here and there and everywhere on business. It'll fall to ruin if I leave him in charge."

While many couples try to convince themselves that staying to-gether in the same house is a workable solution until the division of assets has been negotiated, believe me, it's anything but. I've spoken to many couples who've tried to make it work, and they're almost unanimous in saying it simply doesn't.

Firstly, it clouds the reality of the situation and can keep people in denial, which is a very unhealthy place to be.

Secondly, it compromises the children's emotional well-being. Even if you and your ex can refrain from arguing and name-calling in front of the kids, which is a tall order for most couples, there is often tremendous friction and negative energy between a divorcing couple, and the toll this takes on their children can be immeasurable. However, unfortunately with the growing cost of housing and the financial pressures on families, sometimes this is the only option but should be one of the last options. With my assistance, Adam finally comes to see that moving out will be best for everyone. But he'll take the kids as often as he can—at least three sleepovers a week—to start getting them used to the idea of a future with two separate homes.

As I emphasize strongly to both of them, this is by no means the long-term plan for their family. But for the time being, they both agree it will work.

They also decide to leave the bank account as is. Adam will simply draw the rent for his new living quarters out of the family funds. In addition, apart from the necessities, neither will buy anything new; neither will take any unnecessary trips; and neither will try in any way to siphon funds from the account.

KEY ACTION

Establish a practical plan for the short term—up to around four months. Address money, kids, and anything else that could come up.

Whether we're dealing with short-term plans or long, INR is relentlessly focused on mutually agreeable outcomes. It is grounded in the notion that every problem has a fair solution.

With a solution-driven model like INR:

- You understand how you'll get to where you are going.

- Decisions are not based on momentum-driven panic; they are grounded in mutually understood, mutually agreed-upon facts.

- Reactivity is sidelined as every step is proactive.

- You can trust that the outcome is fair because you arrived at it strategically, not through a parade of chaos, fear, and threats.

No matter how you feel about your spouse when you enter into a divorce, remember that you once loved that person. Honor that in yourself. And honor yourself by not destroying the essence of each other. Good people leave marriages. Good but confused people have affairs. Good people have addictions. Good people make bad decisions.

And good people forgive.

Do not allow anyone or any system to steal the positives of the past from you. Hold tight to pleasant memories, and close that chapter of your life with grace.

I'm by no means endorsing submissive surrender. You needn't take whatever your spouse offers. Be ruthless in your endeavors to be treated fairly and arrive at a fair resolution. But just remember: no matter how dim the outlook may appear, there *is* a win-win outcome.

Even if (right now) you detest your spouse, the best gift you can give yourself and your children is to take the high road and refuse to purposefully create chaos and foster destruction during your divorce.

As you press forward to find a financial resolution that works, you *will* be tested, not to nearly the degree that most people experience in the traditional system of divorce, but there will be ups and downs and tears and frustrations. They're just part and parcel of divorce.

This is exactly the message I impress upon the Cunninghams and the same message I impress upon all of my clients as we prepare to embark upon the next phase of the process, the quest for a win-win resolution on matters related to money.

You'll recall that Independently Negotiated Resolution seeks fair, win-win outcomes. While both parties in a divorcing couple have the same conversations with the same negotiator, they have them at different times. And invariably, each reacts very differently to the issues that need to be discussed and resolved.

As you will see, Adam and Carolyn are no exception.

Carolyn, for instance, reacts almost violently when I inform her that INR addresses the questions of parenting and child support only after resolution is reached on all financial matters.

"But that's crazy!" she exclaims. "How can I concentrate on money matters if I don't know what will happen with the kids?"

"You needn't worry," I assure her. "Remember, with INR, you'll reach an outcome everyone can live with.

"If you're truly concerned about your children, then this is the only logical way to proceed. When it comes to divorce negotiations, money and kids just don't mix. It's too easy for the disputing parties to start using the children as pawns, intentionally or otherwise.

"You need to trust the process, and love your kids more than you hate your spouse."

KEY ACTIONS

Never deal with money and kids at the same time (unless the money matters are very straightforward and you see eye to eye on most of them). It's money first, kids second—always. Do not allow anyone who is representing you or negotiating on your behalf to comingle these two issues. Even if you think you can avoid position bargaining and using the kids as pawns, you cannot.

Only after the financial issues have been dealt with in full will you both be in a place to formulate a plan that's right for you and your children. This is one of the most important, nonnegotiable principles behind INR and its success.

THE FINANCIAL PIE

Once the Cunninghams have agreed on what their lives will look like during the next four months, we are ready to move on to the fair division of money and assets.

My first step in this regard is to familiarize Adam and Carolyn with the legalities surrounding that very process.

KEY ACTIONS

When you arrive at the other end of your divorce, you want to know not only that you were treated fairly but that you made prudent, well-informed decisions all along the way, decisions you won't regret later.

To empower yourself and your decision-making ability, you need to become informed about the divorce laws within your state or province.

What are the laws regarding child support and spousal support? Do the laws specify a 50/50 asset split? What are the laws regarding exemptions, inheritances, and pre-marriage assets? Are there any specific laws pertaining to parenting?

And what does the law have to say about grounds for divorce? Most divorces now are no-fault divorces—that is, divorces in which the dissolution of a marriage does not require fault of either party to be shown, so there is no need for evidentiary proceedings. I strongly recommend this course unless there is an especially compelling reason not to pursue it.

Of course, "no fault" also means how your spouse treated you is pretty much irrelevant, which is another reason to become ruthlessly future-focused.

If you're an eager fact-finder who believes that more is better when it comes to knowledge, you can also look into some precedent cases. But such actions usually foretell a long and vicious battle that may be better suited to the courtrooms.

There are many avenues for learning the laws of your jurisdiction. The Internet is a rich source of information (though you need to make sure you're using credible sources), and local government organizations can provide information and literature. Beware, however: this does not make you an expert; for advice with regards to the law, you need to speak to a lawyer.

If you choose to get legal advice at this point remember that lawyers have a vested interest in encouraging people to pursue the traditional approach to divorce, an approach that may not serve your best interests.

Lawyers will talk about your legal rights, discussions that can lead to acts of chaos and destruction. For some exaggerated examples: If you can prove that it's legally yours, you have the right to take the front door off its hinges and drive away with it. You have the right to burn all your spouse's clothes if they happen to be on your property. And you have the right to hire a private investigator. But does exercising any of these "rights" help you in your quest for a fair, win-win outcome?

Don't confuse lawyers and the law.

While your divorce negotiator does not need to be a lawyer, he or she does need to know what the law says or the "letter of the law."

Once empowered with an appropriate level of knowledge about the law, you are ready to move forward.

The next step is to determine what makes up something I call the "financial pie," the total of all the money and assets a divorcing couple will need to divide fairly, which is often referred to as the "matrimonial assets."

"I am definitely getting the cottage," Adam reminds me after I explain to him this next step in the Independently Negotiated Resolution Process. "It's not even open to negotiation."

"First things first," I tell him.

KEY ACTIONS

Don't even talk about who is going to get what until you know what the "what" is.

If you start dividing assets into "his" and "hers" columns before you've determined the total contents of the financial pie, you will fall into the trap of "position bargaining." As you will recall this is when you put an asset on your side of the balance sheet and then begin bargaining to get it.

Do not allow anyone to take you there as it improperly can inflate or deflate values.

Remember, first things first.

The only way to ensure a fair settlement is to make sure both parties agree on the value of each asset before it goes into the column of either spouse. It's often difficult to exercise the required patience and restraint, but it's imperative for sound decision making.

This method of valuing first and dividing second—a cornerstone of INR— is brilliantly simple. Once all assets have been identified and assigned values, negotiations become academic.

If, at any time, the spouses decide they'd like to make trades, they simply swap the assets in question at face value. It's as easy as trading a quarter for two dimes and a nickel.

This simple process becomes more complicated when businesses or professional practices are involved, but the same principles apply.

If I have a business and it's obvious I'll be keeping it, there is almost certainly a dollar amount I would sell that company for. Determining that number is challenging even for financial experts, because what we could actually get for a business and what we would sell it for are not usually the same, so we need to consider other variables when determining fair market value: lifestyle, future earning potential, personal attachment, dreams for the future, etc. To the individual, these variables have undeniable value, but putting a number to them may seem next to impossible. At the end of the day, though, you can almost always identify a number for which you'd be prepared to sell your company. Arriving at that number is a crucial step not only in the negotiations but in your personal journey. The financials for the company (i.e., the balance sheet, income statements, and cash flow statements) are necessary to determine value. If the financial picture is complicated, using a business valuator is a very good idea.

Once you've settled on a value for your company, negotiations can proceed and you can move ever closer to resolution.

The process will proceed smoothly as long as everyone involved remains committed to a win-win situation. The end result will be a fair outcome.

"First things first," I remind Adam. "And in INR, the first thing necessary for fair financial negotiations is *full disclosure*. Full. That means *everything*. And *that* is nonnegotiable.

"It's the only way to figure out the true size of the financial pie." "So I guess what you're saying is that she'll get half of everything, even though I worked my butt off to support her cushy lifestyle. Does she also get half of my Robert Bateman collection and my Royal Doulton Toby jugs?"

"Well, Adam, if they're of value and you bought them while you were married to Carolyn, they must form part of your financial pie. But you needn't worry. We'll divide home furnishings, art, and collectibles at the end of the financial negotiations, and I'm sure we can find a way to do it fairly. If they're your pride and joy and Carolyn doesn't have the same sense of attachment to them, we can give her other items in lieu of your collections. If she is attached to the same items, we might have to split the collections.

"What we're talking about right now are disclosures of the larger assets—bank account statements, mortgage documents, retirement fund statements, vehicles' values—basically all the backup for the net worth statement."

"Well, don't expect me to give you any cottage documents. As I've already said, my parents left it to me."

"If that's the case, Adam, we'll need the documentation to establish your inheritance. Without backup it's your word against hers, and when we start dealing with perception and selective memory, it's a no-win situation. To avoid any ambiguity and unfair decisions, you need to start pulling all these documents together."

KEY ACTIONS

Next, you need to know the numbers. That is, you need a completed net worth statement.

On the surface this may seem simple enough, but trust me, it's far from simple. Agreeing on the numbers is one of the most conflict-ridden, anger-provoking aspects of any divorce.

For this step in the process, you will definitely need a reliable, unbiased third party. If you are not using Fairway Divorce Solutions, consider hiring a certified divorce financial analyst (CDFA), or enlist the help of an accountant.

Whomever you use, ensure that they follow this progression:

- First, gather all the information.

- Second, put together the net worth statement.

- Third, meet with each party individually to begin the negotiations.

Once again—because it's so very important—I will caution you not to fall into the trap of discussing who will get what until you agree on all the numbers.

KEY ACTIONS

Unless you plan to liquidate all your assets and work only with cash, which is a wholly impractical approach, there are bound to be disagreements on the value of items.

Most often, parties will have different ideas about the value of the matrimonial home. You need to keep reminding yourself that everything has a price, and if the price is fair, each party should—in theory, at least—be indifferent about who gets the home and who gets the equivalent value.

Of course, this highly objective approach doesn't consider your emotional attachment to your home or anything else, but at this stage you just shouldn't go there. Emotions wreak havoc with our decisions in divorce, and deciding to keep an asset that will compromise your cash flow from month to month and keep you in the poorhouse isn't particularly empowering.

But let's not get ahead of ourselves. For now, we're simply trying to agree on the numbers.

So what do you do if you just can't agree? This is where your trained negotiator proves his or her value. If you're working through your divorce without a negotiator's help, you can use third-party appraisals, fair market value (FMV), Realtor assessments, and so on.

One word of caution: just because you get third-party appraisals or valuations doesn't mean you'll both agree with the results. More than one business valuation is likely too expensive, though, so make sure you're both involved in the process, even if you are not both involved with the business.

The valuation for my business, which was ordered by the courts, cost me over $50,000 because it was performed in anticipation of a courtroom battle, where the prospect of cross-examinations and lawyers picking apart every little thing demanded a high level of detail. The valuations we get for clients using INR are just as accurate but, because there's no need for vast pages of details compiled only in anticipation of courtroom arguments, they're a mere fraction of the cost.

KEY ACTIONS

This is also the time to determine if the financial pie is subject to any exemptions according to your state or provincial laws. (Inheritances are just one of many areas where the laws differ from province to province and state to state.)

Again, a trained financial negotiator is a must! A financially savvy negotiator will not only ensure that your outcome is in line with the law but can probably be creative in ways that will maximize the benefits to everyone and keep your assets intact as much as possible.

Whew! That's a lot of Key Actions, and I apologize if it all seems a tad overwhelming. There are, however, a lot of important steps that need to precede the division of assets, and the importance of working with a well-trained, financially astute negotiator cannot be overstated.

Now, while you were working your way through all of these weighty Keys, the Cunninghams were busy providing me with a full disclosure of their financial information.

NET WORTH: SUMMARY
Adam and Carolyn Cunningham

Assets	Amount
Joint bank account	$25,000
House	TBD

Carolyn's value:	$625,000	
Adam's value:	$700,000	
Club membership	$20,000	
Cottage		TBD
Carolyn's value:	$600,000	
Adam's value:	$500,000	
Time-share		$50,000
Retirement savings plans		$450,000
Stock and bond investment account		$125,000
Adam's pension (commuted value)		$225,000
Catering for Status Inc.		TBD
Carolyn's value:	$0	
Adam's value:	$250,000	
BMW (five years old)		TBD
Carolyn's value:	$40,000	
Adam's value:	$34,000	

Honda Odyssey (new)	TBD

Carolyn's value:	$48,000
Adam's value:	$55,000
MGB (Adam's since university)	$3,000

Liabilities

Mortgage	$225,000
Line of credit (including $25,000 for cottage)	$75,000
Credit cards	$8,000
Business loan for Catering for Status Inc.	$50,000

Potentially Exempt

Adam's cottage inherited from parents	$100,000

As you will see, they don't agree on all the numbers, but they don't know that yet because, of course, they shared their numbers with me independently.

From the preceding table, it's easy to see why talking about who gets what before values are agreed upon will probably lead to endless bickering and angry disputes. As long as values remain fluid and unfixed, how can there be any grounds for fair negotiations and fair outcomes? And if we can't even determine the couple's net worth, how can we possibly decide what constitutes an equal half?

Their views on the value of Carolyn's business is a perfect case in point. Whereas Adam feels it's worth at least a quarter million dollars,

Carolyn doesn't even assign a value. Of course by this time I have copies of all the financial statements, so their opinions become less important than a comprehensive understanding of the financials.

The Cunninghams' first attempt at valuing their assets underscores a couple of key points that bear repeating:

1.   Clear-cut agreement on the value of noncash assets is rare.

2.   Parties tend to assign higher values to the assets they expect *the other party* to acquire, thereby increasing the value of their "equal share."

In addition to disclosing their assets and assigning a value to each (or, in Carolyn's case, to all of them except the business), both parties provide me with their income tax returns from the past three years.

In the past year, Adam grossed $275,000, and Carolyn grossed $35,000 (from her board position and her catering business).

While Adam and Carolyn are, thankfully, on the same page with regard to some values, on others they have major differences of opinion, namely, the value of the house, the cottage, Carolyn's business, and one another's vehicle.

They also differ on whether or not the cottage is an exemption. (In the matter of exemptions, the law will prevail, but at this point, Adam continues to maintain that the cottage is "off the table.")

And, it turns out, Carolyn has no real idea how much Adam earns. The value of the pension is also up for debate. Although Adam provided a statement of its value, there's more to pension statements than meets the eye. (I'll address this later on.)

The Cunninghams do agree, however, that there are no pre-marriage assets of any significant value.

This is when I really get to see the differences in the way couples approach decision making.

Adam is clearly the more analytical thinker. He provides me with not only financial documents but his own attempt at a net worth statement. "I think this makes it pretty clear how our division of assets should unfold," he says as he hands me the statement.

"I know you're anxious to move forward, Adam, but I have to re-mind you I'll be using the statements I get from both of you along with your opinions about values that aren't black and white. I'll compile the infor-mation and present it back to you for discussion later on."

Adam grunts disapprovingly while I smile knowingly. It's inter-esting how some people react to nervousness by trying to establish control.

Carolyn presents a completely opposite picture. She arrives at my office with a disheveled heap of documents, which she plops unceremo-niously onto the receptionist's desk. When I come out to meet her, she looks distracted but still very attractive, dressed for tennis and clearly in a hurry to get to the Club. It is clear that she has better things to do than fuss with financial statements.

She asks for a few moments of my time so we go to the boardroom, where she begins to explain the pile. "I don't know, Karen. I did my best. Here's everything I could find. I'm sure Adam will be trying to hide things, so I've attached a list of our personal belongings and some things we need to get statements for.

"I find this all very stressful, you know." I do, and I tell her so before she continues. "I really need to know right now how much he is going to pay me because I need to make some plans."

I reply, "Carolyn, you need to be patient. Coming to the right outcome takes time. I know you're feeling stressed, and that's normal. Perhaps you want to seek some help to get through the emotional part of your journey more quickly, but for this part of the journey, I can't go any faster than we already are."

KEY INSIGHTS

They say that opposites attract, but the differences that brought you together can rip you to pieces in the divorce process.

While there is a win-win outcome to INR, you need to understand that both parties will move through the process and decision making entirely differently in order to get there.

One of you might be analytical and pragmatic, seeing things as black and white and taking a very "step 1, step 2" approach. The other might be more "random abstract," approaching each decision from many different angles; he or she may need to "sleep on things" and might be prone to frequently changing his or her mind.

These differences, which in dating and marriage produced great chemistry and unforgettable passion, can turn divorce into a vicious battleground.

Says one: "What an idiot! The answer's so obvious. Why can't she see it?" And the other: "What a control freak! Why doesn't he just back off?"

Here's the bottom line: although there is a fair way to get through the divorce process, there really is no "right way." That's where Independently Negotiated Resolution differs so much from the traditional approach to divorce: it accepts and accommodates the entire range of individual differences.

With a clear picture of the financial pie, a skilled negotiator can ensure both parties are allowed to move through the decision-making process in a way that works for them. Both will eventually get the same information, but it might be presented in very different ways, and they'll probably process it in very different ways.

This is what I call "empowered decision making." You'll both get to the same endgame, but you get there in the way that suits you best.

This is why the parties move through the INR process independently. Putting two people who approach problems very differently into a room together is a recipe for impatience, sarcasm, name-calling, and button-pushing, especially when you add an unhealthy dose of bitterness and resentment into the mix.

So where are we now? Ah, yes, the slippery numbers for the Cunninghams' assets. From the numbers they first present, we can clearly see that Adam and Carolyn just don't agree on the values of many assets.

Assets	Carolyn's Value	Adam's Value
House	$625,000	$700,000
Adam's pension	?	$225,000
Cottage	$600,000	$500,000
BMW	$40,000	$34,000
Honda Odyssey	$48,000	$55,000
Catering for Status Inc.	$0	$250,000

As I said before, this is normal. In the traditional model of divorce, this is where the debate can get very heated. By contrast, INR gets couples to consensus without dramatically increasing conflict.

Does this mean the participants never get stressed? Of course not. "Stress-free divorce" is an oxymoron of mammoth proportions, but at least they don't get murderous.

I now invite the Cunninghams back in (separately, of course) to discuss their numbers. I show them where we have agreement and where we do not.

We then address each value separately and try to arrive at consensus. As before, I avoid any discussion about who will get what.

Let's address the values one by one.

THE HOUSE

As you'll recall, Carolyn valued the house at $625,000, while Adam's price tag was $700,000.

While I have not yet facilitated any discussion on who will get what, I know from her comments in one of our early meetings that Carolyn desperately wants the house. (Adam said the same thing, but with not nearly the same conviction.)

Even if she didn't do it consciously, Carolyn probably undervalued the house in anticipation that it would end up on her side of the property division balance sheet. This is an almost innate tendency: we tend to over-value items the other person is likely to receive, and we undervalue those that we hope to get for ourselves. It's as if position bargaining were deeply embedded in our collective unconscious.

In my separate discussions with Adam and Carolyn, both endeavor to justify their valuations.

Carolyn: "I should never have told him I refuse to give up the house. He's only saying it's worth $700,000 because he knows how much I want it. If he was ever home long enough to notice, he'd see how much work it needs. I'm sure it needs at least $100,000 worth of renovations."

Adam: "Six-twenty-five is a joke. Not a single house on our street has sold for less than $700,000 in the past year and a half."

Each has credible reasons to support the numbers, so what to do?

The easy answer is to sell the house and split the cash, which is not a palatable option for most couples.

We could also commission an appraisal, look at tax assessments, or solicit opinions on the value of house from a realtor or two. The trouble here is that each approach will usually render a different number, often with many assumptions attached to it.

So again I say, what to do? We need to find some way to get the parties to an agreement.

Here's the good news: when a skilled negotiator is involved, two parties will eventually arrive at a number they agree on so long as:

1. It seems fair.

2. It does not seem arbitrary.

3. It is discussed separately from any other assets to circumvent our natural inclinations toward positioning bargaining.

As negotiations get closer to their conclusion, a little more give and take often becomes necessary, but we're not there just yet.

Although getting them to settle on a fair value for the house takes some time, they eventually agree to approximately split the difference for a final number of $660,000.

How do I get them there?

Well, for starters, I tell Adam that if we can't agree to a number, the highest bidder will get the house.

"But . . . but I'm not so sure I want the house anymore," he stammers, looking more than a little alarmed. "I've been thinking about my 'painted picture,' and I just don't see myself living alone in such a big house. Carolyn really wants it, and since she'll probably have the kids a bit more than me, she should have our family home. Surely there's got to be some value in keeping the home for the kids' sake?"

"I understand how you're feeling, Adam. Having a strong emotional attachment to the home your children have been growing up in is normal. But as I've said over and over, at this stage we need to be very pragmatic. We really need to arrive at a number that works for both of you."

"I honestly don't think $700,000 is unreasonable," says Adam, "I actually thought I was being a bit conservative."

"If you say it's worth $700,000, that's fine. You can have it for $700,000. That's the number I'll attach to it when I put it on your side of the balance sheet."

Suddenly, Adam feels a little more flexible. "Well, Carolyn probably makes a fair point about the house needing work. Maybe that 700 can come down a little."

It's always interesting to see how people respond when a negotiator calls their bluffs!

I call this the "highest bidder trick," and as the tools of divorce negotiations go, it's indispensable, especially because it works from either perspective.

Consider, for example, my subsequent meeting with Carolyn:

I say, "Carolyn, you and Adam are aligned on the value of some assets, but you differ on others—the house, for instance. Your estimate of $625,000 is significantly lower than his estimate."

"Well, he's not around enough to see what kind of shape it's in. I know better than him what it's worth, and I'm not budging from 625."

"Okay," I say matter-of-factly. "Then we'll let Adam have the house for $625,000."

"Wha—no, wait. That's not fair," Carolyn protests. "Not fair? Tell me, Carolyn, what's not fair about it?"

Silence, but I know exactly what she's thinking. ("Because I want it, and I want it at a discount.")

I push her a little. "Come on, Carolyn. If 625 really is a fair number, why can't Adam have it on his side of the balance sheet at that price?"

Thus begins the backpedaling: "Well," Carolyn admits, "maybe I did undervalue it a bit. …"

By using this simple tactic, a savvy negotiator can get agreement on the numbers relatively quickly as it forces people to look beyond emotional attachments and put honest numbers on their assets.

It was without too much trouble, then, that we all managed to arrive (without any tears or gnashing of teeth) at $660,000 as a value for the house.

I then move on with each of them to another point of difference.

THE PENSION

KEY ACTIONS

A word of caution: pensions are extremely tricky. If you've been with a company more than 10 years and are older than 40, it's very worthwhile to have your pension valued. Each pension is unique and to lump them under one umbrella approach could result in a completely unfair number.

Interestingly, most people are very possessive about their pensions, and the thought of sharing them is a tough pill to swallow. The thought of splitting RRSPs doesn't raise nearly as much resistance, which is an interesting phenomenon since both involve the division of funds earmarked for the future.

Most pension administrators can provide a statement of a pension's commuted or liquidation value, but these indicate the value of a pension if the pensioner retired immediately. If an employee has had a long career and is likely to continue working for some time, his or her pension's future value can be substantially more. I have seen commuted and liquidation values of

$150,000 when the true future value is closer to $350,000.

Additionally, many pensions have other benefits (such as medical benefits) layered in—benefits that add value to a pension. Many are indexed with inflation as well, again adding to the value.

Unfortunately, when it comes to pensions, values are never cut and dried. Let's say Spouse A's pension is future-valued at $300,000. That figure now counts toward Spouse A's share of the financial pie.

But if Spouse A later quits before his or her pension is fully realized, he or she will have overpaid to keep an asset that's future-value based.

There are a number of ways to deal with this but note that there are a number of restrictions and it is best to make sure you are well informed:

- Split the present/liquidation value and agree to a future payment when the person actually retires.

- Split the pension (as of today's date) at the time of retirement.

- Have a conversation about options with the employer/pension administrator. You'll then be able to make an informed, empowered decision.

At my urging, the Cunninghams agree to have Adam's pension valued by an actuary. The results show that the commuted value on the statement Adam provided was a bit low, but the difference wasn't significant.

Carolyn, who was obviously paying attention when I spoke to her about the present versus future value of pensions, now decides that it needs to be valued higher.

Adam, in turn, disagrees. He reminds me that he'd been thinking about retiring early, an idea he has since decided to follow through on. "So it wouldn't be fair to inflate the present value," he insists. "Even if I stick around for another six months, my pension isn't going to increase all that much. And since it's already on paper for more than it's worth, I really don't think it should go any higher."

I take Adam's rationales back to Carolyn, and without too much fuss she agrees. The value of the pension, then, is set at $225,000.

Now we move on to one of the really messy ones:

THE COTTAGE

This is where things get intense.

Remember that Adam inherited the cottage from his parents, but with inheritances, even the letter of the law takes on shades of gray.

Adam's desire to get exemption from including the cottage in the financial pie can be affected by any number of questions, which the laws in different jurisdictions will answer differently:

- Was it left for the benefit of the entire family?

- Is there a comingling of assets in it? (You'll recall that profits from Carolyn's company were invested into cottage renovations.)

- Was the asset held in trust?

- Has the asset already been transferred?

- What was the asset's value upon inheritance, and what is its value now?

The answers to these and many other questions will help a nego-tiator determine whether an asset should be considered an inheritance and, if so, whether it is subject to exemption. A clear understanding of the laws in your state or province is crucial and legal advice on this specific issue would be prudent.

When Adam's parents left the cottage to him for him and his family, it probably wasn't their intent that in the case of a divorce, either it would have to be sold and the proceeds split, or Adam would have to buy out Carolyn.

Obviously, Adam argues that this was not their intent. Carolyn, on the other hand, points out during her session with me that their intent cannot be proven, but the fact that they sunk $50,000 from Carolyn's business and an additional $25,000 from their line of credit into improvements for the cottage certainly can.

Suffice to say that of all the hot buttons between Adam and Carolyn, the cottage is far and away the hottest. (The good news is that INR prevents the divorcing couple from pushing those buttons directly, since both parties go through the negotiations independently.)

Adam's stance: "The cottage is mine, and that's that. Mom and Dad left it to me for me and my kids, not for my wife and the boy-toy she dumped me for! You can tell her I said so."

Though he still maintains the cottage should be exempt, he's willing to agree that the $50,000 from Carolyn's company, an additional $25,000 from the line of credit, sweat equity from both of them, and good market conditions have all increased the value of the cottage.

In my conversations with Carolyn about the cottage, she right off the bat takes the position that it ought to be shared equally. She explains it was a gift for both of them and their children. After a few minutes of discussion, however, Carolyn concedes it was really intended for Adam and his family, even if that possibly didn't include her. Ouch! Sometimes such admissions are tough to make and tough to take.

Carolyn also agrees with the numbers but has to get in her two cents' worth: "That man certainly does have a selective memory. What about all those words about our legacy and our hard work and how the money from my business would make it so much nicer? I could have done so many other things with that money."

"Carolyn, I understand this is difficult. I'm not yet sure how this will play out, but I can promise you will get compensated for the money your company put into it."

Carolyn has to have the last word: "The cottage was a dump when we got it. Now it could be in a home and garden magazine. That was all my doing. It's as much mine as it is his, and I still think I should get half."

As for the law's take on the matter: in the Cunninghams' jurisdiction, it is reasonably clear based on some legal advice, that the cottage's original value is exempt, but the upside value as well as any investment into it is jointly owned and needs to be split somehow.

In a case like this, the art of negotiation lies in finding a balance between what the law says and what's really fair to both parties. (There's often a huge disconnect between "legal rights" and "moral fairness.")

Although it requires a good deal of back-and-forth negotiations (and an even greater deal of hotheaded blustering), Adam and Carolyn finally came to some agreements.

Following some persistent negotiations, they ultimately agree that the cottage was worth about $400,000 when Adam inherited it, and since that time both the market upswing and their investment into it have increased its value to $600,000.

Because of her monetary investments as well as her "sweat equity," Adam finally agrees Carolyn deserves an equal share in the increase of $200,000, and this amount should therefore be addressed in the equalization of assets.

He also (more reluctantly) agrees that since the cottage has been a big part of the entire family's life, including Carolyn's, she will get to use it one week each summer for the next three years.

"But only on the condition that I get to pick the week," insists Adam, arms crossed tightly across his chest.

Compared to the cottage negotiations, the negotiations over the family vehicles seem like a piece of cake.

THE VEHICLES

The quickest and easiest way to determine the fair value of a vehicle is to search the Internet, the classified ads, or some similar source of advertisements for pre-owned vehicles. You can almost always find a vehicle similar to yours in year, mileage, and condition.

Especially with vintage vehicles, there may be a little debate and disagreement, but I've always found differences of opinion about the value of vehicles refreshingly easy to resolve.

As I very much expected, neither one of the Cunninghams has any qualms about accepting the average value of vehicles similar to theirs in the local auto trader publication.

If only the negotiations over Carolyn's business proceeded as smoothly!

CAROLYN'S BUSINESS

As you already know, the Cunninghams differ dramatically on the value of Carolyn's business. Adam feels it has significant value, while Carolyn feels its value is negligible.

After inspecting the company's financial statements and balance sheet, I conclude that the company has little value on paper, but its revenue is increasing year over year at a significant rate.

Sometimes it's easy for a financially astute negotiator, especially one with an MBA and many years of experience as a financial advisor, to determine the value of a business. In the case of Catering for Status, given its ever-increasing sales and given how far apart Adam and Carolyn are on its value, I deem it prudent to recommend an independent valuation by a true expert on this matter.

I am a strong advocate of doing things right. The traditional system seems to spend a great deal of money spinning wheels and wasting time; I would rather see couples do whatever it takes to get viable, accurate numbers and then move on. In this case, for just a few thousand dollars, we have a business valuator look into Carolyn's business (visiting the business, interviewing Carolyn, and analyzing sales and financial statements), prepare a short written report, and present his findings to Adam and Carolyn (with me present to moderate the exchange).

At first, my suggestion to have the company valued really spurs Carolyn's ire. "Ridiculous!" she clamors. "It's a bloody hobby—nothing more. This will be nothing but a waste of time and money."

Adam, meanwhile, thinks the valuation is a good idea. He feels a bit sheepish about pushing for it, but he really feels he owes it to himself. After all, it could be argued that he just made a sizable compromise with respect to the cottage.

I always strive to ensure that an outcome will stand the test of time. It bothers me to think that a year or two down the road, someone will look back and lament, "If only I'd asked this or done that." I want to avoid such scenarios, so from my perspective, getting Carolyn's business valued is a necessary call.

Despite her feelings to the contrary, Carolyn at last agrees when I appeal to her sense of fairness. "It was awfully big of Adam to make significant concessions on the cottage. Isn't it fair in return to give him this valuation? Besides, it might just substantiate your stance." After Carolyn gives me the green light, I engage K. Kelly & Associates, a well-established and highly reputed accounting firm. A few weeks later, they present their findings.

According to K. Kelly & Associates, although Carolyn's business has high potential value if Carolyn continues to work hard at it, its present fair market value is only $135,000—a figure that includes some inventory, accounts receivable, and liquid assets with a small weight on future earning (as a going concern). It is impossible, says the valuator, to put a significant value on future earnings.

Following the presentation, both Adam and Carolyn feel well informed and ready to move forward.

OTHER ASSETS

As the Cunninghams agree on the value of all their remaining assets, the time has come to take the next step in the INR process: the divvying up of the financial pie—that is, the asset division.

The Division of Assets: Who Gets What?

	Adam	Carolyn
Assets		
Cash	$12,500	$12,500
House		$660,000
Time-share		$50,000
Hillside membership	$10,000	$10,000
Investment accounts	$125,000	
Cottage	$200,000	
Retirement funds		
RRSPs	$225,000	$225,000
Pensions	$225,000	
Business assets		$135,000
Vehicles		
BMW	$36,000	
Honda Odyssey MGB	$3,000	$47,000
TOTAL ASSETS	$836,500	$1,139,500

Liabilities

Mortgage (house)		$225,000
Line of credit	$75,000	
Credit cards	$4,000	$4,000
Embedded tax on cottage	$50,000	
(**Note:** 25 percent of $200,000)		
Embedded tax on retirement funds		
	$118,750	$50,000
Embedded tax on business if sold		
		$33,750
Total Liabilities	$247,750	$312,750
TOTAL NET ASSETS	$588,750	$826,750

Because Adam ended up with the lion's share of the cottage, both agree that Carolyn should have the time-share.

Both have their hearts set on the Hillside Membership, so they agree to split it. Adam will have to pay an additional $4,000 to split it in two, an expense he doesn't mind paying.

The balance sheet reveals a difference of $238,000 in Carolyn's favor. To equalize the 50/50 split of the financial pie, she owes Adam $119,000.

SOME NOTES TO THE READER

Especially for those who don't have a head for numbers, the table above can be daunting and confusing. The following notes will help illuminate the numbers.

Again, though, I must emphasize: make sure you're 100 percent comfortable and 100 percent confident with your negotiator's ability to crunch the numbers on your behalf.

1. For this example, we assumed a tax rate of 25 percent on everything taxable. In reality, you need to be careful that the correct tax rate is applied. Make sure that whoever is handling your financial negotiations knows what he or she is doing with regard to tax. (You might recall from my story that a tax-related oversight cost me nearly $200,000.)

2. For Adam, $400,000 of the cottage's total value ($600,000) was exempt. At the time of transfer after he inherited the cottage, all tax on its original value ($400,000) was paid by his father, so we calculate tax only on the value above $400,000. Be very careful with matters like this; it's where a lot of mistakes can happen.

3. With respect to the pension and RRSPs: in this case, for simplicity's sake, we have looked at them as being similar— apples to apples. In reality, this is not the case.

4. A pension is much less liquid than an RRSP, making way for a strong argument that an RRSP is actually more valuable. I would far rather have an RRSP than a pension or a LIRA (locked-in retirement account). "Locked in" means just that: until a certain date, the funds are off limits and untouchable.

5. That said, it is very difficult to put an accurate number to the difference in value (since it is very much a perceived value). You may, in the end, treat your apples and oranges as apples alone, but I want you at least to be aware of the differences.

6. This is where things get even trickier. In dividing the financial pie,

you cannot directly compare an after-tax asset to a pretax asset. (In this case, for example, the matrimonial home is an after-tax asset—no tax would be levied if the asset were sold—but the business and the cottage are both taxable if liquidated.)

To come up with a true net worth, we embed tax (even if it is not due now) into the value of the assets. This gives us an accurate picture of total asset values if everything was liquidated right now.

HOW TO DEAL WITH AN EQUALIZATION PAYMENT

As I've already pointed out, the final balance sheet gives Carolyn a $238,000 advantage over Adam. She therefore owes Adam an equalization payment of $119,000.

One approach to settling such a debt is to keep working the numbers until you even out the two columns. If they're even, neither party will owe the other one cash. Sometimes this is possible and sometimes it isn't.

With the Cunninghams, we could perhaps move more RRSPs to Adam's column, but from a financial planning perspective, that may not be a prudent move for Carolyn as she won't be able to make up those contributions again.

A better solution is for Carolyn to increase her mortgage. Because she has a decent income, a viable business, and substantial equity in the house, the bank will likely have no objections to raising her mortgage so she can give Adam a cheque for the full amount of his equalization payment. (Of course, I would have Carolyn confirm this before we settle on such a plan.)

The timing of such events is all set out in the final Fairway Plan—an extensive document that addresses all the decisions, explains why and how they were made, and includes a step-by-step action plan to ensure everything gets done.

It is time now to put the division of assets behind us and move on to what is often the most contentious topic of all: spousal support.

Chapter 21

SPOUSAL SUPPORT

Of all the conversations I have with clients as we progress through Independently Negotiated Resolution, the one about spousal support (a.k.a alimony) spurs the most accusations and arouses the most anger—not always, but a vast majority of the time.

I hear a variety of objections from the prospective payers of spousal support, most of them expressed far more colorfully than the examples I offer below:

"I supported him while he went back to school, started his own business, and then went belly-up. Now I've got to support him? That's a joke."

"So she raised the kids. How hard is that? They're in school seven hours a day. What was stopping her from getting a job?"

"She talks about all her sacrifices. She spends her mornings playing tennis and her afternoons at the spa. Some sacrifices!"

"I've busted my buns for 20-some years and now he gets half my assets *and* spousal support? It just never ends!"

I understand that in times of stress, people are often at their worst. I never judge because I've been there too. And I usually let them vent because once they get all the anger off their chests, I can usually bring them around to seeing the fairness in paying some spousal support because it *is* fair.

KEY INSIGHTS

In Canada, early 2005 brought about new spousal support guidelines. They were put forth by a committee who worked together to see if they could establish guidelines like those used for child support. These guidelines, which you can find on the Internet with relative ease, are exactly that—guidelines. They have not yet been enacted into law.

These spousal support guidelines dictate a range of monthly payments based on several factors, including:

- each spouse's income

- the duration of the marriage

- the number of dependents, and the amount of child support being paid

There has been much discussion regarding the fairness of these guidelines, and while some judges use them, others do not. In any case, they appear to remain a long way from becoming law.

While I like the idea of standardization and do find these guidelines useful, I also believe in the prudent application of common sense, fairness, and keen financial acumen.

Through my experiences with the traditional system of divorce—both personally during my own divorce and vicariously through clients who have come to Fairway Divorce Solutions after the traditional system failed them—I have a good understanding of how spousal support is addressed in the world of position bargaining. Almost invariably, the opposing lawyers start at opposite ends of the range provided for spousal support payments and come to court prepared to fight to the bitter end with a vast and varied arsenal of arguments supporting their respective client's position.

INR respects the fact that each party will probably start in much the same way: digging in his or her heels at opposite ends of the spousal support spectrum. We then help them to understand and agree that the fairest outcome usually resides somewhere between the two extremes. (Not to be confused with "somewhere in the middle," the place that mediation tends to move toward.)

Let's now see where the Cunninghams stand on the question of spousal support, shall we?

In their case, there is a substantial difference between Adam's and Carolyn's incomes.

For the last few years, Adam has earned around $275,000. A big increase in the future is unlikely.

Carolyn, by contrast, has made about $35,000 a year over the last few years, but she agrees that this number is a bit low: she could have taken more money out of the company, but chose not to.

Looking forward, she'll be working more, so $60,000 seems very fair as a projected income for Carolyn, one they are both comfortable using.

Based on their incomes and the number of years they've been together, the government's spousal support guidelines prescribe a range of $0 to $5,000, which takes into account the fact that he'll be paying child support. Clearly, zero is simply not fair, but $5,000 may be a bit steep.

Upon hearing these numbers, Adam is completely overwhelmed and feels like skipping town.

"Are you out of your mind?" he asks me. "You told me this process was fair. I'm not prepared to pay that woman even a penny more. I've already told you I'm quitting my job. I'm sure the tennis pro makes a good living—let him support her."

I let him vent, and in fairly short order he calms down. Kind of. "Okay, Karen. How much do I actually have to pay?"

I explain the numbers. "To be as fair as possible, I applied the latest government guidelines. If we take them literally, you're looking at up to $5,000 a month, probably for a period of eight years since you and Carolyn were married for so long."

I see the color start to rise in his face, and I'm quick to preempt another angry outburst. "But they're only guidelines, Adam. They're not written in stone, and they leave us lots of room to maneuver.

"Since Carolyn has a company that's making good money, we can be a little creative here. I see a few different ways of going about it.

"One is a lump-sum payment. We offer a present value of some future payments to be paid out today—signed, sealed, and delivered with no opportunity for Carolyn to come back for more.

"Or we can offer a monthly amount that is either fixed over a term or fixed and declined over a term.

"Or you can pay her monthly for a couple of years, at which time the situation can be held up to a review. We can specify periodic reviews in your final agreement."

I have found that most people like predictability and gravitate toward plans that will give them a sense of certainty. To these people, fixed payments over longer terms or a lump sum up front tend to be attractive options.

In cases where a spouse's future income is going to change substantially, either up or down, fixed long-term agreements don't make much sense and may not be fair to one of the parties. This might be the case if a spouse owns a start-up business that's just about to take off.

It might also be unfair to establish spousal support today based on historic incomes when a family has sacrificed in the past for the potential future. (Let's say, for example, that the husband has worked doubly hard to support the family while his wife attended medical school, from which she graduated just shortly before the divorce.) In such cases, if spousal support is deemed fair, it is best set for a couple of years and then reevaluated.

In cases where income is not likely to move a lot, I prefer fixed and finalized payments that cannot be altered in the future for any reason.

I often get the question, "What if she (or he) remarries? Can I stop paying?"

My answer is usually no unless the supported wife is a lifetime sugar-daddy pursuer, in which case ending the payments might be fair. Otherwise, I find the argument weak. I like clean deals that allow for clean breaks. *What if*s tend to muddy the waters.

While Adam is convinced that the spousal support numbers are far too high even if we settle on something closer to the middle of the range,

Carolyn wonders how she can possibly live off so little.

"He encouraged my lifestyle while we were married. I don't see why I should have to suffer now."

(What's so great about INR is that neither side ever hears the other side's venting!)

Some back-and-forth dialog eventually softens their attitudes as they both begin to see that life after divorce can be rich even with less cash—another paradox that paves the way to marvelous new beginnings. Naturally, though, Carolyn is concerned about paying her mortgage. She is now beginning to see how her insistence on keeping the house is going to cost her in cash flow and lifestyle.

"Maybe I should look at downsizing after all," she tells me. "I mean, do I really need such a big house? I'm sure I could get a decent condo or a smaller house here in the same neighborhood for a whole lot less."

KEY INSIGHTS

The most empowered way to move through divorce is to ensure you are not attached to specific outcomes. If you are, you may be shutting out other (and perhaps better) alternatives.

From day one Carolyn was attached to keeping the house. Had it made no sense financially, I'd have told her so and recommended a sale, but in this case it was doable, though not without some sacrifices.

Only now is Carolyn beginning to see the lifestyle changes keeping the house will entail. Now that she sees what keeping it will mean, she's suddenly much less attached to it.

After all, what fun is it to be stuck behind four walls with no play money, no matter how big and beautiful those walls happen to be?

As we proceed with discussions about spousal support, we uncover even more opportunities to get creative.

For instance, Carolyn owes Adam an equalization payment of

$119,000, and she's open to exploring the possibility of dissolving that debt in return for a lump sum spousal support payment. (This would save her from refinancing her mortgage and incurring all the additional interest that comes with a sizable mortgage hike.)

The best way to approach this idea is to calculate how the equalization amount compares to the future value of the monthly payments. Are you ready for a little more math?

The present value of the equalization debt is $119,000. If we divide that amount into eight years (or 96 months) worth of payments and apply an annual interest rate of 6 percent to determine future value, we end up with $1,550 per month.

In simplest terms, then, we can say that a lump-sum payment of $119,000 is equivalent to $1,550 per month for eight years at 6 percent. But we must also consider the tax implications. The $119,000 equalization amount comprises after-tax dollars. But spousal support payments are pretax dollars, deductible to the payer and taxable to the payee. In order to net $1,550 a month, Carolyn's payments would need to be "grossed up" to around $2,300 a month. This, then, represents the true value of the equalization payment—eight years' worth of $2,300-per-month payments.

Adam is happy with the lump-sum scenario. He really doesn't need the cash right now, especially since he plans on renting for a while. And Carolyn is thrilled that she might not have to increase her mortgage as cash flow was enough of a concern already.

It's settled, then: in lieu of monthly payments, Adam will forgo his equalization payment, and everything's even steven. (While the range in the guidelines was $0 to $5,000, they were both okay with $2,300 per month being paid to nullify the equalization payment of $119,000.)

As the financial negotiations end, both Adam and Carolyn see that when it comes to divorce, two halves is always less than one whole. Dividing a household costs money, no matter how you slice it.

There were ups and downs and anger and tears, but at the end of it all, they feel they were treated fairly.

And having seen so many friends take the traditional route through divorce, they are astounded by how much they still have between them.

I know what each of them is thinking now: "Will the negotiations over the kids have a fair outcome too?"

PART 3

THE FORGOTTEN ONES

Children of divorce often bear the scars of a double-edged sword. First, they must endure the emotional turmoil that may come as a byproduct of their parents' efforts to prolong dysfunctional relationships "for the children's sake."

Then, when divorce finally becomes unavoidable, they soon get lost in the dust clouds of the ensuing emotional and financial battles; or worse, they become pawns (however unintentionally) in their parents' battles for assets and struggles for control.

In bringing to the world a new and better way to end marriages, Fairway Divorce Solutions has been motivated above all else by a desire to save the children of divorce.

You will see, in my personal story, how the seeds of that mandate were planted. In my Reflections, you'll see how and why that mandate began to take shape. And in the continuing story of Adam and Carolyn Cunningham, you'll see that it's possible to make a clean break while keeping your children's sense of security and self-worth intact.

KAREN'S STORY

Caught up as I was in the emotional turmoil it stirred up, I lost sight of many important things during my divorce: my future, my friendships, my own emotional well-being. One thing I never lost sight of, though, was my children's sense of security.

That isn't to say they weren't affected by my divorce and that I didn't make a lot of mistakes. The process was so protracted and the proceedings were so emotionally charged, to protect them completely and to behave unimpeachably would have been impossible. But I can hold my head high knowing I did the best I could do under the circumstances.

With humility and unabashed honesty, I here relate the story of my divorce as it involved my children. My intent: to show just how vulnerable kids can be to the conflicts between their parents, and to reveal how many different forces can compete against your children's happiness within the traditional system of divorce.

Chapter 22

WATCHING IT ALL FROM A PLACE OF HELPLESSNESS

While the battle for the business raged on, an altogether different (and in many ways, more distressing) matter was also playing itself out.

The inevitable question of child custody—the most important, most heart-wrenching aspect of divorce—had reared its beastly head, and the system charged with resolving the matter threatened to devour my last remaining shreds of hope and dignity.

In the hands of a system where accountability is as foreign as fairness and as unwelcome as change, I was treated like a common criminal: I was *allowing* my marriage to crumble, and for the harm that would do to my children, I had to be punished.

The child custody process as I experienced it was humiliating, expensive, and divisive, effective only in destroying any chance Tom and I might have had to parent cooperatively and collaboratively.

Back when Tom and I were still communicating relatively civilly—around the time he agreed to sell me his share of the business—I had broached the topic of child custody, and he seemed open to discussing the matter. In fact, together we came up with a really good plan: I would have primary residential care of the children, he'd have generous visiting privileges, and we'd split the costs of child care right down the middle. We'd also share in any big decisions on behalf of the children, just the way it should be in most co-parenting relationships.

But then the lawyers got involved, and everything changed.

In the latter part of March 2003, not long after Rebecca Hartman hatched her frivolous plot to unseat me from our company's helm, I instructed Sandra to initiate discussions about parenting and custody with Tom's lawyer.

When, almost two weeks later, I hadn't heard back, I called Sandra at her office.

"So," I said tentatively, honestly unsure whether I wanted to know the answer, "what does he want?"

"I'm not sure, Karen."

"Don't tell me he can't make up his mind about this either!"

"It's not that. I'm not sure because his lawyer won't tell me."

"Won't tell you what?"

"What Tom wants. I've called Rebecca repeatedly, but she won't convey her client's wishes."

"So where does this leave us? How can we find out what he wants?"

"We can't. There's really nothing you or I can do, Karen. We're probably going to have to let the courts sort this out."

"That's absurd. For all we know, he wants the same thing I do." "Sorry, Karen. That's just the way it is."

That's the way it is. That's the system. To hell with collaboration. To hell with negotiation. Just pony up another bundle of dough and we'll leave it to the courts!

Even to this day, I have no idea what Tom wanted. His lawyer never said a word.

THE ASSESSMENTS

I lived in absolute limbo for months after Sandra broached the question of custody with Tom's lawyer. Bewildered by Tom's unwillingness to lay his cards on the table, I passed each long day consumed with panic.

Then, almost out of the blue, Sandra called with news. "I've got good news and bad news," she began.

"Dammit, Sandra, not this again. Just tell me what's going on."

"Well, I've been speaking with Rebecca Hartman, and it's pretty clear she isn't going to give us any answers to our questions about custody."

"Okay, so?"

"So that's the bad news. The good news is Rebecca and I have obtained a court order for a bilateral parental assessment. You and Tom will need to hire an assessor to take stock of your situation."

"An assessor? I don't follow. What do you mean, 'Take stock of our situation'?"

"Don't you remember, Karen? We talked about this last week. I told you we'd probably have to go this route if Tom refused to play nice."

"Yeah, you mentioned it, but I certainly never agreed to it. Now all of a sudden it's a done deal?"

"You should thank me, Karen. This is the best chance you've got of getting a fair plan for the kids."

I simply didn't have the energy to be sarcastic, so I said quietly, "Okay, Sandra. What happens next?"

"As I said, you'll need to hire a third-party assessor. He or she will then interview you and Tom and the kids and anyone else deemed nec-essary to get a clear sense of the family dynamics. There are a number of good ones in the city, but Ms. Hartman and I agreed on Mary Anne Doolittle.** The court has appointed her on behalf of you both."

"Remind me," I said rather impatiently, "what's the point of all this?"

"Well, after conducting all the interviews and carefully weighing her findings, the assessor will render an opinion concerning the parenting of your children."

"I'm sorry. How the—"

I was gobsmacked. Since even before my children were conceived, I had done everything within my power to be the best possible mother, and now a cog in the machinery of a system I could no longer trust was going to determine their fate based on a handful of interviews.

We were no longer dealing with mere financial assets. These were *my children*, and a total stranger was going to decide what was best for them. Who knew what sort of baggage and biases the assessor would bring to our situation?

In the real world, when you hire someone and you're paying the bill, you're allowed to question their tactics. You can take measures to ensure

*   a fictional name

their biases don't hinder their judgment. You have a right to make sure you're getting what you paid for.

But not in the world of third-party assessments. There, I'd have to surrender total control to an intruder in my life, stand by silently as she pried into my life, and foot the bill at the end of it all.

I felt suddenly disoriented; my vision became fragmented and droning filled my ears—a panic attack.

"I can't talk about this right now," I said. The cordless phone fell from my clammy hands and I ran to the kitchen sink, where I bent forward and shut my eyes against the rush of nausea.

Why was this happening? What had I done to deserve this? Everything in my life was slipping away, and just when I thought things couldn't get any worse, there was *this*.

I have no idea how long I stood at the sink, sweat-soaked and trembling, before the telephone rang again.

"Karen? Are you okay?" It was Sandra.

"No, Sandra. I'm not okay. In fact I'm pretty sure I've never been worse."

"Please don't worry, Karen. This'll all turn out. You just need to put your trust in the system."

"I see. And what has the system done for me lately, Sandra? Has it held Tom to his promise to sell me the company? Has it excused me from challenging his ridiculous attempt to force me out? Has it moved me any closer to a settlement with Tom?"

"These things take time, Karen."

"Time? Time is money, Sandra, and your precious system is burning up my money like there's no end of it. Tell me, how much is this assessment going to set me back?"

"It'll be about $20,000." "Total?"

"Each. Twenty thousand for you, $20,000 for Tom."

"Great. I'm hoping that's the last of the bad news. So what's the good news, Sandra?"

"Well, the assessment, of course. Sure, it's kind of expensive, but it'll make sure we get the best outcome as far as the children are concerned. I just can't imagine anyone not finding in your favor."

I could feel a swell of anger beginning to rise in my temples. Once again, my fate was in the hands of a system that had let me down time and again. As I'd already seen, professional titles and designations offer no guarantees of wisdom or common sense.

With my fragile life in her hands, my lawyer was running amok. She sure didn't seem to have my best interests or those of my children at heart. She couldn't have. If she had, surely she would have found the wisdom to put an end to all of this.

No stone unturned.

By all indications, that was the guiding philosophy of Mary Anne Doolittle. She seemed relentlessly determined to find any aspect of my being that could be cast in a negative light.

I vividly recall our first conversation:

"Please remember, Mrs. Stewart, that it's best for everyone involved if you answer each of my questions truthfully."

I had felt fearful and timid in the first place. Her accusatory tone simply made matters worse. "I'm not a liar, Mrs. Doolittle," I said meekly.

It's *Ms.* Doolittle, and I wasn't implying that you are. But I've done enough of these assessments to know that each parent tends to do a fair amount of posturing. And when they lie, it usually comes back to bite them in the behind. If one parent lies and the other tells the truth, my decision usually becomes pretty clear-cut."

I wanted to defend myself against her insinuations. I wanted to tell her boldly that I was a good mother, and what right did she have to question that fact? I wanted to tell her exactly how I felt—bullied and intimidated and entirely distrustful of her and the system in which she operated—but I knew better.

Furthermore, I was full of fear. This woman—this stranger— held incredible power over me, and I'd never before felt so vulnerable and afraid.

In addition to interviewing me and Tom time and again, Ms. Doolittle spent some time (though surprisingly little) observing and interviewing our children.

She also talked to friends, teachers, principals, counselors, neighbors, the nanny, the parents of the children's friends. …

And by the time she'd written up her first 50-page report, it seemed as though everything I'd ever done was out in the open, printed up in black and white for the entire system to peruse and to take out of context.

I pride myself on being a good mother. To be critiqued by a stranger is a horrible, horrible feeling.

I felt violated. So did my children, especially Matthew, who suffered greatly through the assessments.

"I'm going to be asking you lots of questions," she told the kids (as Matthew later told me), "and some of those questions might be scary to answer. But it's important you tell me the truth. That's what your Mommy and Daddy want.

"Just remember your secrets are safe with me. I need you to trust me, okay?"

Among the things Matthew told her was that Tom sometimes had a bad temper—that when he was over at Tom's apartment, his dad would sometimes fly off the handle over the littlest things.

Imagine my disappointment (and Matthew's dismay!) when Ms. Doolittle included his confidential disclosure in her written report, which ended up in Tom's hands and precipitated a very upsetting conversation with Matthew.

With remarkable effectiveness, Ms. Doolittle destroyed my chil-dren's trust not only in her but in the system that should have been protect-ing them.

The report also took some potshots at me—some accurate, and some completely out to lunch. During my legal battles, this kind of misinterpre-tation and misrepresentation labeled as fact seemed to go on and on. To see it now happening with my kids was devastating.

Amazing, isn't it, how in the hands of the system, a victim can be made to feel like such a criminal! Is it any wonder so many victims in our society remain silent? Between letting their perpetrators go unpunished and pros-trating themselves to a system that can't be trusted to hand down real justice, the former often seems the lesser of two evils.

The thing is, people who get divorced aren't criminals. They're usually good people going through an unpleasant journey in their lives.

With her report, Ms. Doolittle merely prolonged my agony. Rather than render a decision, she called for a follow-up report. In the meantime, as a standard part of the bilateral assessment, Tom and I were compelled to undergo psychiatric analyses.

All at our own expense, of course.

In his horrific imagination, Stephen King couldn't have conceived an eerier place.

The driving instructions provided by Mountain View Psychiatrics' receptionist brought me to an old hospital building in the city's east end, a deteriorating gray edifice with grimy tinted windows and a liberal dusting of paint chips along the perimeter pathways.

As instructed, I entered through the south doorway. This bypassed the reception desk and took me straight into a long, dimly lit hallway lined with closed and windowless wooden doors.

Taking my leave of the daylight, I took a deep breath of the corridor's musty air.

I followed the doorways to number 112, which stood slightly ajar. Interpreting this as an invitation to enter, I pushed the door open and stepped inside.

With surprising nimbleness, a lean and ancient figure that had been sitting behind the desk sprang suddenly to his feet.

"You must be Karen." He extended his hand. "I'm Dr. Grey.*" Come in. Make yourself comfortable. Coffee?"

I stepped forward and shook his hand. "No, thank you. I'm fine."

Dr. Grey. How fitting, I thought, as I scanned the room's decor. Gray walls, gray floor, gray ceiling. Dr. Grey didn't have much color, either.

In all, I had three meetings with Dr. Grey.

I spent the first one just filling out forms, signing releases, and sharing a nutshell summary of my life.

That was the easy part.

As I drove to Mountain View the following week, I became suddenly enshrouded in fear.

* a fictional name

I started thinking, "This could ruin everything. If I screw this up, I could lose the most important things in my life. I could lose my children."

The scariest part of the psychiatric analysis was the shocking sub-jectivity of all the tests. For example, we started day two with some inkblot tests, Rorschach's classic windows into the human psyche.

For some reason, I answered each of Dr. Grey's *What do you see?*'s with an animal.

I see a zebra.

That's a butterfly. Elephant.

Walking stick. Unicorn.

Unicorn? That's when the second-guessing started.

What did it mean that all I could see were animals? Was I emotionally immature? Did I have problems relating to people? Did I hate my father for not letting me have a puppy when I was six?

On the last day, Dr. Grey showed me six illustrations that depicted men and women in various situations.

"Look at each picture and tell me what's happening," Dr. Grey said.

The first picture showed a woman in business attire standing before a desk. Sitting at the desk was a man in a suit. I thought he looked angry.

"She's his boss. She's come in to tell him he's underperforming and he'll be fired if things don't improve."

Picture number two showed a man handing a woman a bouquet of red roses.

"He's trying to get out of the doghouse. He made her mad somehow and thinks he can fix it with flowers."

So it went, with me describing the pictures and Dr. Grey scribbling his observations.

Though I tried many times to see what he was writing, his hand-writing was tiny and cryptic. The only thing I was able to make out was something he jotted following my response to picture number four: "issues in her love relationships with men."

Duh! After everything I'd been through with Tom, I'm pretty sure that went without saying.

The last illustration in the series showed a man sitting on the edge of a bed. A naked woman lay spread-eagled beside him. Her eyes were closed, and his back was toward her.

The first thing that sprang to mind was the obvious: they've just had great sex.

But all of a sudden, I was clutched by an irrational fear: What if I say that? Will he write me up as a sex addict?

So I lied. I said, "I don't know. It looks like maybe she's dead. I guess he strangled her and now he's leaving."

Nice one, Karen. So as not to appear "abnormal," you twisted a perfectly happy sexual afterglow into a scene of murderous violence!

The results of my assessment came back two weeks later. In every respect I was normal, normal, normal, except for Dr. Grey's footnote: "She appears to have issues with sex." My one white lie came back and bit me in the behind, just like Ms. Doolittle predicted it would.

To minimize who you are as a person to what you see in an inkblot is completely unfair.

Even more unfair is having a third party with no vested interest in the outcome determine your fate.

In her second assessment of our situation, Ms. Doolittle concluded that "parallel parenting" was the best answer for our family. That meant any major decisions concerning the children would have to be made jointly by Tom and me.

It sounded great in theory, but I wonder if Ms. Doolittle considered how you can make major decisions with someone you haven't spoken to for years—and someone who's vowed never to speak to you again.

Unless you have two communicative, amicable parents, successful co-parenting is difficult at best and can cause stress for all involved, especially the kids. You simply can't force two people to get along, even for their children's sake. And you can't apply a template model to a singular situation with its own unique dynamics. Some kids are best with Dad, some with Mom, and most with both. Each family's perfect scenario is unique, a fact that parenting and custody plans need to (but generally don't) respect.

Ms. Doolittle's recommendations were otherwise acceptable. I would receive primary care and make day-to-day decisions on the children's behalf, and Tom would enjoy liberal access to the kids.

As such, we agreed to accept her report. Mercifully, then, the matter of child custody never had to go to trial.

I was immensely relieved a decision had finally been made and that the outcome, for once, was positive. Because ours had been such a high-conflict case, the final custody report laid out in very specific detail all of the logistics and parameters of Tom's visitations. As such, it has proven immensely valuable as a roadmap for Tom's and my future as parents.

I've become a big fan of detailed parenting plans, which can be invaluable for families trying to map out roles, responsibilities, duties, and schedules. Unfortunately, when they are ordered by the system, the process of arriving at a plan is unnecessarily painful and expensive, and it is grounded in fear. Had Tom and I gone to Ms. Doolittle on our own accord, she would most likely have arrived at her plan much more quickly with input from both parties.

Nevertheless, I was thrilled beyond words that Matthew, Sarah, and Alexandra would live with me while seeing a lot of their father.

At the same time, my resentments toward the system festered. These assessments had for the most part been a waste of time and money because the arrangement at which we finally arrived was no different from the one Tom and I had originally discussed, and because of the manner in which it was conducted, the process inflicted irreparable damage upon the children it was designed to protect.

THE INNOCENT VICTIMS

Looking back on my journey through divorce, I can see that soon after Tom's fateful pronouncement, I became a textbook case of classical conditioning.

Every time the phone rang, my throat would tighten and I'd feel a sudden rush of anxiety.

I was just like one of those lab rats that receive random electrical shocks: their systems remain on high alert, and their over-the-top stress levels never subside.

Naturally, I jumped in my skin when the phone rang at 3:45 on the afternoon of Friday, February 13, 2004.

I'd come home early from work to prepare for Sarah's sixth birthday party the next day and to decorate the fairy princess cake she'd been asking for for the past several weeks.

Swallowing hard, I picked up the phone on the third menacing ring. "Hello?"

"May I speak to Karen Stewart, please?"

The voice was unfamiliar. I swallowed again. "This is Karen."

"Hi, Mrs. Stewart. It's Kathy Tanner,** Matthew's teacher."

Instantly, my body let go of its tension. "Mrs. Tanner, hi. I'm sorry, I thought it might be someone else. What can I do for you?"

"I was hoping we could talk about Matthew for a bit. Do you have a few minutes to spare?"

"Yes, certainly. Is Matthew all right?"

"That's why I'm calling. I'm a little concerned about him." "Why? What's wrong? Has something happened?"

"Don't worry, Mrs. Stewart. He's not hurt. I've just been noticing a few things I thought you should know about."

"Things? What things?"

"When Matthew changed schools a few months back, you mentioned that you and Matthew's father were going through a divorce, and you wanted me to let you know if I noticed any changes in him. Well, I have. He doesn't have his usual spark, and he gets distracted easily. He also seems sullen, and a bit angry. I think the divorce is taking its toll on him.

"Today in Phys. Ed. he got quite emotional over an incident with a classmate. It took me quite a while to calm him down."

"Matthew's been going through a lot lately," I said. "A lot of stuff at home." I wasn't trying to defend his behavior. Or maybe I was. After all, Matthew didn't create the problem. He was an innocent bystander in all of this.

"I appreciate you letting me know, Mrs. Tanner. I'll talk to Matthew," I said. "A real talk."

* a fictional name

My concern for the children was a frequent topic in my discussions with Dr. Dennis Sinclair.

"If you remember nothing else," he told me, "remember this: your children need at least one stable parent in their lives. If they have that, they'll be all right in the end. So your job at all times is to be the best mom you can be."

"I try, Dennis. I really do. But sometimes things get so crazy with work. And with Tom."

"Nobody's asking you to be perfect, Karen. Everybody makes mistakes, and everybody falls down sometimes. The important thing is to be present, to let them know they're an important part of your life and can depend on you always, especially when the going gets tough."

I kept that advice tucked away in my mind and pulled it out whenever I felt myself slipping too far into myself—into the "poor me" place where I felt completely overloaded.

So many times, Dennis's words and my kids kept me from going off the deep end. They inspired me to be the best I could be at the worst time of my life.

Todd was a big help too. For both me and the kids, he was a stabilizing force and a reliable reality check during a time of unpre-dictable, unavoidable chaos.

While I knew I couldn't protect my children from the turmoil of my divorce, I was determined to do everything within my power to help them to get through it with their self-esteem and sense of security reasonably intact.

My thoughts turned back to my conversation with Matthew's teacher, and I took stock of all Matthew had been through.

He had witnessed firsthand the fallout from Tom's affair—my emotional shutdown, my days-on-end sobbing, my catatonic stupors as I sat and stared blankly at the walls.

Children know when something's going on. We, the adult players on this stage of life, play our sordid, twisted roles, and they, the audience, take it all in. To hope or to think otherwise is simply naive.

When the kids spent time with Tom, they tended not to share what he said about me, and I tended not to ask. From the bits and pieces I picked up, though, it was clear his contempt for me was thinly veiled. I badmouthed Tom at times as well, though I tried my hardest not to because I know how harmful it is. Residing within a child is part of each parent: when you attack the parent, the child feels the sting.

If all that wasn't reason enough for Matthew to feel insecure, there was the recent change of schools and the frequent juggling of the children between caretakers, an inevitable consequence of my trying to manage as a working single parent while going through a messy, all-consuming divorce.

Yes, I could see how Matthew might require a little more stability in his life. No wonder he was showing signs of stress at school. What kid wouldn't? But even if things were tough and messy, I was determined to ensure that my children came out the other end confident and empowered. To make that happen, I needed to commit that much more to being there for them, to being the best I could be and to showing through my actions (and reactions) that what happens to us is far less important than how we handle it.

Immediately after his teacher's call, I resolved to have a heart-to-heart with Matthew the next day. While we chatted often and had a very open relationship, I knew this time I needed to delve much deeper. I needed to reach him at the very place where he was keeping all his pain bottled up.

Once Sarah's Saturday birthday party was over, I left the girls with Bram and took Matthew to the mall.

We poked around a few shops for a while, looked at model cars in the hobby shop and Star Wars Lego sets in Toys 'R' Us, and then we stopped in at Starbucks for a quiet chat.

We sat in the corner, as far removed as possible from distractions. And while Matthew jabbed a stir stick at his hot chocolate's whipped cream topping, I asked him how school was going.

"Okay, I guess." He shrugged inside his hoodie and looked completely unconvincing.

"You guess? You mean you're not sure?" I spoke gently, with an air of lightness. I didn't want Matthew to feel any pressure or any hesitation.

"Well, it's kinda boring. Mrs. Tanner's nice. She talks a lot, though.

Sometimes it's annoying, all the talking. I think I liked my old school better."

"Yes, St. Michael's was a good school. But you understand why you had to change schools, don't you? You know Mommy just couldn't afford St. Michael's anymore."

"Yeah, I know. It's because of the divorce."

"Let's talk about that, Matthew. About the divorce. I'd like to hear how you feel about it, and what you think has been going on with Daddy and me."

Matthew spent the next 20 minutes articulating his seven-year-old perspective on what was going on. And it was clear from his first sentence to his last that he knew *everything*.

"Mom, I'm scared. I love you and I love Dad and I don't want you to not be together anymore."

Tears began streaming down Matthew's cheeks and mingling with the hot chocolate ring around his quivering lips.

I reached over with a tissue and dabbed his cheeks, then I gave each corner of his mouth a wipe.

"I need you to know, honey, that none of this had anything to do with you or with Sarah or Alexandra." I felt, at that moment, a profound sadness not only for Matthew but for all children of divorce, so many of whom feel they are somehow to blame for their parents' inability to resolve their differences.

"Then how come when I ask you what's going on, you pretend everything's okay? It's like you don't want me to know it was all my fault."

"Matthew, please listen. If I didn't tell you what was going on, that's only because I didn't want you to worry about me and Daddy. None of this was your fault. I need you to believe that."

I had stumbled inadvertently into a trap laid with irony. In an effort to protect my son, to not burden him with the problems of his parents, I had denied his own intuition, an even greater burden that becomes more difficult to shed the older we get. It's little wonder so many adult children of divorce are out of touch with their intuition: their parents failed repeatedly to validate their children's suspicions, and they repeatedly denied their children's right to know what was going on.

Mind you, it's just as important not to tell children too much. With

Matthew, it wasn't my place to fill in the blanks. All I needed to do was let him know that what he believed to be true really was true.

After the hot chocolate and the heart-to-heart, Matthew seemed happier. He became more comfortable sharing what he thought the truth was, and I tried at all times to validate his perceptions.

It's so easy for us adults to get so caught up in our own pain that we lose sight of how profoundly the kids are affected. Sure, they're resilient, but they need to be reminded of how much they are loved, and they need our reassurances that they are not to blame.

In the current system, there's nothing that can help kids fully understand divorce. But the statistics aren't likely to get any better, and divorce isn't going to go away.

All of my children, especially the older two, have been changed for life because of me, my ex-husband, and the agents of the system, which victimizes children, cannibalizes their innocence, and turns a blind eye to their vulnerability.

The time has come to empower them so they do not bear the negative brunt of their parents' divorce.

REFLECTIONS:
YOUR CHILDREN'S EMOTIONAL WELFARE

Especially within the traditional system, divorce can be a very disempowering process. This is true for the husband and wife, particularly after they relinquish control of their destinies to mat-rimonial lawyers and the system of family law.

It is especially true, though, for the children who must watch their parents' divorce unfold from the sidelines. From that vantage point, divorce becomes a breeding ground for fear, insecurity, self-blame, diminished self-esteem, a profound sense of powerlessness, and any number of other negative emotions that can take root and grow within your children's psyches, often for life.

In the two chapters that follow, I share my Reflections on why the traditional system of divorce fails our children . . . and how a new model can help protect them.

Chapter 23

CHILDREN ARE CHILDREN (NOT PAWNS)

— — — — — — — — — — —

When parents become paralyzed or distracted by fear, their children's lives often become subject to position bargaining.

For most parents going through divorce, "Who gets the children?" is the first concern and "Who gets the assets?" is the second.

Unfortunately, when one party plays a money card, the other party often responds by bargaining with the children.

Few divorcing parents plan, either consciously or unconsciously, for their children to become pawns in the negotiations game. But intentional or not, it happens. Often.

In fact, within the traditional system, it's almost inevitable.

Traditional divorce tends to get so nasty and combative that if there's any way to gain an upper hand, one of the parties will use it, even without direct intent. It's a hardwired instinct: when you're caught unarmed on the field of battle, you grab whatever weapon is near at hand.

In most cases, one parent will hold the balance of power on the financial end of things. This imbalance, even if it's only slight, impels the other side to seek other means of boosting their position bargaining influence, and they may find it in the children.

Regardless of how good a parent you are and how clear you are in your value system, not getting drawn in is next to impossible. Remember, when you're in the system, you're under the system's control. And once you're there, there's no getting out unless you and your partner both agree on it.

We come into this life with nothing, but we leave with a legacy. Our children carry our essence forward. Yet in divorce we often lose sight of this fact, and we turn our children into pawns in an unwinnable contest.

Though I wish I could say otherwise, my children became unin-tentional pawns in my negotiations with Tom. Warped by the fear of losing primary care of my children, my judgment became seriously compromised. From that place of fear, I made many poor decisions and gave in on far too many issues.

I honestly tried to keep them out of it. I tried to spare them from overhearing my conversations about what I thought of their dad. And I tried to appear positive. But in the end, I was far from perfect.

I messed up time and again. I felt constantly drained and I had a short fuse. I was so stressed and caught up in my own mess that I didn't always see their needs as well as I should have. They heard a lot of things they shouldn't have, and I behaved at times like life was over.

But I'm only human, and that's exactly what I remind guilt-ridden parents who ask my advice. "Be good to yourself. It's natural to yell now and then. It's okay to lose your cool. Nobody's perfect. Remind yourself that you're a good person. If you're willing to admit your mistakes, to ask your children for forgiveness, to be honest with them about where your heart and your head are at, your kids will be okay." Positive self-talk can stop negative thinking in its tracks.

As well, make sure you talk to your children to assure them their place in your heart is secure. The dialog is easier than you might expect. "Mommy (or Daddy) is having a tough time right now. It's not about you, and it's certainly not because of you. It's because of me—no one else. You need to know that I love you, that I'm working to be the best I can be for you and me. I'm truly sorry for reacting too quickly and losing my cool. Please forgive me. I promise to try not to do it again."

That's all it takes. Your children, in turn, will learn to accept themselves and take the good with the bad. Your honesty will be a gift.

A fair approach to divorce empowers parents to make the best decisions on behalf of their children. It begins by drawing a clear line of separation between money matters and child-related matters.

Chapter 24

EMPOWERING THE CHILDREN

— — — — — — — — — — —

Everyone making decisions on behalf of you and your
children (judges, lawyers, assessors) has his or her own
biases, which, in the traditional system, can have dev-
astating effects on the outcomes.

Ever the quipster, Oscar Wilde offers us an amusing take on a familiar expression: "It's not whether you win or lose, it's how you place
the blame."

But when I consider this quotation in the context of the third-party
assessment ordered and executed during my custody battle with Tom,
Wilde's wisecrack loses its humorous edge.

From the start of the assessment until its painfully slow conclusion,
I had no idea whether I (and my children) would end up as winners or
losers. And it seemed to be less about what you've done right as a parent
and more about what you've done wrong—an exercise in finding blame.

The process looked something like this: A total stranger was or-dered
by the courts to come into our lives. This person intimidated me and my
children (though I'm sure that was not the intent), asked close friends very
personal questions, and then rendered a decision that would
set a course for the remainder of my children's lives.

And through it all, I felt I was being treated not like a loving, caring, capable mother but like a common criminal.

Courts will often order third-party assessments (also known as bilateral assessments) when rival parties and their lawyers cannot come to an agreement on their own.

In theory, these assessments are a good idea, for they seek to bring an aspect of objectivity to questions about child custody. However, the process has a number of significant drawbacks for the subjects of the assessments.

First, they are completely disempowering, requiring a wholehearted surrendering of control. You must place your children's futures into the hands of the third-party assessor.

Second, the ideal of "objectivity" doesn't stand up very well in real life. Everyone has personal biases, including the person you're paying to evaluate your worth as a parent.

Third, the process is often very expensive, and the responsibility for payment falls squarely on the parents.

Finally, even if neither party is satisfied with the outcome, the assessor's recommendations usually stand.

INTO ACTION

First things first.

That, for so many reasons, is the most resounding mantra of Independently Negotiated Resolution.

Hundreds of people have shared with me their stories of divorce within the traditional system; and over and over, I've heard about the devastating consequences that follow when negotiations over the children get entangled with negotiations over the matrimonial assets.

Dealing with money and children at the same time is a recipe for disaster. And distress.

My most important mandate—to save the children of divorce—is grounded in the non-negotiable practice of dealing completely and conclusively with all financial issues before opening up discussion on the matter of a parenting plan.

It has worked wonderfully well for hundreds of clients . . . just as it does for our fictional couple, the Cunninghams.

Chapter 25

THE CUNNINGHAMS' MOST PRECIOUS ASSETS

The number crunching is done.

Adam and Carolyn Cunningham have divided up their assets fairly, equitably, and to everyone's general satisfaction.

Now it's time to take another giant step forward.

It's time to solve the parenting puzzle.

Although the financial negotiations sparked some conflict and fired up some tempers, that phase of the INR process ended rather peaceably. In the end, neither Adam nor Carolyn feels cheated or shortchanged, so in my view, they are both in a good place to open up dialog about a parenting plan.

My assistant calls each of the Cunninghams to book a planning session and this time, since the financial negotiations are over and done with, I'll see Adam and Carolyn together. (This is not something I always do, but if I feel that it will actually benefit the couple and lay a good foundation for the future, I will.)

KEY INSIGHTS

Once all the financial issues are behind them, many people experience an uplifting sense of freedom from stress, a feeling some of my clientshave described as "miraculous." They suddenly feel that everything's going to be okay, and that they've arrived at a place where they can truly begin to put their children first. (Buyer beware, there is still the underlying divorce sting that can show its ugly head without notice.)

When both parents are in this place, however, INR makes coming up with a great parenting plan remarkably easy. The outcome can be a very creative, highly individualized plan that empowers everyone. It works for the two new single parents and for their children who now have two homes.

Just remember to put first things first. If you try to create a parenting plan before all the money issues are laid to rest, you're going to end up in a long and contentious tug-of-war over the kids and the financial assets. I guarantee it.

KEY INSIGHTS]

It's time for a new way of thinking.

I strongly dislike the word "custody." The term "parenting plan" is far more progressive and empowering.

More importantly, I do not endorse the concept of splitting time with children by percentages. It's very limiting, and it prevents people from seeing and exploring more creative, practical, and beneficial options.

As soon as couples break free from these timeworn clichés and outdated conventions, they seem much better able to rise above conflict and work with a trained negotiator to create a workable plan and a wonderful outcome.

KEY ACTIONS

There are two key issues in any divorce—money and children—and having the same negotiator(s) deal with both offers many benefits as long as they are trained in both areas. The parenting plan has a financial component (namely, the question of child support), so using the same person who negotiated your resolution on the financial assets makes sense. (This is exactly the approach Fairway Divorce Solutions takes.)

If you opt to use a different person for negotiations regarding the children, do your research and enlist a person trained in putting together parenting plans. If yours is a high-conflict divorce, a child psychologist who specializes in children of divorce might be a good choice as your children may benefit from the counseling opportunities while you and your spouse benefit from his or her expertise in coming up with a parenting plan.

INR places high importance on individual needs and will recommend psychological support for our clients and their children when we feel it may help.

KEY INSIGHTS

It's easy to overreact to concerns about "custody". Try not to.

How many days you get the kids matters far less than what you do with your time together. Your love for your children and the strength of your relationship simply doesn't depend on whether they sleep at your house on Tuesdays or Friday or half the time or more or less.

Accept each day together as a gift. In many ways, divorce has the opportunity to improve parents' relationships with their children because they more earnestly treasure their time together. They are more present and in the moment (partly because they want to be and partly because they have to be), which is a gift to the parents and children alike.

When the day arrives for the Cunninghams' appointment, Adam arrives 15 minutes early, and Carolyn comes in a few minutes later.

As Cheryl, my receptionist, later tells me, their meeting seemed awkward at first, but after a few stilted exchanges of "How have you been?" and "Hanging in there. You?" they actually became quite at ease together.

I see this a lot. As they near the end of the INR process and the divorce journey, their energy toward one other changes. It's not yet an emotional freedom, but it's positive movement toward that. Besides, if they were still ready to strangle one another, I wouldn't be bringing them together for the parenting meeting (even though together is always preferable for parenting meetings).

Cheryl ushers Adam and Carolyn into Fairway Divorce Solution's boardroom a minute or two ahead of me. When I arrive, I can sense right away that their energy has changed dramatically since the first time—and the last time—we met. They seem far less stressed and far more relaxed. Even more remarkably, they are chatting to one another. Calmly.

I savor the energy for a moment or two before I initiate the session at hand.

"Welcome back," I say to them both, smiling genuinely at their easy demeanor. "Let me start by congratulating you on the successful resolution of your financial matters. How does it feel?"

Carolyn answers quickly. "It feels pretty good. It certainly is a relief to have it over and done with. I'm so ready to move on."

Adam smiles and nods in agreement. "Ditto," he adds.

"That's super," I say. "It sounds like you're both in a perfect frame of mind to embark on the next phase of the process.

"Adam, you can start us off today. Tell me your ideal outcome with respect to the kids. How has your 'painted picture' evolved?"

"Well, I still want the kids to stay with me one week on and one week off."

Out of the corner of my eye, I can see Carolyn's frown.

"I'd also like the kids to stay in all their activities. And I'd like to be able to communicate with Carolyn about the kids.

"Just the kids, though. No offense, Carolyn, but it's been three months since we started the INR process and I'm really trying to get on with my life. I'm concerned that too much contact between us is going to hold me back."

"At least for now, I'd prefer to communicate by e-mail. We can chat on the phone if we absolutely have to, but I'd really rather avoid it."

"Great. Thank you, Adam. How about you, Carolyn? What's your ideal outcome?"

"Well, I agree with Adam on everything except his one week on, one week off idea. I just don't think it's best for the kids. Adam travels so much, and the kids are used to having me pick them up after school and help them with homework.

"With work, I just don't see how Adam can get home in time to greet the kids after school. And the twins are still too young to be home alone.

"I respect Adam's right to spend time with his kids—I really do—but I just don't want their lives to be totally disrupted. So I'd prefer it if he took the kids every second weekend.

"If Adam can't be there for the kids, I should be."

KEY INSIGHTS

Adam and Carolyn are typical of the divorcing couples I've worked with.

Mom doesn't want to let go, Dad feels a need to step up to the plate, and neither is really sure how to go about it.

In actual fact, both parents need to do some letting go, and both need to do some stepping up. Divorce demands change—much more than most people expect.

Each parent needs to find a way to make his or her new life work. Having to work and being unable to get home right after school shouldn't preclude Dad (or Mom) from having the children stay with him (or her). The working parent can arrange after-school programs or hire a nanny. Meanwhile, the other parent can embrace the opportunity for some precious time alone.

Being a single parent requires compromise coupled with a huge amount of letting go. It's so easy to get hung up on disputes over what the kids are doing or eating or watching on TV at the other parent's home. My advice: as long as they're safe, let it go. Your kids will someday get to choose their own journey. When that day comes, they'll have been blessed with two different homes and lifestyles to learn from. Empower them when they are with you. That is all you can really do.

Say it with me: "Grant me the serenity to accept the things I cannot change, the courage to change the things I can, and wisdom to know the difference."

For one who has seen hundreds of parents struggle with questions of custody, it's pretty easy to guess how Adam and Carolyn came up with their custody numbers. They've heard so much about "one week on, one week off " and "every second weekend" that these formulas have become lodged in their worldviews and they just can't see the infinite other options.

When people start seeing beyond pre-fab percentages and exploring more individualized options, the entire process unfolds far more smoothly.

"Let go of your preconceptions," I tell Adam and Carolyn, "and let's come up with an original, creative plan that really works for everyone, especially the kids."

We spend the next couple hours exploring different options. It doesn't take them long to see that one week on, one week off isn't a practical plan right now. But Adam feels the idea might have some merit down the road, so he wants to keep that option open.

The arrangement currently on the table involves extended week-ends with Adam. Every second week, he'd pick up the kids after school on Wednesday, and they'd stay with him till he took them to school Monday morning. On the alternate weeks, the kids would sleep over at Dad's on Wednesday and Thursday.

Adam likes the plan a lot, but Carolyn has some misgivings. "What's going to happen after school?" she asks, genuinely worried. "Who'll pick them up when Adam has to work late? And who's going to help them with their homework?"

Adam tries to reassure her. "Don't worry, Carolyn. I'll rearrange my work schedule so I can be there on those days, And if I can't for some reason, I'll find someone who can."

"Great. So the kids will have some stranger picking them up from school. If you can't be there to pick them up, I think I should be the one to do it."

At this point, I interject. "Carolyn, it's important after a divorce to set some personal boundaries, and to honor Adam's boundaries as well. If having you help out works for Adam, great. But he deserves the chance to make things work in his new life, so let's give him a chance."

"You needn't worry, Carolyn," adds Adam. "If I'm stuck at work and can't get to the kids, I won't abandon them or send a total stranger. You'll be the first person I ask for help, at least for the first while. So be sure to check your e-mail now and then when the kids are with me."

Carolyn breathes a sigh of relief. "Thank you. I appreciate that. This is really hard for me.

"And what about the kids?" she continues. "How are they going to take it?"

(At some level, Carolyn already knows the answer to this because I educate clients about parenting throughout the mediation process, providing books, seminars, and even counselors' names so that by the time they get to this point, they are well informed. Still, it's human nature to worry.)

KEY INSIGHTS

Kids are remarkably resilient. If they feel loved and cherished and empowered, they'll be just fine. The rest is your stuff, so get over it. (Sorry if that sounds harsh. But believe me, it's the only way to future happiness and personal empowerment.)

KEY ACTIONS

Whether you think you need it or not, put together a detailed parenting plan to lay a foundation for effective co-parenting. If you choose to put it away in a drawer, fine, but I can almost guarantee that at some point you'll need to pull it out and refer to it. And at that time, you'll be very thankful you took the time and spent the money to create a plan.

There are several key areas your parenting plan should address:

1. WEEK-TO-WEEK SHARING

Who gets the kids on which days? From what time to what time? Who picks up and who drops off? Be specific and consistent. Regular and predictable times and places make it easier for everyone to fall seamlessly into the new family's routines.

Once these details are established, write them into your calendar for the next two years. If you have to exchange a weekend every now and then, that's fine, but do not change the rotation—ever. This will ensure a fair distribution of holidays and long weekends, and it will make it much easier for you to plan your life with and without the kids. And trust me, you will get to a point when you cherish both times. . . .

Note that there are some software products on the market that enable divorced couples to share their kids' calendar.

2. HOLIDAYS

Major holidays need to be shared. You might decide to take a "one year on, one year off" approach, or you can plan to divvy up the holidays at the start of each year. Be creative and find a solution that works best for your family.

3. MAJOR DECISIONS

Agree to confer on all major family decisions and expenses—matters related to the kids' education, healthcare, expensive sports and so on.

4. SCHOOL-RELATED ACTIVITIES

Both parents need to attend school plays, parent-teacher interviews, open houses, classroom volunteering opportunities, and so on. Each party should ensure that he or she is on the list to be notified. (Schools are used to communicating with divorced parents, so requesting separate communications will be no bother at all.)

If you're comfortable attending events together, great. It's a wonderful and reassuring show of support for your children.

5. CHILDREN'S CLOTHES AND BELONGINGS

"How much do the kids have to tote back and forth between their two homes? Do we need to buy two of everything?"

Here's how INR answers these questions:

Share expensive items like sporting goods (skateboards, ice skates) and outerwear (shoes, boots, coats). Kids like to have some of their own stuff anyway and do not mind taking some things back and forth. But since packing twice a week gets tiring for everyone, it's best if each child has a good supply of day-to-day clothing at each home.

6. MAJOR EXPENSES

Your parenting plan should specify who will cover such expenses as private school tuition (if applicable), insurance, healthcare needs, post-secondary education, and so on.

If you've established children's education savings (RESPs in Canada), your plan should also outline who will contribute how much.

There are a couple of ways to handle shared expenses:

- One parent pays and the other reimburses on a specified date each month.

- Both parents pay a prorated portion to source (this works best for large amounts like private school tuitions).

7. A MILLION OTHER THINGS

In your parenting plan, try to anticipate the vast variety of situations that might affect your co-parenting roles and responsibilities. For example:

- Birthdays

- Mother's Day and Father's Day

- Travel (domestic and international)

- Passports

- Summer camps

- Tutoring

- Extracurricular activities

- Dangerous sports (e.g., skydiving—what's your threshold?)

- Private lessons

- Special family events

- Emergencies (Under what conditions will the other parent be contacted?)

- How will you and your spouse communicate? (e-mail, phone, passing notes?)

- Phone privileges (children's access to the other parent)

- Parent-teacher interviews (together or separate?)

- And on and on and on. . .

Canada has clear child support guidelines. And unlike its spousal support guidelines, they've been established on the recommendation of the Minister of Justice and are used by lawyers and judges to determine child support payments. You can access these guidelines online, and the associated tables will tell how much you have to pay or how much you will receive. Payments are a function of your income and the amount of time you have your children. (Here, you have to specify your custody arrangement as a percentage.)

If both spouses have the same incomes and they split the child care 50/50, it's a break-even proposition. No child support is payable to either parent. (Sorry to use those percentages again, but that's how the tables work. I'll just have to do it a few more times.)

In a 50/50 arrangement where the spouses' incomes are substantially different, child support will be payable.

Whenever the arrangement is something significantly different from 50/50, the parent who spends the least percentage of time caring for the kids must pay child support. The amount owing will depend on that parent's income.

Sadly, some parents push for a 50/50 arrangement solely to minimize their child support payments. I encourage you at all times to have the moral fortitude to do what's best for your children, not your spending account.

On the flip side, I've heard accusations that the other parent wants a half-on, half-off arrangement only to pay less child support. I don't know which upsets me more: the person who makes such accusations or the thought that a parent would want kids more only because it costs less.

In the United States, approaches to child support vary from state to state. Be sure to work with a negotiator who's well versed on the applicable statutes and guidelines.

KEY INSIGHTS

Extraordinary expenses above and beyond child support are shared based on prorated income.

However, the concept of an extraordinary expense is relative to a person's income. What's "extraordinary" at $70,000 per year—new hockey equipment and a full year of ice-time fees, for example—may be perfectly "ordinary" to someone earning $300,000 a year.

Lawyers love to debate these sorts of things.

As for me, I encourage parents who are able to gladly pay these expenses (or at least a share of them) whether they seem extraordinary or otherwise.

This is about your children, not some shallow opportunity to make your spouse beg for money.

During our intensive work session, Adam, Carolyn, and I are able to craft a plan that addresses all of the issues outlined above.

Adam is still a little uncomfortable about the child support number of just over $4,800 per month, but it's what the jurisdictional guidelines dictate.

He understands, though, how great their plan will be for the entire family, so in the end he accepts the outcome.

KEY INSIGHTS

As I mentioned earlier, a recent trend in co-parenting involves a movement toward splitting children 50/50 between the two parents' homes. While this is a positive step in honoring both parents' rights to be involved with raising their children, sensitivity to the impact on the children is crucial.

In some cases, having two homes causes confusion and lack of grounding. Some experts believe that having one place to call "home" is extremely important to children, while others say not. One thing is certain, though: 50/50 arrangements work best when the parents respect and support one another.

I am not biased either way as long as the best interests of the children are top of mind at all times.

KEY INSIGHTS

In many divorces, one of the most tearful, emotionally wrenching experiences is the selling of the family home. Many parents lament, "But what about my children—their friends, their school, their bedrooms? They'll be devastated!"

Not quite. More often, it's the parents who are devastated, and the children experience devastation vicariously through them.

Here's what you need to keep in mind: a house is merely a possession, and the dreams and activities associated with that home can be recreated in an even better way within another set of walls, even if those walls contain fewer square feet.

Kids, as I've said, are resilient, and your children are going to be just fine. So are you. Why not make this a positive adventure? Focus on the advantages, not the drawbacks. Now you won't have to spend your weekends doing work around a big place. Instead, you can spend them riding bikes or flying kites or climbing mountains with your kids.

Sure, you'll have a smaller space, but you can make it just as beautiful as a big space. You'll have less upkeep. You can build a new life in every way, and your kids can do the same.

KEY ACTIONS

Jot down every positive thing that might come out of all the changes in your children's lives. A new neighborhood to explore. New challenges in the classroom. Opportunities to make new friends. . . .

Most healthy kids adapt to new situations with little difficulty. You'll probably find that although they loved your old home, they weren't attached to it. Their real attachment is to the concept of a home with a loving parent in it, something they never lost.

A fair approach to divorce empowers parents to make decisions that serve their children's best interests. This begins by drawing a clear line of separation between money matters and child-related matters.

As you have seen, Independently Negotiated Resolution is grounded in the notion of "first things first." We first see this concept in action during the financial pie identification, and the same principle holds true in matters relating to the children.

Financial issues and parenting issues both need to be addressed before your divorce can be finalized, but always deal with the money first. Get the financial issues off the table in the most pragmatic way possible. Much of the fear and conflict in divorce revolves around money issues, so put them behind you before you even consider discussing the kids.

This way, you will never be able to use the children as pawns in your negotiations, intentionally or otherwise. The process simply won't allow it.

Life is tough enough for our children without the added emotional burden of divorce and their parents' inability to come to resolution fairly.

My mission is to protect the children, eradicate the word "victim," and empower the children of divorce to see that anything is possible.

I pray this book makes meaningful steps in that direction.

Chapter 26

A VISION OF HOPE

In the days following my final meeting with Adam and Carolyn, each of them rings me at my office to let me know everything went well with the lawyers they individually hired to prepare and finalize their divorce agreements.

I ask how each of them is feeling now, and their answers are vir-tually identical: "Tired, Karen, but really ready to move on with my life and my children's.

"It was tough, and at a few points I was really ready to pull the plug, especially when we were negotiating over the house. But I'm glad I stuck it out. I've shared my experience with friends who got divorced the tradi-tional way, and they keep telling me I really don't know how lucky I was to get through it all so quickly. And inexpensively!"

I wish Carolyn my best for the future, just as I did Adam when I spoke with him.

A few days later, while attending a large garden party hosted by a prominent local businessman, I am approached by a familiar face.

I know her instantly, though her aspect has altered dramatically since the last time I saw her almost 10 months ago. Her eyes are full of life and love, and she carries herself with an easygoing confidence that just wasn't there last time we met.

That isn't surprising, since last time we met she had just come through a divorce of her own, a divorce that Fairway Divorce Solutions helped her and her ex-husband negotiate.

Her name is Kathy Holmes. And as we meet, she throws her arms around me and gives me a long and heartfelt hug.

"How are you, Kathy? Wow! You look great!" She is exuding an aura of joy.

"I feel great. And everything's going just…well, great. There's no other word for it!"

At her side is a well-dressed fellow probably five years her senior—salt-and-pepper hair, steely blue eyes, and a broad smile that makes a matching set with Kathy's.

"Karen, this is Brad, my fiancé," says Kathy, turning her gaze from me to her companion. "Brad, this is Karen—Karen Stewart—the woman who helped me get through my divorce."

"I've heard a lot about you. Kathy's so thankful for everything you did for her and her children. So am I," says Brad, his manner warm and sincere.

Kathy and her husband Jim started the INR process a little over a year before, an act of sheer desperation. When they came to Fairway Divorce Solutions, they had already incurred over $150,000 in legal bills and their situation had only gotten messier. Kathy described it at the time as a feeling that they were sinking further and further into a frightening abyss that neither she nor her husband was sure they'd ever escape from.

The couple had a lot of assets, and they were fighting over every-thing, including their three young children. On her lawyer's advice, Kathy had even obtained a restraining order against Jim. They had decided to divorce because they'd fallen out of love, but six months into the divorce pro-ceeding, they passionately detested one another. They were already deep into the traditional process, much like

I was, but they had a choice to stop the madness. And (unlike me!) they did just that.

They fired their present lawyers, came to Fairway Divorce Solutions, and never looked back. Three and a half months later, their divorce was done and they, believe it or not, were back on speaking terms.

"Karen, you have no idea how good things are," Kathy gushes. "Apart from being engaged to this great guy, my family's never been happier. You won't believe this: last weekend, Jim and Brad and I sat out on my back deck and had a glass of wine together. We talked about your process and how great it was and how far we have come. And our kids are absolutely thriving!"

As I listen, my skin tingles and a joyful tear finds its way down my cheek.

Driving home after the party, I reflect again on the destruction caused by my own divorce. The entire debacle drained me not only emotionally but financially. The lawyers' fees and assorted costs of survival in the vicious battle consumed well over half a million of my dollars, and who knows how much was spent on Tom's side?

The issue of money, though, paled against the abuses on my sense of dignity. I was dragged through the wringer of my ex-husband's indiscretions and the traditional legal system, yet all the while I felt I was in the wrong for letting it end in divorce, for not forgiving his trespasses and fighting harder to hold my family together. Through every aspect of the ordeal, I felt like a criminal, a traitor not only to her family but to the highest ideals of Western society for taking the so-called easy way out.

It's time to change the way we think.

I reflect on the highly paid professionals who profit from people's desperation and their misplaced trust, and on my own denial and the complete breakdown of my intuitive wisdom. As soon as I got lured into the system, I felt trapped. And as my intuition became weaker and weaker, I became easier and easier prey.

I reflect, too, on the costs of divorce as we know it today—not only the exorbitant financial costs, but the toll it takes on people's time, on self-esteem, on children's security.

Even in the midst of all my emotional, financial, and legal turmoil, I began, in the summer of 2003, to visualize a different approach to divorce, one that brings resolution rather than destruction. So deep are the flaws of the system, I knew I couldn't change it.

No one can. But I knew I could reveal a better way, an alternative that will change the way people think about divorce.

And here I am today, knowing—thanks to the feedback I get from clients like Kathy Holmes—that my nasty divorce wasn't in vain, and that the universe had a reason for having me endure so much pain. Once my rose-colored glasses came off—and stayed of: my gift and my challenge was to do my best to make a difference

There is a better way, and I, like others am striving to educate others to use it.

I know the Cunninghams are tired right now and probably not regarding INR from a place of gratitude. They were spared from the ravages of the traditional system, but divorce always has its sting. Often, it takes months to be able to reflect back and be thankful for a process that kept your integrity intact and your assets in your family; that was concluded quickly relative to the traditional route; and that did all it could to protect your kids. In time, the Cunninghams will get there.

The role of mediator or negotiator is to help couples reframe themselves, each other, and their new reconfigured family. Doing so gives me immense satisfaction and no small measure of happiness.

But I also carry with me a sense of sadness I know will never leave me. The cost of this journey for me was the fact that my ex and I have not spoken since. As with so many couples, the damage that was done—the ashes that remained after all the lawyers, affidavits, notices, court appearances, suits, and applications—left wounds too deep to heal or, at the very least, to forget.

To the lawyers we were just another file and another billing. But the experience changed my life and those of my family forever. My children were young and remember only bits and pieces of the actual events, but the outcome remains a powerful force in their lives today. They just do not have what the Cunningham and Holmes children have: a mom and dad who can still work together to help their kids grow up happy and independent.

Today, Fairway Divorce Solutions is a thriving business that has helped thousands of couples through the daunting journey of divorce. I pray that those who must cross the path of divorce hold the traditional system accountable or, better yet, choose an alternative that promises accountability and treats the things dearest to them—their children and their assets—with the utmost care and protection.

An alternative like Independently Negotiated Resolution.

May your personal journey and the journeys of those dear to you be filled with as many insights and gifts as my own. Be true to your heart, and never stop loving yourself.

Appendix

12 RULES FOR MAKING A CLEAN BREAK

1. **Accept your situation.** The past is behind you and the present is just the way it is. Seize this opportunity to embrace a new beginning.

2. **Put your children first.** Making them your top priority is what they deserve. Never let them be used as pawns.

3. **Have no regrets about your past decisions.** Remember that you were always doing the best you knew at that time.

4. **Take charge of your emotions.** Allow your feelings to be felt, and then let them go. And remember that you would never be given anything that you could not handle. Rational decision making is a must.

5. **Be an empowered decision maker; shed fear.** The future is yours to create from this day on. Take your power and keep moving forward.

6. **Trust and act on your intuition (spider senses).** Watch for subtle signs and listen. Let your heart and soul be your guides at all times.

7. **Choose to be proactive, not reactive.** Find strength in self-discipline and in taking action ahead of time.

8. **Pay attention to details.** In your situation, little things can have large ripple effects.

9. **Demand accountability from your advisors.** Keep the professionals you hire on their toes.

10. **Never give up.** When you feel overwhelmed, remember: this too shall pass. There is light at the end of the tunnel.

11. **Take responsibility—do not blame.** Realize without judgment that we each create our own lives, and we attract all the people and events that show up.

12. **Love yourself first.** You will draw new joy into your life.

Make your Notes Here

About the Author

Karen Stewart B.Sc., MBA, C.Med, RFM, CDFA,
Founder & CEO, Fairway Divorce Solutions®

Karen Stewart has had over 25 years of experience building companies in the Financial Industry. She has been either a founder or co-founder of eight different businesses. Combining Karen's personal divorce experience with the financial acumen she's developed over the years as an MBA, entrepreneur and financial company founder, Karen created Fairway Divorce Solutions in 2006. Fairway is a national divorce mediation company, focusing on providing clients with an alternative to the traditional system of divorce. Fairway offers a step-by-step process that dramatically reduces time, costs, the emotional pain of traditional divorce and, most importantly, protects the children during the process.

Today Fairway Divorce Solutions has offices across Canada and Karen has made many media appearances discussing the effects of divorce in today's society. These appearances include The Globe and Mail, The Social, Slice TV, Breakfast Television, ABC Money Matters, Entrepreneur Magazine, PROFIT Magazine, Canadian Business, Alberta Venture, More Magazine, Financial Times, BNN, USA Today, Reader's Digest, CTV, Slice™ and Breakfast Television. Karen is also a featured blogger on Huffington Post Canada and Divorce Magazine.

Karen is a sought-after speaker; known for her inspiring and informative presentations. She has spoken at Vancouver's Annual Wellness Show, Edward School of Business, Victoria Breathe Now Conference and Canadian Institute of Financial Planners. Karen was awarded the Woman of Vision Award in Calgary and PROFIT Magazine's Top 100 Business

Women in 2010.

To find an office near you, visit www.fairwaydivorce.com
or call the head office at 1-866-755-FAIR (3247).

CPSIA information can be obtained
at www.ICGtesting.com
Printed in the USA
LVOW11s2243250618
581631LV00002BA/2/P